THE CULTURAL G
OF EARLY MODEF
1620–165

CW01424530

Literary geography is an exciting new area of interdisciplinary research. Innovative and engaging, this book applies theories of landscape, space and place from the discipline of cultural geography within an early modern historical context. Different kinds of drama and performance are analysed: from commercial drama by key playwrights, to household masques and entertainments performed by families and in semi-official contexts. Sanders provides a fresh look at works from the careers of Ben Jonson, John Milton and Richard Brome, paying attention to geographical spaces and habitats such as forests, coastlines and arctic landscapes of ice and snow, as well as the more familiar locales of early modern country estates and city streets and spaces. Overall, the book encourages readers to think about geography as kinetic, embodied and physical, not least in its literary configurations, presenting a key contribution to early modern scholarship.

JULIE SANDERS is Professor of English Literature and Drama at the University of Nottingham. She is the author of *Ben Jonson's Theatrical Republics* (1998), the editor of *Ben Jonson in Context* (Cambridge, 2010), and has recently edited *The New Inn* for *The Cambridge Edition of the Works of Ben Jonson*. She has appeared several times on the BBC Radio 4 programme *In Our Time* talking about early modern literature and drama, and has advised on theatre and radio programmes as well as giving talks for playhouses and theatre companies in the UK and USA.

# THE CULTURAL GEOGRAPHY OF EARLY MODERN DRAMA, 1620–1650

JULIE SANDERS

CAMBRIDGE
UNIVERSITY PRESS

# CAMBRIDGE
## UNIVERSITY PRESS

University Printing House, Cambridge CB2 8BS, United Kingdom

Cambridge University Press is part of the University of Cambridge.

It furthers the University's mission by disseminating knowledge in the pursuit of education, learning and research at the highest international levels of excellence.

www.cambridge.org
Information on this title: www.cambridge.org/9781107463349

© Julie Sanders 2011

This publication is in copyright. Subject to statutory exception and to the provisions of relevant collective licensing agreements, no reproduction of any part may take place without the written permission of Cambridge University Press.

First published 2011
First paperback edition 2014

*A catalogue record for this publication is available from the British Library*

*Library of Congress Cataloguing in Publication data*
Sanders, Julie, Dr.
The cultural geography of early modern drama, 1620–1650 / Julie Sanders.
p.   cm.
Includes bibliographical references and index.
ISBN 978-1-107-00334-7
1. English drama – 17th century – History and criticism.   2. Landscapes in literature.
3. Space in literature.   4. Setting (Literature)   5. Masques, English – History and criticism.
6. Theater – England – History – 17th century.   7. Cultural landscapes – England – History.
I. Title.
PR658.L35S36   2011
822'.4 – dc22      2011006851

ISBN 978-1-107-00334-7 Hardback
ISBN 978-1-107-46334-9 Paperback

Cambridge University Press has no responsibility for the persistence or accuracy of URLs for external or third-party internet websites referred to in this publication, and does not guarantee that any content on such websites is, or will remain, accurate or appropriate.

*For John,* angelo dell'orto.

in our lived experience, the self is not locked in the body but open to its surroundings; thus the mind overflows into the environment. And so, too, the life of inhabitants overflows into gardens and streets, fields and forests . . .

Tim Ingold, 'Buildings'

a culture's most cherished places are not necessarily visible to the eye – spots on the land one can point to. They are made visible in drama – in narrative, song, and performance.

Barry Lopez, Arctic Dreams

# Contents

.     *Illustrations*

For kind permission to reproduce the images and for supplying photographs, I would like to thank the following libraries and institutions: the Bodleian Library, Oxford University; the British Library; the Devonshire Collection, Chatsworth House; and the London Metropolitan Archives. All maps were produced by Tracey Mooney. Every effort has been made to secure necessary permissions to reproduce copyright material in this work. If any omissions are brought to our notice, we will be happy to include appropriate acknowledgement in any subsequent edition.

# *Acknowledgements*

Monographs are always narratives of personal journeys and I have many companions from the road to thank here. I first put together an interdisciplinary panel on 'The Cultural Geography of the 1630s' for the North American British Studies Conference in Pasadena in 2000 at the suggestion of Ann Hughes. She was, then as now, an inspiration and she is a presence in these pages in more ways than I can explain. My thanks also to my fellow panellists, Ian Atherton, Tom Cogswell, James Knowles, and Matthew Steggle, who rightly tested my use of the term then and have since helped to set me on the way towards this study. En route I have been influenced by others working in parallel ways, in particular, Kate Chedgzoy, Andrew McRae, Philip Schwyzer, and Garrett A. Sullivan Jr.

I joined the University of Nottingham in 2004 with the dream of this book in my head. Fundamental to its eventual realization and shape have been the geographers with whom I have had the honour and pleasure of working: Michael Heffernan, David Matless, Alex Vasudevan, Charles Watkins, and, most of all, Stephen Daniels, who has been my fiercest critic and greatest inspiration throughout the researching and writing of this book. I hope that he regards the eventual product as having the integrity of practice he rightly demands. Fellow members of the Landscape, Space, Place research group that Steve and I co-founded at the University have all been important allies; my thanks especially to Neal Alexander, Nicholas Alfrey, Daniel Grimley, Richard Hamblyn, David James, Jemima Matthews, Jo Robinson, and Daniel Weston, and to the University of Nottingham for the research funding that has made the work of the group possible. Thanks also to my Dean, Alan Ford, for enabling research leave at a key time and for access to the Dean's Fund to secure the images for this publication. Sarah Grandage offered gracious research assistance on the pictures and Tracy Mooney created the maps with great patience and skill. All my colleagues in the School of English Studies have been co-workers in this project, but special mention must go to Ron Carter for his belief and encouragement from the beginning and at every crucial step along the way.

Presentation of early stages of work in research seminars helped enormously and I must therefore thank audiences at King's College, London; the Universities of Warwick, Edinburgh, Auckland, and Calgary; various gatherings of the Shakespeare Association of America and the Renaissance Society of America; and, especially, the University of Queensland for the space and time afforded by the Lloyd Davis Visiting Professorship of Shakespeare Studies in the summer of 2009. The University of Calgary was equally generous in inviting me as a Visiting Scholar in 2008 and again in 2010 and in allowing me to share with them their wonderful manuscript play. To Susan Bennett, Jacqueline Jenkins, and Mary Polito, as well as the entire research team, I owe a great debt of gratitude and I must also acknowledge generous financial support from the Social Sciences and Humanities Research Council of Canada. Susan will also find herself written all over the lines, pages, and ideas in this book; I can only say that she has been my role model, my best critic, and my great friend in the thinking on space and place presented here.

Research libraries and archives at the British Library, National Archives, Hereford Cathedral Library, National Library of Wales, National Library of Scotland, the Bodleian, the Cambridge University Library, the University of Nottingham Manuscripts and Special Collections, and the University of Calgary Special Collections all offered much needed assistance and access to materials.

Individual inputs came from Martin Butler, Dan Brayton, Richard Cave, Kate Chedgzoy, Elizabeth Dutton, Georgina Harding, Gordon McMullan, Andrew McRae, Alison Scott, Lauren Shohet, Mimi Yiu, and Adam Zucker. Stephen Daniels, Ann Hughes, and David Matless all read sections in the early stages. Thank you also to my supportive and attentive Cambridge University Press readers. My ideal critic and reader, however, was Lucy Munro who, with spectacular insight and generosity, commented over the course of a year on the entire book in draft. It is much the better for her input and all remaining mistakes and infelicities are wholly mine. It is once again an honour and a privilege to be working with Sarah Stanton and the team at Cambridge University Press who are a model of their kind.

Finally, there is the person to whom the book is dedicated, John Higham, 'gardiner'. Thank you. For everything.

# Abbreviations

| | |
|---|---|
| *Brome Online* | Richard Cave (ed.), *The Complete Works of Richard Brome Online* [www.hrionline.ac.uk/brome/] |
| *CWBJ* | David Bevington, Martin Butler, and Ian Donaldson (eds.), *The Complete Works of Ben Jonson* (Cambridge University Press, forthcoming 2011) |
| *DNB Online* | *The Oxford Dictionary of National Biography Online* (Oxford University Press, 2004) [www.oxforddnb.com/] |
| *OED Online* | *The Oxford English Dictionary Online* (Oxford University Press, 2000) [www.oed.com/] |
| *REED* | *Records of Early English Drama* (University of Toronto Press, 1975 onwards) |
| *Shakespeare* | Stanley Wells and Gary Taylor (eds.), *William Shakespeare: The Complete Works*, 2nd edn (Oxford University Press, 2005) |

NOTE ON EDITIONS USED

All references to Richard Brome are from Richard Cave (gen. ed.), *The Complete Works of Richard Brome* (www.hrionline.ac.uk/brome/). All references to Ben Jonson are, with kind permission, from the forthcoming David Bevington, Martin Butler, and Ian Donaldson (gen. eds.), *Complete Works of Ben Jonson* (Cambridge University Press, 2011). All references to Shakespeare are from Stanley Wells and Gary Taylor (gen. eds.), *William Shakespeare: The Complete Works* (Oxford University Press, 2005).

# Introduction
## Entering the bear pit
### Cultural geography and early modern drama

Accessed by the highly symbolic contemporary space of a garden centre in the village of Wentworth in Yorkshire can be found the physical traces of that site's historical past and usage and, along with those traces, some very particular ideas about the practices of theatre in the early modern period and after. A 1630s stone gateway marks the point of entrance to a bear pit (see Figure 1). The visitor enters through a tunnel to a circular area containing small chambers which most likely formed the cages that would have held the poor incarcerated animals which were kept there for the amusement and grisly entertainment of visitors in centuries past. The historical record remains ambiguous as to just how long the site was in operation as a bear pit, although a bear is known to have been kept there as recently as the early twentieth century.[1] There is certainly a traceable tradition of eighteenth- and nineteenth-century bear pits in this region (another extant from 1836 is in the Sheffield Botanical Gardens) and many historical accounts suggest that the 1630s doorway which provides the splendid portal to the Wentworth example was relocated there when the Jacobean household and estate were demolished to make way for the new high-profile eighteenth-century property complete with its landscaped gardens by Humphrey Repton.

The Jacobean property at Wentworth Woodhouse, to give the estate its proper name, although now reduced to mere traces on the landscape, has a significant story of its own to tell, however, in the context of a local and a national political and cultural geography. It was one of the first significant brick houses in the county, constructed for the purposes of displaying individual, family, and state power by Thomas Wentworth, Lord President

---

[1] Paula Henderson, *The Tudor House and Garden: Architecture and Landscape in the Sixteenth and Early Seventeenth Centuries* (New Haven: Yale University Press, 2005), p. 148, implies that the pit was in use for holding bears as early as the 1630s, but tourist information relating to the site today suggests that the doorway was moved there from the Jacobean property as part of eighteenth-century reworkings of the site.

Figure 1: 1630s entrance to the bear pit at Wentworth Woodhouse. Photo: John Higham.

of the Council of the North in the 1620s and later Lord Deputy of Ireland and Earl of Strafford (he would be executed in 1641 following a high-profile trial in the months leading up to the outbreak of the English Civil War).[2] Wentworth was not alone in making such architectural statements in the region; his colleague in the Council, Sir Arthur Ingram, embarked upon similar high-profile building projects in York (on the resonant site of the former Archbishop's Palace) and in the nearby villages of Temple Newsam and Knottingley in the 1620s and 1630s, respectively.[3] It is through the link to Ingram that we gain a hint that Wentworth himself might have been interested in the use of bears for performance sport on his estate grounds, if not necessarily proving that he built a 'theatre' for the purpose. In a political metaphor deployed in a letter to Christopher Wandesford in 1624, Wentworth declares that the situation 'represents unto me the Sport of whipping the Blind Bear (not that of Sir Arthur Ingram's, but the other of Parish Garden) . . . '.[4] Several things are revealed to us in this instance; we learn of Wentworth's awareness of bear-baiting traditions both in the provinces and in the capital (the Paris Garden site had been in operation from as early as 1562 and was by 1624 better known as the site of the Hope Theatre);[5] we learn that he was a man not without empathy for the animal's condition in the context of such 'sports'; and we learn that a member of his Yorkshire peer group was actively involved in either the keeping of bears for performance or the hiring of itinerant bearwards and their animals.

Participation in performances involving 'bear theatre', from rural bait-ings of blind bears to the more extravagant and circus-like displays of the London bear-baiting arenas, via the more restrained appearances of bears within the context of the early Stuart court, was just one tiny part of Wentworth's strategic self-fashioning within the specific geopolitics of the different locations through which his career required him to move. The semiotics and significance of his Yorkshire estate begin in this way also to tell a story about the semiotics of the 'North' in the early modern period: Wentworth was acutely conscious of his Yorkshire origins, a point which rival courtiers highlighted when referring to him pejoratively as the

---

[2] On Wentworth's political career, see J. F. Merritt (ed.), *The Political World of Thomas Wentworth, Earl of Strafford, 1621–1641* (Cambridge University Press, 1996).

[3] Intriguingly, Knottingley is the site of the last recorded bear-baiting to have taken place in England.

[4] Letter, 17 June 1624 in William Knowler (ed.), *The Earl of Strafford's Letters and Dispatches with An Essay Toward his Life*, 2 vols. (London: 1739), 1: 22.

[5] Erica Fudge, 'The context of bear-baiting in early modern England, 1558–1660', University of Sussex Ph.D., 1995, pp. 171–2.

'Northern clowne'.[6] The area of the country north of London and north
of the royal and governmental centres of Whitehall and Westminster was
in itself a significant spatial and geographical concept in this period, a way
of bringing into being a cartographic understanding of the nation. The
political map of the country contributed to these kinds of constructions by
determining key administrative roles and jurisdictions geographically, not
least by their placement north or south of the River Trent: Wentworth's
Council of the North was located, as its name suggests, on the northern
banks of that all-important riverine boundary (which will be the focus of
further discussion in Chapter 1). Wentworth was a figure for whom the
local and the national were 'integrally linked' in exactly the ways that early
modern historians have suggested we need to understand in order fully to
appreciate the relationship between early modern politics and culture.[7]

Wentworth's reshaping of his Wentworth Woodhouse estate in the 1620s
and 1630s (there are further tantalizing references in contemporary correspondence to his involvement in building works in York, which was his
official location as Lord President)[8] was undoubtedly part of establishing a northern power base as an extension of the authority of the crown,
but it was also a conscious performance of the self. In Wentworth's case
it is significant that this complex political and social persona was one
that he frequently chose to enact through the medium of drama and not
least through the formal and institutional space of the playhouse. Richard
Dutton, for example, has detailed the various engagements with theatre,
both in a private and public playhouse context, that Wentworth made
while resident in Dublin during his stint as Lord Deputy of Ireland from
1633 onwards.[9] What we also interpret from the particular reference in
Wentworth's correspondence is, at the local and personal level, his highly
conscious comparison of provincial and metropolitan experiences of bear-
baiting and their intrinsic differences. What the single example of an extant
1630s Yorkshire gatehouse, however ambiguous its meanings, provides us

---

[6]  National Archives C115, m35/8406; cited in Merritt (ed.), *The Political World of Thomas Wentworth*,
   p. 129. The remark was made by the Earl of Pembroke in 1632.
[7]  The phrase is Peter Lake's from his concluding essay to Merritt (ed.), *The Political World of Thomas
   Wentworth*, 'Retrospective: Wentworth's political world in revisionist and post-revisionist perspective', pp. 252–83 (p. 275).
[8]  Sir William Pennyman to the Lord Viscount Wentworth, Lord President of the North, 12 March
   1630; in Knowler (ed.), *The Earl of Strafford's Letters*, p. 55.
[9]  Richard Dutton, 'The St Werburgh Street Theater, Dublin', in Adam Zucker and Alan Farmer (eds.),
   *Localizing Caroline Drama: Politics and Economics of the Early Modern English Stage, 1625–1642* (New
   York: Palgrave Macmillan, 2006), pp. 129–55 (130–1). On the established theatrical identity of York at
   this time, see Alexandra F. Johnston and Margaret Rogerson (eds.), *REED: York*, 2 vols. (Manchester
   University Press and University of Toronto Press, 1979).

with, then, is an entry point into something other than the literal bear pit; it enables us to start to reconstruct, albeit partially, the cultural world in which a key figure such as Wentworth moved, (re)locating him in the space of his Yorkshire estate and its adjacent neighbourhoods, and restoring him in the process to a more quotidian set of practices and behaviours. In turn we gain access to a fuller understanding of what theatre and performance constituted in the cultural life of England in the decades leading up to the civil wars (this study will focus, in particular, on the 1620s–1640s). It is through this kind of methodology that I hope in this study to indicate the ways in which cultural geography as both a disciplinary field and an approach might prove insightful for literary criticism and theatre history. We are already beginning in this single example to think about the role of the individual within wider networks: of patronage, politics, local identity, manuscript and artistic and theatrical circles, neighbourhoods, and the potent domain of the estate itself, and these ideas will all play a crucial role in the cultural geography I am attempting to limn for the early seventeenth century and, in particular, for its drama.

The early modern estate is one prime spatial means of exploring cultural geography and in its variant forms it will prove an important conceptual and material site throughout this study. Thomas Wentworth's engagement, however partial or tangential, with the particular form of theatre that was represented by performing bears in the early seventeenth century provides us with yet another fruitful point of access to the cultural geography of the age in which he lived. The remarkable archive that has been provided for us by the Records of Early English Drama project (henceforth REED) offers considerable evidence for the frequency of visits to country estates and towns by performing bears with names such as Tarleton, Robin Hood, Will Tookey, and Mad Besse, sometimes transported in carts and sometimes walked there on foot by their keepers and wards; and the vibrant cultural context of Yorkshire in the 1620s would have been no exception to this rule.[10] Blind bears appear to have been a particular subcategory

---

[10] Payments to bearwards can be identified in the records in the early 1600s; see, for example, House Books York, 1606, p. 521 and City Chamberlain's Rolls, 1611 (*REED: York*, 1: 521, 539). Ingram's house is also notably a site for the reception of King Charles I on entry into York in 1641 (1: 611). On the phenomenon of itinerant bearwards, see Mark Brayshay, 'Waits, musicians, bearwards, and players: the inter-urban road travel and performances of itinerant entertainers in sixteenth and seventeenth century England', *Journal of Historical Geography*, 31: 3 (2005), 430–58. For reflections on the theatrical naming of bears, among many other things, see Barbara Ravelhofer's fine article, '"Beasts of recreacion": Henslowe's white bears', *English Literary Renaissance*, 32: 2 (2002), 287–323 (293), and also John Taylor's contemporary pamphlet *Bull, Beare and Horse* (London, 1638), sig. D3r, in which he specifically discusses those of Paris Garden.

of this cruel form of drama but bears more generally prove a vibrant
means of engaging with the relationship between the physical and cultural
landscapes of England at this time. As indicated by the quotation from
Wentworth's correspondence, these creatures were an established part of
popular amphitheatrical theatre in London, regularly displayed and baited
on the Bankside where they were also housed.[11] By the 1620s they were part
of the performance lexicon of elite courtly entertainments and masques;
as well as the infamous stage direction in Shakespeare's *The Winter's Tale*
(1611) – '*exit pursued by a bear*' (3.3. s.d. 57) – which may or may not have
indicated the use of a real bear or an actor in a bear costume, masques by
Ben Jonson included the display of polar bears (*Oberon* in 1611, *Masque of
Augurs* in 1621).[12] Two polar bear cubs transported to England from a Muscovy Company expedition to Greenland in 1609 are known to have been
presented to King James VI and I at Whitehall but appear to have ended
up residing in the Bankside bear houses, suggesting a definite crossover
between high and low culture, between the private consumption of courts
and aristocratic country estates and the public commercial space of the
Paris Garden, in much the same way that Wentworth's ursine allusions
implied.[13]

If the early modern provenance of the Wentworth Woodhouse bear pit
is in doubt, we do know for certain that there were private bear houses in
England at this time. Sir Sanders Duncombe, a renowned traveller credited
with the introduction of sedan chairs to London from France in the early
1630s (sedans will feature in later discussions of mobility), had by 1639
been accorded a royal patent for the 'sole practising and making profitt
of the combatynge and fightynge of wild and domestic beasts within the
realm of England for fowertene years'.[14] We know that he kept some of
these creatures – specifically bears – on a private property in Islington,
because in 1642 a sensational account of a killing by one of the bears was
published:

---

[11] Ravelhofer, 'Beasts of recreacion', recounts the fact that in the 1610s Philip Henslowe and Edward
Alleyn held the Mastership and Serjeantship of the Bears from the Crown. They issued licences to
bearwards as well as breeding mastiffs for baitings (p. 288). Bearhouses stood adjacent to the Hope
Theatre at least into the 1620s (p. 292). See also S. P. Cerasano, 'The master of the bears in art and
enterprise', *Medieval and Renaissance Drama in England*, 5 (1991), 195–221.

[12] Cf. Ravelhofer, 'Beasts of recreacion', p. 298.

[13] Ravelhofer, 'Beasts of recreacion', starts with the anecdote of the polar bear cubs transported from
Cherry Island in 1609. See the account published in Samuel Purchas, *Hakluytus Posthumus or Purchas
His Pilgrimes*, 20 vols. (Glasgow, 1906), 13: 281.

[14] J. Leslie Hotson, 'Bear gardens and the bear-baiting during the commonwealth', *PMLA*, 40: 2
(1925), 276–88 (283).

Strange and horrible newes which happened betwixt St Johns Street, and Islington on Thursday morning . . . Being a terrible murther committed by one of Sir Sander Duncomes Beares on the body of his Gardner, that usually came to feed them, where thousands of people were eye-witnesses.[15]

The pamphlet informs us that Duncombe, 'This worthy Knight', had so liked the site that he had built a bear house there some two years earlier 'betwixt the Red Bull and Islington'; we know that this was a private small-scale enterprise owing to the pamphlet's observation that it was 'not quite furnished in the full manner of a beare-garden . . . '.[16] On this particular day in October 1642, a strong storm blew down the bear house, causing two of its inmates to escape with disastrous consequences. The pamphlet's account of the huge audience that gathered to witness the gardener's demise (there is grim detail of how his bowels were torn from his body) is striking, not least for the implicit parallels it draws between this grisly spectacle and the mainstream theatrical entertainment of the kind that would have been seen on a daily basis at the nearby Red Bull theatre. Pamphlets such as this will prove to be a crucial non-dramatic source of primary material in this study and we will, on countless occasions, witness rich interplay and cross-fertilization between the public theatres and print culture in the manner suggested in this instance. Here, though, we also have contemporary description offering us access to the ways in which theatre and performance were woven deep into the contemporary psyche and, not least, the experience of specific spaces and places like the Bankside.

The Bankside was also the locale in 1623 for the spectacular sight (if deeply distressing to a modern sensibility) of a polar bear swimming in the Thames, the poor beast having been 'turned' into the water to be baited by dogs.[17] The association of polar bears, in particular, with swimming was clearly potent in the early modern imagination and John Taylor's reference to the 'white swimming Beares' in his 1638 pamphlet *Bull, Beare and Horse* suggests either that this kind of occasion was a repeated occurrence or, perhaps, that the bear houses, which like many cages for exotic animals at this time, do appear to have doubled as miniature theatres for visiting and, often, paying spectators, contained some kind of space for

---

[15] *Strange and Horrible News* (London, 1642), sig. A1r.
[16] *Strange and Horrible News*, sig. A2r.
[17] The sight is recounted by John Chamberlain in a letter to Sir Dudley Carleton, cited in G. E. Bentley, *The Jacobean and Caroline Stage* (Oxford: Clarendon, 1968), 4: 211. This event is also discussed in Fudge, 'The context of bear-baiting', p. 176, and Ravelhofer, 'Beasts of recreacion', p. 295.

swimming.[18] These London spectacles may have been very different in tenor and tone to the regional displays of individual bears at properties such as Sir Arthur Ingram's, but the link between the kinds of cultural activity, habits of thought, and structures of belief to which they appealed can tell us much about the early modern period. If bears, though, were part of surprisingly everyday spectacles on the roads and common highways of England, they also formed part of a complex flow of bodies and cultural practices around the nation, acting as a bridge between metropolis and region, and between those smaller 'circuits of knowledge' constituted by those regions themselves.[19] All of these ideas of flow, of circulation, and of network and mobility paradigms which are so resonant in contemporary cultural geographical practice will have their influence on the particular narratives of space and place and their integral relationship to early modern theatre that I seek to recount here.

There are a host of ways, then, in which the Wentworth bear pit proves a suggestive example of the built environment and the practical theatre in the focus decades of my study – a period stretching from the latter years of James VI and I's reigns to the end of the English Civil Wars and the onset of quasi-republican government in 1649. This period was selected partly because of the obvious potential of a holistic study of Caroline theatrical culture in this regard, focusing on drama produced during the reign of Charles I from 1625 to 1649, and encompassing the particular cultural moment of the Personal Rule from 1629 to 1640 when the King governed without summoning any parliaments. By extending the focus beyond the somewhat arbitrary time frame of a particular monarch's reign, we are also able to account for continuities of practice, and for evidence of performance beyond the frequently perceived endpoint of the closure of the commercial theatre houses in 1642 at the outbreak of the civil war.[20]

---

[18] Taylor, *Bull, Beare and Horse*, sig. C4v. Ravelhofer, 'Beasts of recreacion', reproduces a later seventeenth-century engraving of a bear compound in Dresden that clearly depicts swimming areas as part of the architectural design.

[19] The phrase is actually Iain Sinclair's in application to the perambulations and poetry of John Clare and delivered as part of his presentation to the Arts and Humanities Research Council (AHRC) Landscape and Environment conference on Art and Environment held at Tate Britain in June 2010, but seems equally resonant in application to my early modern subjects. Jason Scott-Warren, who refers to theatre and bear-baiting as 'culturally isomorphic events' at this time, describes 'bearwards wearing the liveries of their lordly patrons [taking] their masters' animals on tour to the country houses of the kingdom' ('When theaters were bear-gardens: or what is at stake in the comedy of humor?', *Shakespeare Quarterly*, 54: 1 (2003), 63–82 (65, 64)).

[20] On the Personal Rule as an organizing category, see the editorial introduction to Ian Atherton and Julie Sanders (eds.), *The 1630s: Interdisciplinary Essays on Culture and Politics in the Caroline Era* (Manchester University Press, 2006), pp. 1–27. On the topic of post-1642 theatrical practice, see the pioneering work of Susan Wiseman in *Politics and Drama in the English Civil War* (Cambridge University Press, 1998).

Facilitating examples of this kind enable us to think about a number of the connecting lines of thought between literary criticism, theatre history, and cultural geography that will form the basis of my methodology here when trying to unlock new ways of approaching and understanding early modern drama as form and practice.[21]

It is necessary at this point to define what I mean by the term 'cultural geography' in this context. Mike Crang has spoken helpfully of geography's capacity as a discipline to look at cultures as 'locatable, specific phenomena' and how this in turn helps us to understand not only 'how cultures are spread over space but also . . . how cultures make sense of space'.[22] It is my opinion that drama was one of the key means by which early modern English society strove to make sense of space and that attending not only to the spaces and places represented in plays written both for household and commercial performances but also to the agency those representations held in contemporary society in terms of what Henri Lefebvre termed the 'production of space' can be a highly fruitful exercise.[23] Cultural geography 'looks at the ways different processes come together in particular places and how those places develop meanings for people'.[24] This driving idea of 'process' is key to my approach throughout and my aim in bringing together literary criticism, theatre history, and cultural geography in an early modern context is to reveal several of these processes at work in different spaces and places and on different levels and scales: in the region, in the city, in specific habitats and milieux such as forests and wetlands, in the 'micro-geography' of the household or estate, and in the early modern playhouse itself.[25] I am interested in the complex interactions that take place between people and the spatial structures and concepts (it should be stressed that my aim throughout is to interweave natural and built environments in the

---

[21] The work of fellow scholars who are working in parallel ways with ideas and practices derived from cultural geography requires acknowledgement here; see, for example, Andrew McRae, *Literature and Domestic Travel in Early Modern England* (Cambridge University Press, 2009); Philip Schwyzer, 'Purity and danger on the west bank of the Severn: the cultural geography of *A Masque Presented at Ludlow Castle, 1634*', *Representations*, 60 (1997), 22–48; and Kate Chedgzoy, 'The cultural geographies of early modern women's writings: journeys across spaces and times', *Literature Compass*, 3/4 (2006), 884–95.

[22] Mike Crang, *Cultural Geography* (London and New York: Routledge, 2002), pp. 1, 2.

[23] Henri Lefebvre, *The Production of Space*, translated by Donald Nicholson Smith (Oxford: Blackwell, 1991 [1984]).

[24] Crang, *Cultural Geography*, p. 3.

[25] In making these interdisciplinary accommodations, I am keen to stress that many cultural geographers have themselves been pioneering in bringing together the consideration of space and place as material and measurable phenomena with their textual and aesthetic histories of representation: seminal work in this respect includes Denis Cosgrove and Stephen Daniels (eds.), *The Iconography of Landscape: Essays on the Symbolic Representation, Design and Use of Past Environments* (Cambridge University Press, 1989).

discussion as much as possible) that shape their understanding and practice of the world and how behaviours, to quote James Sutton, 'imbricate with place'.[26] It is my view that literary forms and genres are one key way in which these accommodations take place and in this respect I am able to benefit from recent moves in geography as a discipline to embrace ideas of text, representation, and performance as central to its own evidence base.

The natural meeting ground or space of encounter that is the so-called subfield of 'literary geographies' can be seen in areas like mapping, chorography (a seventeenth-century form with crucial overlaps with antiquarian practice), and cultural cartographies, as well as in more phenomenologically informed theories of sensory geographies and embodied landscapes.[27] Through this kind of multidisciplinary work – which embraces not just literature, performance studies, and geography as subjects but also adjacent and complementary disciplines such as archaeology and anthropology and, of course, social and environmental history – landscape and environment have come to be viewed not simply as static texts to be 'read' but as dynamic sites of enactment, re-enactment, and performance.[28] As a consequence, theatre can provide key terms for describing and articulating this kind of research as well as its raw materials in terms of buildings, sites, places, texts, performances, and practices. The raw material of that drama itself needs to be considered as part of this process of investigation – to that end, pamphlet culture will be a particularly prevalent printed source throughout this study, alongside letters and correspondence, which altogether provide a key to contemporary mindsets as well as that difficult-to-reconstruct sphere of spoken discourse. As will already be clear, my intention is to stress throughout the agency of the artistic form as much as its reflective or representational power.

In the context of the recent so-called 'spatial turn' in a range of disciplines, literary criticism and theatre history not least, certain key theorists

[26] James Sutton, *Materializing Space at an Early Modern Prodigy House: The Cecils at Theobalds, 1564–1607* (Aldershot: Ashgate, 2004), p. 11.
[27] See Mary Floyd-Wilson and Garrett A. Sullivan Jr (eds.), *Environment and Embodiment in Early Modern England* (London and New York: Palgrave Macmillan, 2007).
[28] Key influences in this context would include Christopher Tilley's work in the sphere of archaeology on the value of walking sites and attending to phenomenological experience in the act of historical reconstruction; see his *The Materiality of Stone: Explorations in Landscape Phenomenology* (Oxford: Berg, 2004) and *A Phenomenology of Landscape: Places, Paths, and Monuments* (Oxford: Berg, 1994); see also the interdisciplinary collaborations of Mike Shanks and Mike Pearson in *Theatre/Archaeology* (London: Routledge, 2001). Work on landscape and environment in the literary sphere has benefited hugely from earlier publications by James Turner, *The Politics of Landscape: Rural Scenery and Society in English Poetry, 1630–1660* (Cambridge, MA: Harvard University Press, 1979) and Garrett A Sullivan Jr, *The Drama of Landscape: Land, Property and Social Relations on the Early Modern Stage* (Stanford University Press, 1999).

have emerged. A virtual canon now exists, at the head of which sit the afore-mentioned theories of the cultural production of space by Henri Lefebvre, as well as Michel de Certeau's influential ideas of practised space, and Pierre Bourdieu's notions of *habitus*. From these canonical writers, in turn there has emerged a lexicon of keywords for scholars operating in this area and these terms have certainly provided a helpful working vocabulary for my arguments. Criss-crossing the chapters and case studies presented are a series of spatial terms which help to suggest the ideas of practice and process that I wish to invoke and promote when making my central case about the social agency of drama in the early modern period. As well as thinking about theatre's role in a Lefebvrian 'production of space' or in telling the kinds of 'spatial stories' that are central to de Certeau's notion of how we both understand and practise space, I deploy central concepts from their writings that engage with ideas of group practice and ideas of community, thinking en route about ensembles and networks, and finding in the process parallel and contiguous concerns deriving from the field of social history.[29] The centrality of history as practice and method will be self-evident from these observations. My interest in bringing together some of the pressing concerns of research in more contemporary fields of knowl-edge – performance studies and site-specificity, urban studies on mobility and networks, and book history's new awareness of manuscript culture and the sociology of the text, to name just a few of the most pertinent examples – needs to be allied with a historicized understanding of milieu and environment. How did early modern people think about particular kinds of habitat, space, and environment, constructed or otherwise?; how were the ways they practised or inhabited these landscapes, and indeed 'taskscapes', to deploy Tim Ingold's helpful and suggestively active phrase, reflective of the ways in which the literary and imaginative texts of the day thought about and represented them?[30]

---

[29] See, e.g., Lefebvre, *The Production of Space*; Michel de Certeau, *The Practice of Everyday Life*, trans. Steven Rendall (Berkeley: University of California Press, 1984); Pierre Bourdieu, in Randal Johnson (ed. and intro.), *The Field of Cultural Production: Essays on Art and Literature* (Cambridge: Polity Press, 1983). For some key works of early modern scholarship deploying this material, see Jean Howard, *Theater of a City: The Places of London Comedy 1598–1642* (Philadelphia: University of Pennsylvania Press, 2008); Adam Zucker, *The Places of Wit* (Cambridge University Press, forthcom-ing 2011); and Janette Dillon, *Theatre, Court, and City, 1595–1610; Drama and Social Space in London* (Cambridge University Press, 2000). One salient example from the vibrant field of social history and early modern urban studies is J. F. Merritt, *The Social World of Early Modern Westminster: Abbey, Court and Community, 1525–1640* (Manchester University Press, 2005).

[30] Ingold reconstrues landscape as dynamic 'taskscape' from an anthropological perspective in his *The Perception of Environment: Essays on Livelihood, Dwelling, and Skill* (London: Routledge, 2002).

I am able in the process to benefit from and to collate a range of advances in recent early modern scholarship – building on new attention to the material conditions of performance, to the sites and spaces of performance, and not least to their connection to force fields of memory and collective belief, and, indeed, to a widening of our understanding of what constitutes performance to embrace not just purpose-built playhouses but other sites and spaces adapted to and for theatrical purposes – including households, gardens, estates, city streets, rivers, and forests, which are all the focus of individual chapters.[31] My aim is not simply to depict these particular sites as stand-alone constructs, or even communities, but rather, to stress the endless interaction between them. As the editors of a recent collection of short essays on geographical concepts suggest: 'Sites are mutable, porous, and covered in flows'.[32] Flow theory will prove a major undertow to many of the arguments here which seek constantly to connect so-called province with metropolis, domestic with public space, and homeland with colony, as well as imaginative geography with material site, not least in terms of the exchange of ideas and practices, as well as literal objects and commodities.[33]

The organization of material in this book is in itself an attempt to respond to and reflect on many of its central working practices. I have made a deliberate decision not to start in London or at least not to commence only in London. There has been much fine scholarship on the spatial histories

[31] Key works for me in this respect would include: Natasha Korda's 'thick description' of the material conditions of the early modern theatre in, for example, Jonathan Gil Harris (ed.), *Staged Properties in Early Modern English Drama* (Cambridge University Press, 2002) and her forthcoming study of female labour; Lucy Munro and Gordon McMullan's ground-breaking arguments in the sphere of repertory studies; see, for example, Munro's *Children of the Queen's Revels: A Jacobean Theatre Repertoire* (Cambridge University Press, 2005) and McMullan's 'What is a "late play"?' in Catherine M. Alexander (ed.), *The Cambridge Companion to Shakespeare's Last Plays* (Cambridge University Press, 2009), pp. 5–28 (20–1); Deborah Harkness's ethnographic studies of scientific neighbourhoods in early modern London in *The Jewel House: Elizabethan London and the Scientific Revolution* (New Haven: Yale University Press, 2007) and forthcoming work on site-specific theory, not least by Susan Bennett.

[32] Stephen Harrison, Stephen Pile, and Nigel Thrift (eds.), *Patterned Ground: Entanglements of Nature and Culture* (London: Reaktion, 2004), p. 130. See, also, Tim Ingold's contribution to that volume on 'Buildings', pp. 238–41, which provides one of the epigraphs to this book: 'in our lived experience, the self is not locked in the body but open to its surroundings; thus the mind overflows into the environment. And so, too, the life of inhabitants overflows into gardens and streets, fields and forests' (p. 239).

[33] I have been deeply shaped in this thinking by the work of William Cronon on nineteenth-century Chicago in his *Nature's Metropolis: Chicago and the Great West* (New York: Norton, 1991); see, also, the fine collection of essays edited by Lena Cowen Orlin, *Material London c. 1600* (Philadelphia: University of Pennsylvania Press, 2000), which offers a broad spectrum of the kinds of research practice and attention to flow, not least between metropole and region, that I am attempting to deploy in my own work.

of the capital and their reflection in early modern drama, but I wanted to place London in a bigger cultural geographical context by thinking about models of flow and interaction, and notions of multidirectional influence as well as overlapping and interacting communities.[34] Therefore, in Chapter 1, we begin with the particular challenges and ambiguities of the riverine landscape. Aquatic landscapes prove a necessary and insightful way to think about landscape practices, leading us immediately into thinking about habitats as *habitus*, in Bourdieu's terms, that is, as sites of practice and use.[35] Drama *on* rivers was a landscape practice in itself in the early seventeenth century and with its courtly and civic pageants, the River Thames is, of course, already a rich field of study. In turn, this connects with the country at large – the seventeenth-century city relied on rivers for access to the suburbs and the constituent parts of the regions. London at this time had only a single bridge (London Bridge) and for that reason, key workers on the water also formed a crucial part of its cultural geography; in this case, the watermen who figure in the mental and literary landscapes of the day, as several plays explored in the course of these pages indicate. As well as the Thames, however, this chapter looks at the Trent and the Severn as equally potent riverine spaces in the cultural and political imaginary. All three of these rivers serve to make manifest the ways in which literary and material ideas of landscape operated, often simultaneously, in early modern life and, as a result, this chapter ranges across the geographies of London pageants to Ludlow masques.

The milieu that is the focus of the next chapter – forests – provides a similarly 'worked' landscape to the Thames in early modern studies, not least from a historical and historical-geographical angle. But my aim in entering into the woodlands is to deploy the work of social historians such as Buchanan Sharp, Steve Hindle, and Daniel Beaver, and their explorations of the operations of communities of commoners who claimed customary rights to the royally controlled forests and deer parks that dotted the landscape of seventeenth-century England. The aim is to release an interest in these highly topical notions of particular sites in dramatic texts that are usually interpreted in the context of more purely literary notions of woodland geographies. An unfinished late drama by Ben Jonson, *The Sad Shepherd* (1637) and John Milton's *A Masque Presented at Ludlow Castle*,

---

[34] See, for example, Howard, *Theater of a City*; Dillon, *Theatre, Court and City*; James Mardock, *'Our Scene is London': Ben Jonson's City of London and the Space of the Author* (London: Routledge, 2007); and Adam Zucker, 'London and urban space' in Julie Sanders (ed.), *Ben Jonson in Context* (Cambridge University Press, 2010), pp. 97–106.

[35] I am grateful to Jemima Matthews for discussions on this topic.

*1634* are the central foci of the analysis, having already figured in the preceding chapter's discussion of watery settings; court masques are also bought into the frame. What these diverse texts are seen to engage with is the question not only of woodlands as political and judicial spaces but the woodland ecology itself and the hugely contested issue of natural resources. Contemporary landscape theory and cultural geography has developed a particular fascination with 'wastelands', but waste and spoil in the context of the king's forests in the seventeenth century was not about neglected or despoiled areas. These were, instead, sites of contestation and dispute, leading to a wave of popular protest throughout our focus decades. We will look at the ways in which commercial drama, and masques and entertainments both in provincial and courtly contexts (since another central premise of this study is to keep as many kinds of performance text and as wide a notion of performance sites as possible in play; the stress here is on plurality, and on the inter-theatricality and inter-textuality of cultural practice[36]) responded to these social issues as they arose and were in part conditioned by the spatial and the geographical. This is a chapter about the battle for access to resources as much as it is about particular resonant landscapes.

Chapter 3 continues the attention to the resources, social and material, of particular bounded domains by turning to the powerful locale of the early modern estate and the variant forms of performance that took place there during the late Jacobean and Caroline eras. There have been important recent research findings on related topics of hospitality, patronage, estate management, and, indeed, the implications of these for issues of gender and community.[37] What I want to offer, building on this seminal research, is a specific case study of Midlands theatrical culture, centring on Nottinghamshire and its manuscript and printed theatre, as well as the social productions of space it fostered and encouraged. Household drama, but also its impact on London commercial plays (not least by Jonson, Shirley, and Brome, often seen as key playwrights of the city at this time), will be interrogated. In turn, this helps to challenge simplistic ideas of directions of flow – of influence and travel – between the capital and the countryside.

Chapter 4 continues to test ideas of direction of travel, but here, modes of mobility themselves become the focus of analysis. Looking at key concepts

---

[36] I am deploying Jacky Bratton's theory of 'intertheatricality' as expounded in *New Readings in Theatre History* (Cambridge University Press, 2003).

[37] See Felicity Heal, *Hospitality in Early Modern England* (Oxford University Press, 1990) and Alison Findlay, *Playing Spaces in Early Women's Drama* (Cambridge University Press, 2007).

from cultural geography and the adjacent discipline of anthropology, I explore mobility and dwelling in a series of juxtaposed contexts connecting back to the households of the preceding chapter and projecting forward to the parish neighbourhoods and networks that are the focus of the chapter to follow. We move from open highways and a focus on the vagrants, strolling players, beggars, and migrant labourers who paced their rutted surfaces, to new modes of technology and transport, such as the coach, and their impact on social relationships.[38] Particular attention here will be paid to the infrastructure and networks that bring certain kinds of space into being: here, in particular, the inns, taverns, and ordinaries that formed the nodal points on a national network.[39] These nodal points frequently operated in conjunction with emergent institutional formations such as the postal system, but were themselves active in making visible new urban and suburban spaces, communities, and behaviours. In a wider discussion of peripheries and edge-cities in an early modern context, the chapter will consider the transitional spaces of parks as a particular form of 'contact zone'.[40] In turn, perambulation proves helpful for thinking about new urbane practices of the city and its hinterlands and in this way we begin to operate at 'street level', to use Roy Porter's and Deborah Harkness's resonant ideas, as we see the space of the city understood, and, to a certain, extent created by the process of walking.[41]

Continuing the method advanced in this chapter, of thinking about the particular localities of the city by focusing in on specific neighbourhoods and wards, Chapter 5 looks at a range of networks and neighbourhoods within the city as well as in nearby rural parishes. From Jonson's *A Tale of a Tub* (1633) to carefully situated plays by Richard Brome and Thomas Nabbes, we will look at ways in which different kinds of professional practice as well as leisure activity shaped ideas of neighbourhood, focusing in particular on the medicalized communities located on the edges of the metropolis. These discussions will, in turn, lead us into the focused analysis

---

[38] Cf. Susan Whyman, *Sociability and Power in Late Stuart England: The Cultural Worlds of the Verneys 1660–1720* (Oxford: Clarendon Press, 1999); Merritt, *The Social World of Early Modern Westminster*, pp. 169–73; Julie Sanders, 'Domestic travel and social mobility', in Julie Sanders (ed.), *Ben Jonson in Context* (Cambridge University Press, 2010), pp. 271–80.

[39] My thinking in this respect was inspired by comments made by geographer Matthew Gandy at the aforementioned AHRC conference on Art and Environment held at Tate Britain in June 2010.

[40] The phrase is James Clifford's from *Routes: Travel and Translation in the Late Twentieth Century* (Cambridge, MA: Harvard University Press, 1997).

[41] See Roy Porter, 'The patient's view: doing medical history from below', *Theory and Society*, 14 (1985), 175–98; and Harkness, *The Jewel House*, which deploys this idea at the heart of its methodology.

in the final chapter of two specific areas or 'contact zones' of the capital that were evolving in our period of study: The Strand and Covent Garden. The latter was actually constructed in the decade of the 1630s and plays by Brome and Nabbes will provide direct access to contemporary thinking about the development and its spatial and social practice. Plays by Shirley and Brome centred on the Strand and its environs in the West End of the city similarly help to underline the changing orientation of Londoners towards the new town districts that these sites encompassed. The ways in which all these plays suggest modes of behaviour as well as reflecting them proves central to the argument. We close, then, with an active example of the way in which drama not only reflected and represented cultural geography, but made direct contributions to the public understanding and practice of the same.

It will already be clear that I have deliberately not organized this material around particular authors. In the course of this volume a range of playwrights will be discussed – including Jonson, Brome, Shirley, Heywood, Nabbes, and Massinger – but all of them are consciously discussed as part of a wider context of networks, neighbourhoods, repertory, repertoire, and ensembles. Theatre is presented as an essentially collaborative enterprise, a community practice with all the tensions and internal conflicts that tend to accrue around such entities.[42] There is not necessarily a hierarchy of types of theatre advanced in this study; commercial theatre from the 1620s and 1630s proves an important evidence base for the discussions but equally resonant in many respects are amateur household plays performed in the regions. Drama is witnessed very much in conversation with itself, as these variant forms are seen to interact and overlap in productive ways, but also as a genre in dialogue with other kinds of text and discourse: pamphlets, travel writing, medical manuals and herbals, royal edicts, newsletters, and private correspondence. What becomes important here are ideas of circulation, networks, and gatherings, textual and social.

This study is necessarily selective – I have made facilitating choices not only of focus texts but also of the particular environments and spaces whose stories I wanted to tell. It is absolutely my intention, however, that the methods and approaches adopted here are open to appropriation and can be redeployed to look at other kinds of cultural landscape: for example, the Scottish and the Welsh communities that operated on the edges of the mainstream at this time; the mountains of the Peak District and North

---

[42] On the notion of literary coactivity, see James P. Bednarz, 'Between collaboration and rivalry: Dekker and Marston's coactive drama', *Ben Jonson Journal*, 10 (2003), 209–34.

Wales as particular kinds of ecosystem and cultural community; the early modern court, both as a resonant set of spaces and sites and, equally, as a peripatetic space when in progress; and, further abroad, the negotiations of new colonial settlements in New England, not least the newly formed Massachusetts Bay Colony in the 1630s, with its novel landscape and new ways of understanding land use.[43] What I hope, nevertheless, to have demonstrated from my particular and personalized sample is the potential of cultural geography as a series of ideas and practices to unlock early modern understandings of space, place, and landscape in productive and challenging ways and to reaffirm the agency and cultural centrality of drama as a social and aesthetic form in the process.

---

[43] There was a spate of texts reflecting on the New England colonial experience in our focus period; see, for example, Edward Winslow's *Good News from New England* (1624), Christopher Levett's *A Voyage into New England* (1628), the Reverend Francis Higginson's *New England's Plantation* (1630); Edward Johnson's *The Wonder-Working Providence of Sion's Saviour in New England* (1630); and William Wood's 1634 publication *New England's Prospect*. Nick Bunker's *Making Haste from Babylon: The Mayflower Pilgrims and their World: A New History* (London: Bodley Head, 2010) is admirably attentive both to the cultural and physical geographies from which the settlers came and to which they travelled.

CHAPTER I

# *Liquid landscapes*
## *Water, culture, and society in the Caroline period*

The significance of water to the everyday experience of someone living through the Caroline period is perhaps best exemplified by imagining the sights and sounds of London in the late 1620s and 1630s. The River Thames was a dominant presence on any formal map of the metropolis; both cartographic representations and more three-dimensional visual panoramas placed the river as their central point (see Figure 2). Londoners and visitors to the capital would have regularly come into sight, smell, and sound of the Thames. I stress this plural aspect to the sensory perception of the river because that helps to drive home the centrality of water in the everyday early modern urban experience. Not only was the river a focal point in terms of activity – trade and transportation were hugely dependent on it – and a major sight on anyone's journey through London, but the sonic, olfactory, and haptic, as well as optic, experience of it would have struck the imagination forcefully.

Urban historian Mark Jenner has described the 'moral economy of water' in the capital at this time.[1] Recounting several law court hearings revolving around water-related disputes, he identifies pumps and conduits as prime gathering sites in the city: 'Water sources were centres of neighbourhood life and were thus the forum of gossip, ribald commentary, and collective sanctions'.[2] Bruce Smith stresses that water was one of the soundmarks for both urban and rural communities. In London that keynote sound was frequently provided by the Thames. It could often be incredibly noisy; multiple contemporary pamphlets attest to the river's 'roaring', and not

[1] Mark S. R. Jenner, 'From conduit community to commercial network?: Water in London, 1500–1725', in Paul Griffiths and Mark S. R. Jenner (eds.), *Londinopolis: Essays in the Cultural and Social History of Early Modern London* (Manchester University Press, 2000), pp. 250–72 (254).
[2] Jenner, 'From conduit community to commercial network?', p. 255. His first example of a water access dispute dates from our focus period: in 1629/30 Frances Humfrey found her route to a Thameside water collection point blocked and complained to her landlord. Heated exchanges followed and ended up in the courts (p. 250; and see *London Metropolitan Archives* DL/C 233, fos 141v–2, 154).

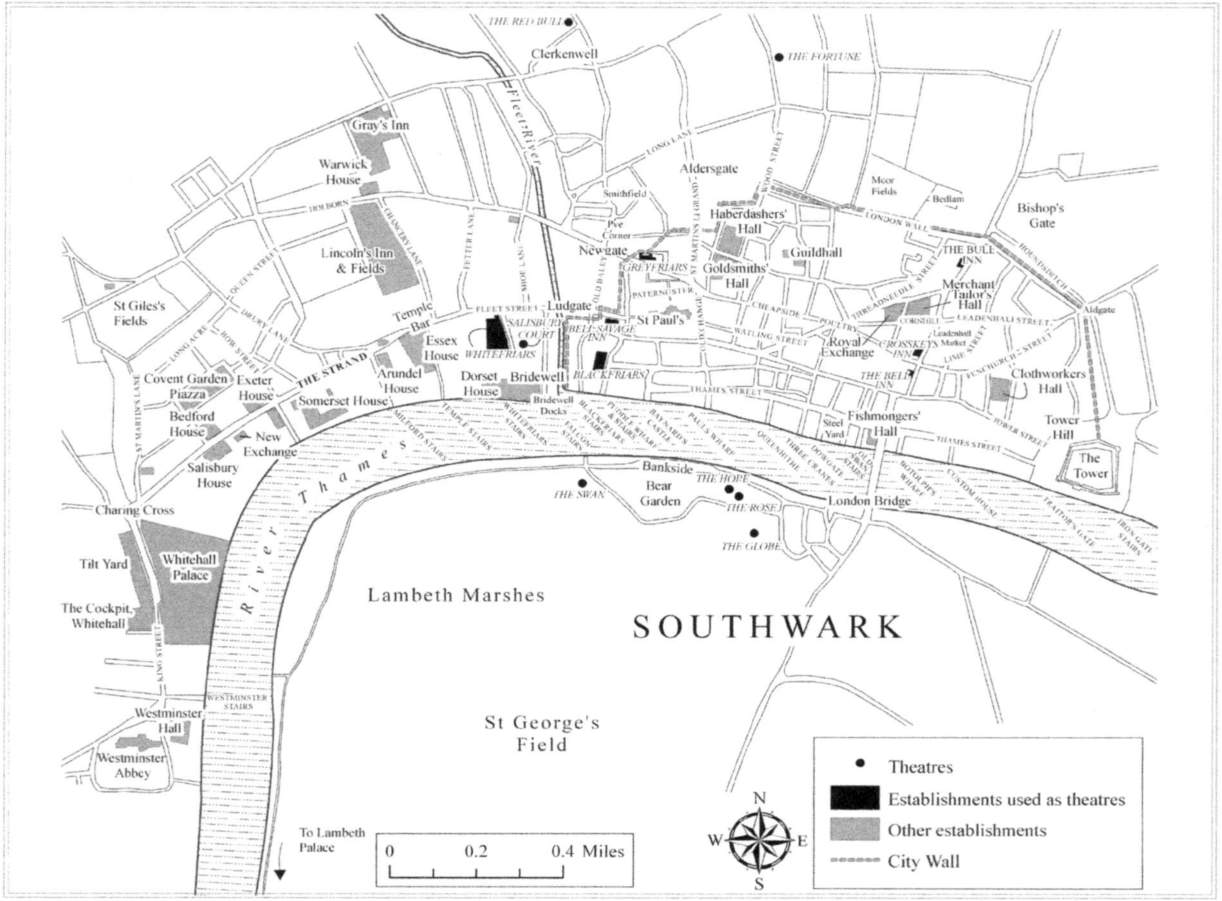

Figure 2: Map of London and its environs, c. 1630s.

just at the specific moment of a storm surge (of which there were several
notable examples in the 1620s and 1630s, as we shall see). The river and
its tributaries ran quite literally through, and sometimes under, the built
environment of the city: 'In several places', notes Smith, 'the running
water of built-over rivers could be heard through iron gates'.[3] There were
also dominant landmarks that produced their own water-induced sound
such as the Great Conduit in Cheapside, a playing fountain of sorts;[4] and
those who plied and worked the water added to its sensory effects. The
cries of the watermen who ferried people across the river – often to the
Bankside theatres, a popular fare from Blackfriars wharf – contributed to
this diverse sonic landscape; as Wye Saltonstall reflected in his 'character'
of a waterman in *Picturae Loquentes* (1635): 'When you come within ken of
them, you shall heare a noyse worse than the confusion of Bedlam'.[5] The
watermen's calls found their way into artistic representations, not least in
the various 'Cries of London' that were composed in the early seventeenth
century. The business of the Thames was in these ways being reworked
quite self-consciously into art.

The importance of the river in Early Stuart London is attested to in
the specific chapters that Anthony Munday added to John Stow's *Survey of
London*, in editions issued in 1618 and in 1633 (the latter emerged in print
just a few months after Munday's death). Those additions indicate to us the
sheer weight of traffic on the Thames, from the 2,000 wherries and small
boats noted by Munday to the 3,000 watermen whose livelihood depended
on it.[6] The river was, then, hugely important in cultural and geographical
terms and yet, to talk about water in the context of the theatrical culture
of Caroline London provokes something of an ironic response in that, in
the practical confines of the commercial stage at least, this key element is
often only figured, imagined, and represented, rather than literally staged.
There are occasional moments in which water becomes literally present
onstage in the form of characters entering dripping wet because they have
been subject to a dousing, often in the Thames; examples of such scenes
include the drenched arrival of the vain gallant John Littleworth in 5.2 of

---

[3] Bruce R. Smith, *The Acoustic World of Early Modern England: Attending to the O-Factor* (University
of Chicago Press, 1999), p. 57.
[4] On fountains in early modern culture more generally, see Hester Lees-Jeffries, *England's Helicon:
Fountains in Early Modern Literature and Culture* (Oxford University Press, 2007).
[5] Wye Saltonstall, *Picturae Loquentes, or Pictures Drawne Forth in Characters* (London, 1635), sig.
D2r.
[6] John Stow, *The Survey of London*, with additions by Anthony Munday (London, 1633), p. 18, sig.
C3r.

James Shirley's *The Lady of Pleasure* (1635) – we soon learn that he fell into the Thames and was left to struggle by his friend Alexander Kickshaw, who, reluctant to ruin his newly acquired fine clothes, declares: 'Let the watermen alone; they have drags and engines' (12–13) – or those that take place in a tavern wash-house in Thomas Nabbes's *Tottenham Court* (1633), which involves George receiving a soaking in a washtub in which he has hastily concealed himself (3.[4] 3.[5]). Even a moment such as that involving Littleworth's literal drenching in Shirley's carefully embodied play-world entails a scene-stealing entrance that necessarily gestures towards the larger world of the river, its watermen, and its industry offstage.

In this way, often through economical stage directions such as '*Enter X wet*', the soundscape and riverscape of London, as well as of other regions, became a veritable feature of the richly suggested, yet never quite present, world just off-stage in the commercial theatres – literally so, presumably, in the case of the open amphitheatres on the Bankside, such as the Globe, where the sound of the Thames could be heard as an undertow to theatrical performances. In a 1640 comedy, *The Court Beggar*, Richard Brome makes witty play on this fact in a trenchant satire on the fervour for projections and get-rich schemes at the contemporary Caroline court. A projector announces plans for a water-based playhouse:

> a new project
> For building a new theatre or play-house
> Upon the Thames, on barges or flat boats
> To help the watermen out of the loss
> They've suffered by sedans.     (1.1.100)

The specific reference is to William Davenant's and John Suckling's contemporary plans to build a new theatre in Fleet Street. The men were granted a royal patent for this purpose, which indicates not only that they envisaged a far larger playhouse than existent theatre buildings, but also one that would enjoy multiple usage, housing 'Action, musical Presentments, Scenes, Dancing and the like'.[7] The scheme fell through, but Brome pushes Davenant's and Suckling's extravagant aims even further by locating their project as a floating theatre on the Thames. He further allies it to another contemporary hot topic, the watermen's company's complaints about a recent influx of coaches and sedan chairs into the city. The watermen petitioned that this was taking away trade as well as contributing to

[7] See Matthew Steggle, *Wars of the Theatres: The Poetics of Personation in the Age of Jonson*, English Literary Studies Monograph 75 (University of Victoria Press, 1998), pp. 118–20.

noise pollution and increased accidents. Brome's play proves an instructive example of the ways in which the element of water found its course, in however roundabout a fashion, onto the stage. The aim of this chapter is to unpack further examples, and, by means of their complexity and diversity, to reconsider the ways in which inhabitants of London, but also the nation at large, responded to and thought about the rivers, waterways, and oceans that surrounded them.

The introduction to this book suggested that scholarly considerations of early modern drama frequently commence in London because their starting point is the commercial playhouse. The metropolitan locale of that particular institution cannot be avoided, but this chapter, like the study as a whole, seeks to reorientate more conventional approaches whereby early modern events and even artefacts are frequently seen only through the prism of the early modern metropolis. Admittedly, the goods that decorated the country estates of the gentry and the nobility in this period were largely produced by, or passed through, the trading mechanism that was London. However, although London's emergent spaces and cultural geographies will be a major interest in later chapters (Chapters 5 and 6), earlier chapters consider more elemental features such as water, or particular kinds of habitat such as forests, in an attempt to demonstrate that early modern London existed in a far more symbiotic relationship to the nation and its natural and manufactured resources as a whole than accounts of dramatic culture at the time have tended to indicate.[8]

The Thames was a transporter of many of those aforementioned goods and commodities that found their way from the city streets into provincial households. The river functioned both internally through the networks of canals and inland waterways that led into the regions, and externally leading out, as it did, towards the wider oceans and maritime spaces of trade and export. The trajectory of this chapter will be to move from the idea of the river, exploring actual waterways such as the Thames, the Severn, and the Trent in the process, to the coastline and, from there, out to the open sea. The aim is to perform a series of cultural interventions and engagements that will encompass subjects and landscapes as diverse as the ceremonial staging of the river in royal and civic performances, the drained fenlands of East Anglia and Lincolnshire, even further abroad to the icy wastes of northern whaling stations, and, eventually, to piracy on the high seas.

---

[8] I am reapplying the methodology of Cronon's ground-breaking work in *Nature's Metropolis* here.

PART I: STAGING THE RIVER: FROM THAMES TO TRENT

*Riverscapes and real estate*

The curtains raised on the opening scene of *Britannia Triumphans*, a masque co-created by Inigo Jones and William Davenant in 1637, to reveal the following:

English houses of the old and newer formes, intermixt with trees, and a farre off a prospect of the Citie of London, and the River of Thames, which being a principall part, might be taken for all great Britaine.[9]

The London-centric assumptions of this quotation – that the City and its river might be taken to represent the whole country, being its 'principall part' – is still a point debated in British culture, but Davenant's description (provided for the printed version of the text in the same year as its performance) captures the centrality of the capital and, not least, of the River Thames to the national imaginary. The panoramic depictions of Wenceslaus Hollar and others produced in the early to mid seventeenth century are cartographic evidence of the centrality of this 'riverscape' to understandings and interpretations of the city. As C. V. Wedgwood pointed out, London was in the Caroline period 'the centre of maritime and mercantile England' and many of the central emphases of Davenant's masque underscore this.[10]

As well as being central to the political, maritime, and mercantile fortunes of the nation, the Thames was a site of expansion. There was notable development along its edges in the late 1620s and early 1630s, creating some of the suburbs that are so pertinently depicted in Inigo Jones's designs for *Britannia Triumphans* with its 'English houses of the old and newer formes' neatly suggesting this period of architectural transition. Notable among these riverside developments were extensions and alterations to the great houses of the nobility along The Strand, many of which developed both their frontage onto the street and their landing stairs onto the river (see Figure 3). This atmosphere of febrile development was, naturally, not without its controversies – James Hay, Earl of Carlisle, was embroiled in a decade-long legal dispute over nine properties built on the Wapping mudflats. Carlisle sought the property rights to these houses. In 1631 he was finally granted these, by right of their inhabitants' having encroached on 'the King's Waste'; that is to say the mudflats were adjudged to be part of

---

[9] William Davenant, *Britannia Trumphans* (London, 1637), sigs. A3r–v.
[10] C. V. Wedgwood, *The King's Peace, 1637–1641* (London: Collins Fontana, 1970 [1955]), p. 27.

Figure 3: View of Durham House, Salisbury House, and Worcester House from the River Thames, *c.* 1630.

the river and therefore in the possession of the monarch rather than any landowner. There is considerable irony in the fact that Carlisle sought this legal judgment precisely so that he could pull down the said residences and build his own properties on the site (a scheme he, at least partially, saw through to completion). Nevertheless, the legal judgment gave Carlisle the right to do with these properties as he pleased 'under a title of concealment called *per presture*, that is to say, encroachment upon the King's Waste, as if they had won the ground their houses stand upon out of the river of Thames, which belongeth to none but his majesty'.[11] Wasteland had become a site of desire for property developers and it was an aspect of the capital's riverside real estate that would characterize its development up to the present day.

## Drowned lands

The notion of property ownership in the fluid waterlands of mudflats and estuaries is an intriguing concept. A vast swathe of the tidal waters of the

[11] Mr Pory to Sir Thomas Puckering, 1 December 1631, in Thomas Birch, *The Court and Times of Charles I*, 2 vols. (London: H. Colburn, 1848), 2: 148.

Thames was, for example, deemed to be under the legal jurisdiction of the Lord High Admiral, a post held in the early years of the Caroline reign by George Villiers, Duke of Buckingham. Another waterscape of unpredictable qualities, prone to seasonal flooding and mobile parameters, was the vast tracts of Fen land and wolds in East Anglia, Lincolnshire, and the Somerset Levels. Robin Butlin has written about the localized economies of Fen-edge communities and the possibilities of 'use' to be found in these 'waste' lands became of deep interest – and eventually sites of investment – to the property developers and financial projectors of the early Stuart courts.

Fenlands are places in which we can witness (as with the forest domains which are the focus of our next chapter) the fierce defence of customary practice and common land use.[12] As Butlin indicates, 'At the beginning of the seventeenth century, the Fenland was essentially a largely undrained medieval landscape'; drainage schemes threatened or placed pressure upon more traditional use-rights to the natural products of the fens such as fish, eels, birds, timber, turf, reeds, and sedge.[13] These were serious 'conflicts of interest'.[14] While earlier Jacobean efforts to drain the levels proved only partially successful, in the 1620s and 1630s plans to drain the Fens of East Anglia became more advanced under the particular attentions of landowner Francis Russell, Earl of Bedford, and the Dutch water engineer he employed to undertake the work, Cornelius Vermuyden.[15] Bedford is today best remembered for his creation of Covent Garden piazza in the 1630s. Located in an area of former pastureland to the west of the city, where Bedford himself had his house, Covent Garden would become one of the most well known of the Caroline metropolitan building projects and subject of several playtexts of the period, most notably Nabbes's eponymous 1633 drama and Brome's 1632 *Covent Garden Weeded*.[16] These plays, discussed in greater detail in Chapter 6 in relation to Covent Garden, locate their opening scenes amid the building site that was the Long Acre area, the

[12] Robin Butlin, 'Drainage and land use in the Fenlands and Fen-edge of north-east Cambridgeshire in the seventeenth and eighteenth centuries', in Denis Cosgrove and Geoffrey E. Petts (eds.), *Water Engineering and Landscape: Water Control and Landscape Transformation in the Early Modern Period* (London and New York: Belhaven Press, 1990), pp. 54–76 (58).

[13] Butlin, 'Drainage', p. 57.    [14] Butlin, 'Drainage', p. 54.

[15] For a succinct but fascinating account of Bedford and his complex personal politics in this period, see John Adamson, *The Noble Revolt: The Overthrow of Charles I* (London: Weidenfeld & Nicolson, (2007)), esp. pp. 141–3 on the Fen drainage and Covent Garden schema. Denis Cosgrove links these hydroengineering advances to Protestantism in his introduction to Cosgrove and Petts (eds.), *Water Engineering and Landscape*, p. 6.

[16] Brome's play is also known as *The Weeding of Covent Garden*, but I have opted throughout for the title used in *Brome Online* to which all references are tied.

newly emergent 'Town' of Caroline fashionable society. This would all seem at first glance to be a very long way from the Fen lands and reed beds of East Anglia, but it is a fact that Covent Garden was constructed largely on the proceeds and moneys raised for, or at least promised to, Bedford as income from his Fen-land initiatives. In this way, then, we can see the watery environments of Norfolk, Suffolk, Lincolnshire, and Cambridgeshire having a direct impact on London topography.

Brome appears to have entertained a special fascination with the fenland environments of England and the financial and imaginative speculations that accrued around them.[17] In the final act of *The Court Beggar*, Sir Andrew Mendicant, a bankrupt knight turned projector, enters the court in a state of distress, performing an anti-masque that suggests several of the real-life contemporary schemes about which Charles I was being approached. The stage direction tells us: '*Enter Mendicant attired all in patents, a windmill on his head* [ . . . ]' (5.2. s.d. 1104). Martin Butler rightly observes that a windmill was 'the commonplace satirical badge of mad or fanciful enterprises' in this period and yet the reference seems more located than the notion of commonplace suggests.[18] The precise semiotics of Mendicant's windmill headdress would surely have conjured up the East Anglian landscape and all its association with Caroline courtly ambition. That working landscape, with its Dutch-style windmills and watermills working the energies and resources of the region to create both power and produce, was simultaneously a scene of deprivation. Only the nation's elite would benefit from the newly harnessed potential of the Fens; in the process many more localized communities, of sedge-cutters, thatchers, and reeders, to name just a few, would be deprived of centuries of common rights and customary practice. Fen drainage was, understandably then, a major grievance during the period of the so-called 'Personal Rule' and

---

[17] Brome's plays acknowledge the potent landscapes and habitats of the Fens on several occasions. The aptly named Walter Wigeon (wigeons being common wetland habitat ducks) in *The Northern Lass*, although a Cockney born and bred, is quick to remind everyone of his Lincolnshire 'Crowland' provenance. There are further Fen-land allusions in *The Court Beggar* and *The Demoiselle*. Brome, more than Shirley or other contemporaries, appears to have a peculiar fascination with the fens. In this, as in so much else, he may have been influenced by his mentor Jonson who had made the Fen-land projections of the Jacobean court the subject of trenchant satire as early as 1616 in *The Devil is an Ass*, where Merecraft persuades Fitzdottrel that he can become a 'Duke of Drowned Land', albeit at some cost to his person. For a more detailed discussion of Jonson's engagement with Fen-land issues and disputes and land rights debates in general, see my *Ben Jonson's Theatrical Republics* (London: Macmillan, 1998), pp. 117–22; and Helen Ostovich, 'Hell for lovers: shades of adultery in *The Devil is an Ass*', in Julie Sanders with Kate Chedgzoy and Susan Wiseman (eds.), *Refashioning Ben Jonson: Gender, Politics and the Jonsonian Canon* (London: Macmillan, 1998), pp. 155–82. For more on Brome and fen drainage disputes, see also Matthew Steggle, *Richard Brome: Place and Politics on the Caroline Stage* (Manchester University Press, 2004), pp. 76, 132.

[18] Martin Butler, *Theatre and Crisis, 1632–42* (Cambridge University Press, 1984), p. 226.

would feature heavily in the citations of the Short Parliament in 1640 as a policy in need of immediate redress. It is no coincidence that Brome's play, with its negative and cynical appraisal of courtly activities, was written and performed while the Short Parliament was in session. Here, we witness a direct synergy between drama and everyday understandings of landscape and its related cultural practices. Each shapes the other in a series of mutually informing gestures and events.

## *Docklands*

In the early seventeenth century, the Thames was in part made up of the built environment that was established on its edges. It was partially defined by the docksides of Woolwich, Blackwall, and Deptford, which were the locations for shipbuilding and launches. Equally significant were the wharves of Blackfriars and beyond, which were sites for trade and the loading and unloading of goods as well as the physical departure and arrival of merchants, visitors to the city, and explorers of newly imagined geographies such as the north-west passage or the even busier whaling stations in Spitsbergen. Reflecting this world of trade and goods, wharves, departures and arrivals, and exploration and return, a number of plays feature dockside scenes, such as Philip Massinger's 1632 *The City Madam* which opens on the Thames wharfside, inviting audiences in the Blackfriars Theatre, where the play was first performed, to imagine the multiple ships and vessels embarking for foreign lands and disgorging the products of their adventures and trading networks in the so-called 'Pool' zone of the city – that stretch of the Thames that fell between London Bridge and Limehouse Point.

At first glance, Brome's 1635 play *The Sparagus Garden* takes place in a series of rather more landlocked sites and spaces. The 'Asparagus Garden' of the title is, quite literally, a market garden producing fashionable food and plant-stuffs for the discerning and wealthy Caroline market, not least the seasonal delicacy of asparagus – variously presented in this play as both fertility treatment and aphrodisiac as well as must-have fashion item – but also strawberries, artichokes, and tulips, which in 1635 were on the verge of becoming a collecting craze that would sweep Europe, the 'tulipomania' of popular imagination.[19] One of the central knowing jokes of the play is that the garden is attached to a residence that is selling these foodstuffs along

---

[19] See, for example, Mike Dash, *Tulipomania: The Story of the World's Most Coveted Flower and the Extraordinary Passions it Aroused* (London: Phoenix, 2000). Though, for an important corrective, see also Anne Goldgar, *Tulipmania: Money, Honor and Knowledge in the Dutch Golden Age* (University of Chicago Press, 2008).

with alcohol to visiting members of the public but which also offers rooms for rent by the hour. The Asparagus Garden starts to look by the middle of the play, to all intents and purposes, like an upmarket brothel; the entire third act is located in the Garden, its episodic structure swinging audience views around from arbour to arbour and exposing them to the whole range of the clientele as well as the tenant-proprietors, Dutch immigrant Martha and her unnamed gardener-husband in the process. Essential to a full understanding of Brome's central location is the fact that this pleasure garden is a riverside establishment, the rationale for which we will explore in more detail in the next section.

Another intriguing way in which the river is 'staged' to the audience's imagination in Brome's play is via the plotline relating to china-shop co-owner Rebecca Brittleware. Her name is a literal reference to the commodities for sale in the family business but also alludes to the supposed impotency of her five-year-old marriage. When we first encounter her onstage, Rebecca seems to be experiencing deep 'cravings', prenatal, in fact pre-pregnancy, cravings, much to the despair of her exhausted and vilified husband John. John's only relief in the face of her ever more excessive demands is that nothing she requests can harm her unborn child, since she is not yet pregnant: 'The best is the loss of your longings will not hurt you unless you were with child' (2.1.192). Rebecca stresses that her cravings are so strong they precede even the fact of getting pregnant: 'I must have my longings first; I am not every woman, I, I must have my longings before I can be with child, I' (2.1.193). It is the list she provides of her longings that is of particular interest here: 'One of my longings', she says, 'is to have a couple of lusty able-bodied men to take me up, one before and another behind, as the new fashion is, and carry me in a man-litter into the great bed at Ware' (2.1.197). Asparagus in this context is part of a wider field of social (and sexual) aspiration, in which the new mode of travel that is those sedan chairs so opposed by the London watermen for the threat they represented to their trade also plays a role. Rebecca continues: 'I do long to see the new ship, and to be on the top of Paul's steeple when it is built, but that must not be yet; nor am I so unreasonable but I can stay the time. In the meantime, I long to see a play, and above all plays *The Knight of the Burning* – what d'ye call it?' (2.1.199). There is some fairly unsubtle sexual innuendo in this exchange. Rebecca leaves the title of the well-known Jacobean play by Francis Beaumont (*The Knight of the Burning Pestle*) incomplete only for another character, Moneylacks, to finish the phrase for her. '*Pestle* is it? I thought of another thing [ . . . ]' (2.1.201), suggests Rebecca, silently punning on pestle and 'pizzle', a slang term for a penis. This is all part of Rebecca's self-presentation in the early scenes of the play as a woman desperately craving sexual satisfaction from an impotent husband. There is, however, also something apposite about her choice of play in that we might read Rebecca as a version of the ambitious citizen's wife from *The Knight of the Burning Pestle*, which had recently enjoyed a successful revival in the London theatres of the 1630s.

It is, however, Rebecca's mention of the 'new ship' as part of her list of demands and desired-for experiences that most concerns me here. Brome never explains the detail, though I presume he expected it to be easily comprehensible to a Salisbury Court audience in 1635. Rebecca's almost throwaway line in a busy play becomes a means of unpacking the complex ways in which the Caroline community both staged events upon the river and staged the idea of that river back to the public gaze in the form of commercial, courtly, and civic theatre, pageants and entertainments. It is likely that the ship Rebecca refers to – the lexical gap that the audience is asked to fill just as Moneylacks finished off the play title in the previous exchange – is the *Sovereign of the Seas*, intended by Charles I to be the jewel in the English naval crown. On 26 June 1634, Charles I had come to Woolwich to inspect work on the *Leopard*, the latest warship in his revamped fleet, and, impressed at that sight, he then spoke privately to Phineas Pett, the naval architect and builder, who agreed to build another new ship of even grander proportions.[20] That ship was to become known as the *Sovereign of the Seas*, the flagship, quite literally, of Charles's new maritime policy, the financing of which would lead in turn to the controversial taxation policy, Ship Money. In order to show off his ambitious plans, Charles had a full-scale model built in 1634 by Pett himself which he placed on display at Hampton Court. Ambassadorial dispatches from the time indicate the pride with which Charles drew the model to visitors' attention.[21]

What is so witty about Brome's allusion to the 'new ship', however, is not just its topicality but the fact that Rebecca's craving is so premature that the ship is not yet even built; the only thing available to see is the model, a simulacra and marker of the monarch's aspirations and intentions (the reference to Paul's Steeple is comparable, since the funds to complete the renovation works were still being raised). Rebecca has caught the public excitement and sense of theatricality that was being whipped up around the idea of the *Sovereign* and its ongoing construction on the Woolwich

[20] Alan R. Young (ed.), *His Majesty's Royal Ship: A Critical Edition of Thomas Heywood's 'A True Description of His Majesties Royall Ship'* (London and New York: AMS Press, 1990), p. xiii.

[21] See Richard Cust, *Charles I: A Political Life* (London: Pearson Education, 2005), p. 190. See also Brian Quintrell, 'Charles I and his Navy in the 1630s', *The Seventeenth Century*, 3 (1988), 159–79.

docksides in the middle of the decade. By 1635 the timber for the ship was being felled in County Durham and by 21 December the keel was laid.[22] Charles I visited the site a few weeks later and again to view progress on 28 March 1636. He visited yet again on 3 February 1637, and on 17 June that year brought Henrietta Maria to view the warship.

Even as early as this in the ship's history, then, when the wood was only just being assembled for building purposes, Brome catches the atmosphere of expectation and the attendant sense of spectacle that would continue to accrue around the vessel, not least at the time of its launch. The initial launch date was set for Monday 25 September 1637 and the King, the Queen, and many courtiers were intended to be on board, but this piece of royal theatre was scuppered due to high tides until October, and then a huge storm whipped up at the last moment. It did eventually launch but with a much scaled-down audience (the diminished theatre of the event perhaps recalling similar problems around Charles's coronation, when London was beset by one of the worst plague epidemics of the early Stuart period). It would not be until 12 May 1638 that the *Sovereign of the Seas* would sail to Greenhithe to take on ordnance. My point is that, by 1635, when Brome's play is staged the general public, as well as courtiers and ambassadors, would already have known a great deal about this ship; it was firmly planted in the public psyche. Historian Alan Young has called it 'the most complex industrial production that [the] nation had ever produced'.[23] It was also one of the more complex works of 'theatre' in the period. It is hard to overestimate the overlap between Caroline courtly masquing culture, the complex theatrical semiotics of civic pageantry, and this vessel as it was presented to a consuming public audience. As well as being vast in size and ordnance, the *Sovereign* was elaborately decorated inside and out with ornately carved emblems and *imprese*, many lifted straight from publications such as Cesare Ripa's *Iconologia*, and with copious mottoes and inscriptions.

Seven thousand pounds was spent on the interiors alone.[24] This decorative programme was provided by an artistic team with an established track record in Caroline theatrical circles. The carvers were members of the Christmas family, John (1599–1654) and Matthais (1605–1654), sons of Gerard Christmas (1576–1634), who had before them been appointed carver to the Navy in 1614, with particular responsibility for decoration of ships. The men usually divided the work between the shipyards and themselves,

[22] Young, *His Majesty's Royal Ship*, p. xv.      [23] Young, *His Majesty's Royal Ship*, p. xiii.
[24] Young, *His Majesty's Royal Ship*, p. xvi.

with John taking responsibility at Deptford and Woolwich and Matthais at Chatham, but the *Sovereign* was such a vast project that they worked in tandem. It is the Christmas family's simultaneous close involvement in manual work for high-profile theatrical events of the day, as so-called 'pageant artificers', that really draws the working world of the docks and that of theatrical spectacular, not least river-based in this period, closer together than we might have imagined at first glance. As the *Dictionary of National Biography* tells us, 'From 1617 onwards [Gerard] divided his time between this office and the work of designing, making, and arranging the sets and stage properties that were required for the annual lord mayor's pageant in the City of London'.[25] Gerard served an increasingly important role in the pageants as well as undertaking one-off commissions as a sculptor, including decoration of Cecil's New Exchange in the Strand.[26] In 1620–1 Gerard also worked on a masque that was performed by the Gentlemen of the Middle Temples before the King at Whitehall. All this serves to suggest that Gerard himself would have known Jonson, among other playwrights, possibly including Brome, reasonably well, thereby blending the worlds of craft and poetry in new ways. The other important link to theatre and pageantry comes in the evidence that the written inscriptions and mottoes for the *Sovereign*'s decorative programme were produced in a collaborative effort with the Christmas brothers by Thomas Heywood, himself a prolific pageant author in the period in focus, despite already being a mature man with some 200 textual creations under his belt. Heywood worked on the 'body' of the pageant, as it were, writing all the speeches, then publishing them in booklet form as *A True Description* with the same publishing house which produced the text versions of his city pageants.[27]

The text, published in London in 1638, begins with mention of Noah's Ark and copious classical authorities. 'Shipping hath bin of old', Heywood tells us, and proceeds to describe all kinds of other boating vessels used over the years before getting to its ostensible subject.[28] He talks en route of great mariners like Drake and Frobisher and finally on page 26 we get to the 'Great Ship, lying in the Dooke at Wool-witch'.[29] This offers us the ship aestheticized in every sense. The various decorative schemes on the stern

---

[25] Adam White, 'Christmas family (*per. c.* 1610–*c.* 1640)', *DNB Online*.

[26] Christmas also produced an equestrian figure of James VI and I for the Aldgate entry to the City in 1617 and a garden sculpture for Robert Cecil at Hatfield house in 1612.

[27] See Alan Young, 'Thomas Heywood's Pageants: New Forms of Evidence', *Research Opportunities in Renaissance Drama*, 30 (1988), 129–48. See also David M. Bergeron, *English Civic Pageantry, 1558–1642* (London: Arnold, 1971).

[28] Thomas Heywood, *A True Description of His Majesties Royall Ship*, p. 6, sig. B3v.

[29] Heywood, *A True Description*, pp. 23, sig. D4r; 26, sig. E1r.

head are described, unpacking the classical iconography, emblems, and devices relating to the art and practice of navigation as well as to classical mythology. These combinations would have been familiar to an audience accustomed to the strategies and aesthetics of civic and royal pageantry. We might also see kinship in the propaganda element and the references to Ship Money as well as the implicit defence of Charles's controversial maritime policies: 'it should bee a great spur and incouragement to all his faithful and loving Subjects to bee liberall and willing Contributaries towards the *Ship-money*', certainly if we place it alongside a later court masque text such as Davenant's 1640 *Salmacida Spolia*, which erected a belated defence of the controversial tax.[30]

Heywood's text offers a kind of apology for the failed first launch of the *Sovereign of the Seas*. This could simply be regarded as a moment of failed theatre in which there was a 'contrary Wind' and lots of cables broke, but I am particularly interested in thinking about the status of the pamphlet publication as a record of a theatrical experience.[31] In this, the pamphlet is akin to the printed versions of pageant and masque texts that were popular in the reading culture of the day. The pamphlet serves as a veritable guide to the exterior and interior decorations of the ship, a substitute for, or even supplement to, an actual physical tour. Were there guided tours around the ship when still in dock? Certainly, we would imagine that the royal couple would have been given a walking tour of the vessel on their 1637 visit when it was so close to completion. Alan Young suggests that the booklet operates as an 'interpretative key', akin in its functions to the guidebooks we might purchase in the present day at the ticket entry point to a stately home or heritage site.[32] The explanatory nature of the booklet was crucial to a full experience of the ship on a walking tour simply because the interpretative schema was so complex; says Young, 'Without Heywood's booklet or without the help of the purser-guider, Philip Ward, I very much doubt that this particular "pageant" would have been understood'.[33]

It is an interesting thought to imagine this as an alternative kind of water-based theatre or pageant available to the consuming public.[34] Is Rebecca

---

[30] Heywood, *A True Description*, p. 46, sig. G3v.
[31] Heywood, *A True Description*, p. 49, sig. H1r.
[32] Young, *His Majesty's Royal Ship*, p. xxv.    [33] Young, *His Majesty's Royal Ship*, p. xxiii.
[34] There were contemporary poems written on the ship, too. These are included in an appendix in Alan Young's edition, including Richard Fanshawe's 'On His Majesties Greatt Shippe lying almost finisht in Woolwich Docke Anno Dom 1637 and afterwards called The Soveraigne of the Seas' (*His Majesty's Royal Ship*, pp. 77–9), which describes the 'sacred Oakes' that built it and that she seemed a 'floating isle', which would again appear to confirm a link to masque imagery in contemporary perceptions and understandings of the ship.

Brittleware in that case aspiring to a royal guided tour in her desire to 'see the new ship' in *The Sparagus Garden*? This would certainly confirm the stereotype of the ambitious citizen's wife implicit in the knowing allusions to *The Knight of the Burning Pestle*. Certainly, if we think of plays such as the second part of Thomas Heywood's *The Fair Maid of the West*, performed and published in 1631, which features lengthy sequences of action on board a ship in which the boards of the playhouse would have readily substituted for the decking of the vessel, it seems obvious that Caroline audiences were not averse to imagining theatres as ships or vice versa. What Rebecca's fleeting reference to this particular craving suggests is that the docklands areas, usually regarded purely as a site of industry, are here reconfigured as potential spaces for theatre and spectacle – a reconfiguration confirmed by the hybrid professional identities of the Christmas family members themselves. In turn, we have our attention drawn to a new way of configuring urban and riverine topography, a new way of 'staging the river'.

## Gardens and marshlands

Before moving on to explore in more detail some of the civic pageants in which Heywood and the Christmases were involved, it is worth pausing to consider other aspects of riverside life that *The Sparagus Garden* packages up for contemporary audiences. As already noted, one obvious focus of attention in the play is those pleasure-houses and gardens that were fast establishing themselves on the river's edge, selling the latest in food and drink alongside a commodification of the desire for luxury and excess. The Asparagus Garden, the property at the heart of the play's imaginary, is just such a residence. The gardens attached to the property furnish its tenant landlords with the asparagus for sale. As well as being a very visible source of wealth (and its expenditure), the river was, then, a site for other kinds of practical activity, not least the growing of foodstuffs to serve the ever-expanding population of the capital. Many market gardens were established along the Thameside, not only owing to the proximity of excellent irrigation and easy means for transportation of produce, but also to the ease of delivery from the dung boats that regularly plied the waters. Asparagus, one of 1630s' London's favoured delicacies, required a large input of manure into the Lambeth marshlands, where it was grown in considerable quantities. In this way, the development of the pleasure gardens which became such a feature of mid seventeenth-century urban life, making their presence felt in Caroline and Restoration drama, can be linked to practical hydrography and the simple matter of resources.

As *The Sparagus Garden* attests, the popularity of the seasonal vegetable that is asparagus had a specific impact on the built environment of the city, encouraging as it did the further development of market gardens such as that staffed by the Gardener and his Dutch wife Martha in Brome's play, and also of the frequently adjacent tavern and supper rooms with their lodgings or rooms for hire:

GARDENER: What did the rich old merchant spend upon the poor young gentle-man's wife in the yellow bedchamber?
MARTHA: But eight and twenty shillings, and kept the room almost two hours. I had no more of him.
GARDENER: And what the knight with the broken citizen's wife (that goes so lady-like) in the blue bedchamber?
MARTHA: Almost four pound.
GARDENER: That was pretty well for two.
MARTHA: But her husband and a couple of servingmen had a dish of asparagus and three bottles of wine, besides the broken meat into one o' the arbours [ . . . ]                                                                                      (3.1.416–21)

Examining a range of references to asparagus gardens in Caroline plays (including Massinger's *The City Madam* and Shirley's *Hyde Park*), Matthew Steggle has speculated that they could be those 'sparagus gardens' marked on maps of the Lambeth Marshes region later in the century.[35] My purpose here is not to conduct a detective hunt to pin down an actual locale as the definitive site of Brome's play; what interests me, rather, is the cultural landscape in which the play operates. An intriguing connection between place and politics in Brome's text exists between the marshlands on which the asparagus intended to feed the London elite was grown and the aforementioned Fen lands that were such a topic of dispute in the 1630s. The Gardener of *The Sparagus Garden* draws a direct comparison between the land he works and the land he hopes to purchase by his labour. This land purchase would, it seems, be a product of Fen drainage schemes similar to those being perpetrated by Martha's countryman Vermuyden in East Anglia:

[35] Steggle, *Richard Brome*, pp. 72–3. The Lambeth setting should not, however, preclude us from considering simultaneous real-life sources for Brome's imaginative geography. There were a number of such pleasure gardens at the time. Cuyper's Gardens, for example (its title later corrupted to 'Cupid's Gardens'), opened in 1634. It stood on lands sold off for the purpose by Thomas Howard, Lord Arundel, one of the chief property developers, along with his wife Alathea, in the previously mentioned locale of the Strand and is probably one of the sites on which Brome's dramatic (and hybridized) recreation is partly based.

GARDENER: [...] two or three years' toil more while our trade is in request, and fashion will make us purchasers. I had once a hope to have bought this manor of marshland for the resemblance it has to the Low Country soil you came from – to ha' made you a Bankside lady. We may in time be somewhat. But what did you take yesterday, Mat, in all; what had you, ha? (3.1.414)

The Gardener vocalizes his desire to make Martha a 'Bankside lady' and there is in this a knowing joke for members of the audience. That phrase was a byword for a prostitute, although there is no reason to believe from the text that the Gardener means it anything but sincerely – the joke is entirely for sceptics in the audience to produce for themselves. Place and landscape are made here to speak on the stage both in a localized sense (with serious and humorous import) and metaphorically to invoke national issues and concerns, not least about land management.

## Theatre on the water

As the previously cited opening to *Britannia Triumphans* indicated, the Thames was significant on both local and national levels. It was undoubtedly a river to think with and imagine, just as all rivers functioned as actual and symbolic geography in the Caroline cultural imaginary. Andrew McRae has written of the long literary tradition of river writing, not least river poetry, which favoured the trope of the wedding or ceremonial unification of rivers as a means of thinking about the relationship between major rivers and inland waterways and the more complex network of tributaries and estuaries in which they participated.[36] Naturally, the centrality of the Thames to that literary mythology has been well documented and its presence can be felt in Munday's aforementioned additional chapters on the river in the later editions of Stow's *Survey*: 'Our famous River being thus brought to *London*, and hasting on apace, to meete with *Oceanus* her amorous Husband [...]'.[37]

By the late 1620s and 1630s the literary tradition of river weddings had become an almost hackneyed trope. Court masques, however, remained absurdly fond of such images and ideas of water. This was not surprising, perhaps, since processions on the river were a standard feature of royal ceremonials. There are striking contemporary descriptions, for example, of a waterborne progress along the Thames by Charles I and his new French Catholic bride Henrietta Maria in the early months of his reign:

[36] McRae, *Literature and Domestic Travel*, pp. 21–66.
[37] Stow, *The Survey*, pp. 14–15, C2r–C2v.

The last night, at five o'clock, (there being a very great shower) the king and queen, in the royal barge, with many other barges of honour, and thousands of boats, passed through London bridge to Whitehall; infinite numbers, besides those in wherries, standing in houses, ships, lighters, western barges; and on each side of the shore, fifty good ships discharging their ordnance, as their majesties passed along by, as last of all, the Tower did . . . the king and queen were both in green suits. The barge windows, not withstanding the vehement shower, were open.[38]

The postscript to this letter offers a vivid impression of the throng of people who served as spectators to this public performance of the royal union – a performance that was to be repeated in many guises and often in dramatic contexts. The correspondent, Dr Meddus, was apparently part of a waterborne section of the audience: 'Our ship, whereupon stood above a hundred people, not being balanced nor well tied to the shore, and they standing all upon one side, was overturned and sunk – all that were upon her tumbling into the Thames, yet was not any lost that I can hear of.'[39]

A pamphlet authored by John Taylor, the waterman-poet, in 1625 in response to a particularly horrendous outbreak of plague in the capital that year offered a grim revisionist version of this image. In the summer months of 1625, temporarily stationed in Oxford with the court, which had made one of its traditional seasonal escapes from the worst of the plague, Taylor chaperoned Henrietta Maria on a trip up the Thames. The royal barge was gliding past key monarchical sites such as Runnymede and Windsor Castle, producing itself in turn as a kind of elegant history lesson for the queen consort, recently married and recently arrived from France. However, the spectators for this river journey as described by Taylor in his pamphlet called *The Fearful Summer, or London's Calamity*, offer a haunting inversion of the usual riverbank audiences for royal barge processions. Crowds of starving homeless people lined the banks; they were emaciated Londoners fleeing the city. These refugees from the plague met with what Taylor describes as a 'bitter wormwood welcome', and were turned back by rural communities for fear that they carried the contagion with them, many of them as a result dying of starvation or exposure to the elements.[40] The full aesthetic and emotional impact of Taylor's text relies on its readership being only too familiar with the more conventional form of royal river theatre; once

---

[38] Dr Meddus to the Reverend Joseph Mead, 17 June 1625 (Birch, *The Court and Times of Charles I*, 1: 29–30).
[39] Birch, *The Court and Times of Charles I*, 1: 30.
[40] John Taylor, *The Fearful Summer, or London's Calamity* (Oxford, 1626), sig. A3r. Cf. Benjamin Woolley, *The Herbalist: Nicholas Culpeper and the Fight for Medical Freedom* (London: HarperCollins, 2004), pp. 86–7.

again the gaps being filled through the act of reception are indicative of the everyday relationships with water and social performance that were part and parcel of early modern experience.

The civic as opposed to monarchical ritual that was still regularly playing out the cultural significance of the Thames for the population of London at this time was the Lord Mayor's pageant. These pageants tended to be a blend of water- and land-based ritual and, not surprisingly, the precedent of Venetian republican ceremonial was regularly invoked. One rich example of this in action is Thomas Dekker's *London's Tempe, or The Field of Happines* (1629), staged for the installation of James Campbell as Mayor on 29 October. Despite its land-locked title, the entertainment was deeply invested in the spaces and symbolism of water and, in particular, the River Thames, down which part of the mayoral procession journeyed.[41] It was traditional in these ceremonies for barge processions to be ordered in the strict hierarchy of the sponsoring guilds (as is stressed at the end of the published version of *London's Tempe*). The barges were dressed in the ceremonial insignia of those guilds such as coats of arms.[42]

In *London's Tempe*, the first presentation was a 'Water-worke', presented by Oceanus, King of the Sea or 'King of Waues' as he is also titled in the entertainment.[43] He appeared riding on a marine chariot, which was intended to resemble a 'siluer Scollup', led by two sea horses. Oceanus talks of how his oceans and seas are full of:

> *Horrid Sea-fights, Nauies Ouerthrowne,*
> *Hands half-drownd in Bloud, Pyrates pell mell,*
> Turkes *slauish tugging Oares, The* Dunkerks *Hells,*
> *The* Dutchmans *Thunder, And the* Spaniards *Lightning.*[44]

This constitutes a highly topical glance at Caroline fortunes at sea. Between 1625 and 1631, Charles I's fleet had suffered indignities at the hands of French and Spanish ships, in particular the Spanish squadron at Dunkirk (the 'Dunkerks Hell' alluded to here), which took over three hundred ships in the first five years of his reign, equating at that time to at least one-fifth of

---

[41] Tracy Hill makes the point that the river metaphors, of weddings and ceremonials, deployed by Munday in his added chapters on the Thames in the 1618 and 1633 editions of Stow's *Survey* were directly inflected by his own role as a maker of these mayoral pageants (*Anthony Munday and Civic Culture: Theatre, History, and Power in Early Modern London, 1580–1633* (Manchester University Press, 2004), p. 177).

[42] James Knowles, 'The Spectacle of the Realm: Civic Consciousness, Rhetoric, and Ritual in Early Modern London', in J. R. Mulryne and Margaret Shewring (eds.), *Theatre and Government under the Early Stuarts* (Cambridge University Press, 1993), pp. 157–89 (166).

[43] Thomas Dekker, *London's Tempe, or the Field of Happiness* (London, 1629), sig. A4r.

[44] Dekker, *London's Tempe*, sig. A4v.

the fleet. The same ships also suffered from the 'slave-raids of the Barbary corsairs'.[45] This is the world of the open sea that we will discuss later in this chapter, but Oceanus invokes them here to stress all the things that the Thames is *not*. Not only does the Thames far excel these tumultuous seas, but it beats European rivals in a competition for power and splendour. Oceanus invokes the Nile and the Ganges as well as neighbouring European rivers such as the Rhine and the Volga in this context. He then looks to the maritime republic of Venice. As already noted, London's mayoral pageants were frequently placed in direct comparison with that city's water-based civic ceremonies, not least the annual marriage to the sea performed by the Doge:

> That Grand Canale, where (stately) once a yeare
> A Fleete of bridal Gondoletts appeare,
> To marry with a golden Ring (To us Hurld Into the sea).[46]

Oceanus, now happily steering his hyperbolic course of praise to London and the Thames, suggests that Venice is nevertheless a poor match for this event; Venice, he states, 'A poore Lankscip is, / To these full Braueries of Thamesis'.[47]

The second presentation is of a 'Proud swelling Sea' bearing a sea lion. This section of the pageant is intended to represent the East India Company, one of several established trading companies that worked the seas and of which James Campbell himself was a member. Tethys, wife and queen consort to Oceanus, rides the sea lion attended by a merman and a mermaid (the longstanding masquing credentials of this particular character stemming from Samuel Daniel's *Tethys Festival* in 1610). At this point, the presentational barges head for the shoreline and for dry land. This amphibious masque, in a sense reflecting the dual geographical identity of the city, returns to the river at its close for both practical and symbolic reasons when the guests all return to their barges to make the journey homewards. That water frames the festivities in this self-conscious way was felt to be something exceptional even at the time, as is recorded in

[45] N. A. Rodger, *The Safeguard of the Sea: A Naval History of Britain, 660–1649* (New York: Norton, 1997), pp. 361–2; see also Claire Jowitt, 'Introduction: Pirates? The politics of plunder, 1550–1650', in Claire Jowitt (ed.), *Pirates? The Politics of Plunder 1550–1650* (London: Palgrave Macmillan, 2007), pp. 3–19 (12).

[46] Dekker, *London's Tempe*, sig. B1r. Dekker had deployed this form of allusion in previous pageants, including that co-authored with John Webster in 1624, *Monuments of Honour* (ll. 40–3); see Knowles, 'The Spectacle of the Realm', p. 166. Dekker's 1612 *Troia-Nova Triumphans or London Triumphing* also makes complex use of ship and shipping imagery as a central imaginative trope (Knowles, 'The Spectacle of the Realm', 168).

[47] Dekker, *London's Tempe*, sig. B1r.

the published version of the pageant, which comments that 'this yeere, gives one Remarkable Note to after times, that all the Barges followed one another (every Company in their degree) in a stately and Maiesticall order'.[48]

James Knowles has stressed that these pageants were performances of the body politic that emphasized citizen participation.[49] *London's Tempe*, for example, mentions the 'Thronges of People' attending the 1629 event and Heywood's 1631 pageant *Londons Ius Honorarium* in honour of George Whitmore of the Haberdashers' Company (one of the masques in which he collaborated with the Christmas family on the production) acknowledges that the streets of London were full with the mayor's 'Children' or 'issue' by means of the beautiful description of all the main buildings being 'Tyled with faces'. (Compare Figure 4 which depicts the street audiences for the entry of Henrietta Maria's mother Marie de Medicis into the streets of Cheapside in 1638.[50]) Consequently, Kathleen McLuskie sees these pageants as a 'kind of street theatre [ . . . ] not fully dramatic in form', although she stresses that *London's Tempe* is one of the more fully realized entertainments.[51]

*London's Tempe* further indicates that some of these pageants were not only street theatre, but also maritime or riverine theatre, a quasi-dramatic form in which the river represents a weird mixture of the symbolic and the actual. The tension between those two states in contemporary Caroline perceptions of the Thames is beautifully embodied by a pamphlet printed in 1641 under the title 'A Strange Wonder or, The Cities Amazement, Being a Relation occasioned by a wonderfull and vnusuall Accident, that happened in the River of Thames, Friday February 4. 1641'. The pamphlet records that on that day, 'two tydes' were seen flowing at London Bridge.[52] The pamphlet, which, intriguingly, records the soundscape that accompanied this meteorological event, 'the last coming with such violence and hideous noyse', weaves between material description and spiritual interpretation of the happening.[53] A text that closes with the message that the double tide

[48] Dekker, *London's Tempe*, sig. C2v.   [49] Knowles, 'The spectacle of the realm', p. 158.
[50] Dekker, *London's Tempe*, sig. A3r; Thomas Heywood's *London's Ius Honorarium* is cited from Kathleen E. McLuskie, *Dekker and Heywood* (London: St Martin's Press, 1994), pp. 78–9 and derives from J. Pearson (ed.), *The Dramatic Works of Thomas Heywood*, 6 vols. (New York: Russell & Russell, 1964), 4: 275.
[51] McLuskie, *Dekker and Heywood*, p. 75.
[52] Brief mention of this particular pamphlet is made in Peter Ackroyd, *The Thames: Sacred History* (London: Chatto & Windus, 2007).
[53] 'A strange wonder or, the cities amazement' (London, 1641), sig. A1r.

Figure 4: Scene in Cheapside during the visit in 1638 of Marie de Medicis, with detail of left section depicting spectators watching from nearby buildings.

ENTRE ROIALLE DE LA REYNE MERE DU ROI TRES CHRESTIEN DANS LA VILLE DE LONDRES

was a harbinger from God to warn against dealing with papists is elsewhere almost naturalistic in its depiction of the scene:[54]

it was high Water at one of the Clocke: at noone, a time (by reason so accommodated for all imployments, either by Water or Land) very fit to afford witnesse, of a strange and notorious accident, after it was full high Water, and that it flowed its full due time as all Almanacks set downe, and Water-men the unquestionable Prognositicators in that affaire, with confidence mainetaine it stood a quiet still dead Water a full houre and halfe, without moving or returning any way never so little, yea the water-men flung in Stickes to the streame, as neare as they could guesse which lay in the Water as vpon the Earth, without moving this way, or that.[55]

The watermen continue to test this strange spectacle by trying to set sail dishes and wooden buckets on the surface of the water, but to no avail. At this point they launch out in their boats, but find themselves completely stilled: 'the water seeming as plaine, quiet even, and stable, as a pavement under the Arch'.[56] Then, the loud roaring that announces the tidal surge is heard as it races from Greenwich to the bridge itself, 'tumbling, roaring, and foaming in that furious manner that it was horror unto all that beheld it'.[57]

This pamphlet is an indicator of the way in which Caroline people chose to articulate physical weather events. The 1620s and 1630s were a period of deeply unsettled weather patterns and that fed into the mindset of those already febrile with thoughts of religious controversy and battered by economic hardships.[58] By 1641, when the 'two tydes' pamphlet was authored, the possibility of civil war was beginning to loom. What is actually being described is a storm surge – high onshore winds which effectively blow water toward the coast, but, having nowhere to go, it mounts up (the great flood of 1953 in East Anglia in the UK was just such an example). There appear to have been several of these during the period of Charles I's reign. An unidentified writer to Reverend Joseph Mead notes on 13 December 1626: 'On Thursday last week at two in the afternoon was high water here, and at eight at night, high water again, and so a double tide',[59] and again in 1629, when Mead himself writes to Sir Martin Stuteville: 'The great tide in the Thames did more than £10,000 damage in

---

[54] 'A strange wonder', sig. A3v.    [55] 'A strange wonder', sig. A3r.
[56] 'A strange wonder', sig. A3v.    [57] 'A strange wonder', sig. A3v.
[58] On the significance of weather in the context of almanacs produced and annotated in these years, see Adam Smyth, *Autobiography in Early Modern England* (Cambridge University Press, 2010), pp. 15–56.
[59] 13 December 1626; Birch, *The Court and Times of Charles I*, 2: 42.

Thames Street, in cellars, shops, and warehouses, and made 3 or 4 breaches from Blackwall towards Gravesend, whereby much cattle and sheep were drowned, grain and corn spoiled. They say it was near three feet higher than any man can remember'.[60]

In 1626, Mead had written to Stuteville of another comparable Thames 'weather event': 'We have had here much talk ever since Tuesday, of a dreadful tempest of thunder and lightning at London, with such a storm of hail, as made the streets like channels of rivers, and drowned many cellars, &c; and in the concussion, a strange spectacle on the Thames near Whitehall drew the eyes of many with amazement to behold it'.[61] The image here of Thameside itself as a form of theatre, audiences gathering on its banks for spectacles, both organized and happenstance, is inescapable (the appearance in the Thames of a stranded whale in 2006 and the large crowds that gathered to witness the rescue attempt provides a modern comparison).[62] Mead says he received a letter from a (unidentified) friend who had been eye-witness to the event and quotes that verbatim in the middle of his own correspondence (letter dated 13 June 1626; the phenomenal water event itself was on Monday 12 June):

['Yesterday, being Monday, we beheld a strange spectacle upon the Thames; for in the great storm of thunder, lightning, and hail, about three o'clock in the afternoon, the water began to be much troubled hard by the garden in Lambeth parish, over against Sir H. Fiennes's stairs. A sculler (being then tide of ebb) creeping along under the shore, was fallen into this troubled place before he could espy it, which was then so strong, that it turned his boat six times round, yet, with hard labour, he and his fare escaped, and ran ashore among the willows, presently the water very much rarefied like a mist, began to rise into the form of a circle of thirty yards compass, and ten feet high. The inside was hollow, and white with froth; without, there was a lett of water (as those that will be wise call it, for you must not say prodigious) ran very impetuously down the water, as far as the point, then took her course, crossing the water, and beat itself amain against the walls of York House Garden, at the very place where the duke is building a pair of new stairs closer by the House. Therewith beating, it broke itself, a thick smoke, like that of a brewer's chimney, ascending from it as high as a man could discern. All this time, the weather being very black, there appeared right over above it, as the beholders thought, a very bright cloud to the amazement of Whitehall, and many

[60] Christ College, 7 November 1629; Birch, *The Court and Times of Charles I*, 2: 42.
[61] Christ College, 17 June 1626 (Birch, *The Court and Times of Charles I*, 1: 113).
[62] An early modern parallel to the phenomenon of beached whales is found in the 1645 pamphlet 'A Great Miracle at Sea'. See also Dan Brayton's unpublished paper 'Beached Whales and Providence: English Literary References in the Sixteenth and Seventeenth Centuries', given at the 34th Annual Whaling History Symposium at the New Bedford Whaling Museum in October 2009. I am grateful to Dan for sharing forthcoming work in advance of publication.

very great courtiers, who beheld it out of their windows, as did many hundreds more. During the storm, the wall of St Andrews Church in Holborn was beaten down, and many of the coffins of the dead, which lay there buried, discovered'.][63]

That it should be the residence of the Duke of Buckingham, the Lord High Admiral himself, who had supposed jurisdiction over the Thames tides, and that his property is presented as chief victim of this warning event – a localized tornado, judging by the descriptions – is telling. The Duke's ambitions are quietly delineated (and punctured) in the image sketched of his damaged building works. York House, locale for the Duke's expansionist tendencies, becomes the central site in the story, as if it has been singled out for the attention of the tide. Buckingham would, of course, by a strange quirk of fate, be the victim of portside assassination by John Felton, a disgruntled sailor, later that year. Mead confirms in a later letter to Stuteville of 24 June that the eye-witness report he proffered earlier of the tornado has been confirmed by many others: 'I hear of a whirlwater upon the Thames confirmed by all I speak with', as if such an aberrant happening required the confirmation of multiple eyes.[64] In turn, that requirement for shared spectatorship cannot help but lend the narratives of these occasions a certain inherent theatricality.[65]

The ways in which the river was associated with theatre, spectacle, and performance in this period were, then, many and diverse and extended far beyond formal subgenres of the dramatic such as the pageant, to encompass everything from ceremonial to plague, from celebration to punishment (secular and divine), and from civic ritual to storm. Drama was able to rely on a multifaceted understanding of the theatrical potential of rivers on the part of its audiences when restaging these liquid landscapes in the form of play, entertainment, and masque.

### Inland waterways

It is clear from letters and pamphlets of the period that the actions of water were frequently understood in wider national and spiritual contexts.[66]

---

[63] Birch, *The Court and Times of Charles I*, 1: 114.

[64] Birch, *The Court and Times of Charles I*, 1: 114.

[65] Cf. discussions of theatrical and performative events and narrative accounts in John McGavin's thought-provoking work on early modern Scotland; see John J. McGavin, *Theatricality and Narrative in Medieval and Early Modern Scotland* (Aldershot: Ashgate, 2007).

[66] For a more detailed discussion of the significance of water to the cultural imaginary of the island nation of Britain, see Maggie Kilgour, 'Writing in water', *English Literary Renaissance* (1999), 282–305 (284).

McRae has made persuasive arguments for rivers as emblems of mobility in this period, linking this to emergent ideas of national identity and practical arguments for increasing the navigability of canals and waterways. Related concerns surfaced in dramatic texts of the day, not least in provincial performative contexts. In one play, whose 1636 title page declared that it was 'diuers times' presented in Nottinghamshire 'with great applause', possibly in a private household context (this aspect will be further discussed in Chapter 3), William Sampson used his fifth act to stage the case for improved navigability in the region in which the play was set as well as performed. *The Vow-Breaker or The Fair Maid of Clifton* ostensibly takes place in the recent Elizabethan past and brings the queen herself onstage in a remarkable sequence towards the close.[67] There, we see Elizabeth rewarding brave Nottinghamshire soldiers who have fought on her behalf and in turn are receiving conventional gifts and praise from the Mayor of Nottingham.[68] The Queen decides to reward the Mayor's loyalty by answering his 'former motion made for the Trent' (5.1. sig. I4v).[69] 'You'd have it navigable to Gainsborough / So to Boston, Kingston, Humber, and Hull' (sig. I4v), she notes. Her reference occasions a speech of historiographical recollection by the Mayor, who notes that Elizabeth first made the Trent 'navigable'. The Mayor then revisits the further past, recalling the reigns of Richard II and Henry IV and how Owen Glendower had stopped 'the water-courses of the flowing Trent / [and how] By that meanes our navigable course was stop'd' (sig. K1r). Mary Hill Cole has indicated how frequently local civic and regional concerns of this kind were staged as part of the ceremonials surrounding royal progress.[70] Petitions relating to local improvements such as harbours, silting, and fishing rights in coastal communities and canals and navigation in inland towns and cities were regularly presented to the monarch. Sampson's play shows Elizabeth I responding positively to the Nottingham Mayor's request and may in the process have offered a model of good practice to the monarch of the day. The slippage between historical representation and an awareness of being 'in the moment', typical of the subgenre of household theatre, makes it difficult to draw any clear distinction between historical fact and contemporary aspiration in this scene.

[67] Alternative understandings of this ambiguous title page are part of a further discussion of this play text in the context of household and regional theatre in Chapter 3.

[68] On the traditional gift-giving ceremonies of royal progresses, see Mary Hill Cole, *The Portable Queen: Elizabeth I and the Politics of Ceremony* (Amherst: University of Massachusetts, 1999), e.g. pp. 73, 101.

[69] William Sampson, *The Vow-Breaker or The Fair Maid of Clifton* (London, 1636).

[70] Cole, *The Portable Queen*, pp. 107–9.

Navigability of inland waterways was certainly a pressing concern in the decade when Sampson's play was written and performed. Munday spends a considerable section of the additional chapters on the Thames in his 1633 edition of Stow's *Survey* reflecting on the illegal fishing taking place in the river and the perils to both livestock and passengers posed by the placing of traps and nets.[71] Related concerns surface in the decade's newsletters. One written in February 1637 notes the case of William Sandys versus Sir William Russel, in which Russel was accused of blocking Sandys's attempts at improving navigation in his region:

Sandys hath undertaken to make the river Avon, in the counties of Worcester, Gloucester, and Warwick navigable, by an invention he hath, and was encouraged to do it by the general approbation of the principal men of those counties, and of the towns corporate through which the river of Avon runs, it being eighty miles deep in a vale, counties most part of the year not passable with carts.[72]

Russel was eventually found by the King to have hindered the work and was sent to the Fleet prison to consider his actions, but the concerns expressed in this epistolary account of the hearing confirm an interest in rivers as routes *into* places as well as through them, a means of opening up counties to better access.

## Severn and Trent: written on water

As well as being trade routes and routes to places, as noted in the Introduction, rivers were potent political boundaries. The River Trent marked a border, in the cultural imaginary at least, between a notional north and south, a fact that was underlined by the area of the Council of the North's jurisdiction. Similarly, the Council of Wales and the Marches regarded the Severn as a potent watery marker of the troubled borders between the English shire countries, notionally in its control, and the nation of Wales.[73] In this section, I single out the Severn and the Trent for analysis, partly because of their relationship to these significant councils. They functioned as symbolic extensions of the Caroline arm of policy in the regions. Both the Severn and the Trent became subjects for work by major

---

[71] Stow, *The Survey*, p. 19, sig. C4r. Munday also spends time on the official role of the Water Bailiff who patrols and polices the waterways and on the meetings of court sessions for the hearing of matters related to unsustainable fishing practices.

[72] Mr E.R. to Sir Thomas Puckering, Bart, 21 February 1636–7, in Birch, *The Court and Times of Charles I*, 2: 283.

[73] See David J. Baker, '"Stands Scotland where it did?": Shakespeare on the march', in Willy Maley and Andrew Murphy (eds.), *Shakespeare and Scotland* (Manchester University Press, 2004), pp. 20–36.

early modern authors, even though critical history has not always articulated these authors' careers with these particular texts at their centre. John Milton, accredited at least as author in 1634 of the collaborative production that was *A Masque Presented at Ludlow Castle* (also known as 'Comus'), and Ben Jonson, responsible for *The Sad Shepherd*, an unfinished play located in the Vale of Belvoir and on the riverbanks of the Trent in 1637, offer their own politicized and localized versions of liquid landscapes respectively early and late in their literary careers.[74] Both of these texts form part of the analysis of forest habitats in the following chapter, so my examination of them here is restricted to those passages and performative moments which deal expressly with the theme of rivers, and the cultural and literary tradition of water.

*A Masque* is for a large part forest-bound, but in its closing sections it opens outwards not only towards the castle itself, where the symbolic journey of the masque terminates, but to the region in which it was located. In this gesture, the children of the Earl of Bridgewater, who have performed the central children's roles in the masque, are reunited with their father at the castle that is also to be the locus of his installation as the new Lord President of the Council in the Marches.[75] The river that flows not particularly near Ludlow but which represented the symbolic river in Bridgewater's new political jurisdiction was the Severn and one of its tributaries, the Teme, flowed very visibly at the base of the castle, which is located high on a promontory in the town. In a seminal article, Philip Schwyzer has stressed the ways in which the performance text of the *Masque* responds to the Severn's role in political and literary tradition as a crucial boundary or frontier.[76] The goddess associated with that river

---

[74] For a more detailed exposition of rivers as political boundaries, and the relevance, for example, of the Tay and the Tweed to notions of Scottish geopolitics in this period, see Lisa Hopkins, *Shakespeare on the Edge: Border Crossing in the Tragedies and the Henriad* (Aldershot: Ashgate, 2005).

[75] The Council had jurisdictional power in the region and was an extension of the powers of royal prerogative courts such as the Star Chamber and Chancery into the provinces. Bridgewater had been appointed as Lord President as well as Lord Lieutenant of the counties in the region in 1631 but 1634 was the date of his first physical appearance there. On the relevance of the presidential progress he conducted around the region with his family and Lawes that summer, see Cedric C. Brown, 'Presidential travels and instructive augury in Milton's Ludlow masque', *Milton Quarterly*, 21 (1987), 1–12, and his *John Milton's Aristocratic Entertainments* (Cambridge University Press, 1985). See also Chapter 5 of Gordon Campbell and Thomas N. Corns, *John Milton: Life, Work, and Thought* (Oxford University Press, 2008) for a useful summary of Brown's pioneering research. For the performance implications of this experience, see also Susan Bennett and Julie Sanders, 'Rehearsal across space and place: rethinking *A Masque Presented at Ludlow Castle*', forthcoming in Anna Birch and Joanne Tompkins (eds.), *Performing Site-Specific Theatre*.

[76] Philip Schwyzer, 'Purity and danger on the West Bank of the Severn: the cultural geography of *A Masque Presented at Ludlow Castle, 1634*', *Representations*, 60 (1997), 22–48 (24).

was Sabrina, daughter of Locrine, who, as the story goes, was drowned, along with her mother, by the forces that had beaten her father, first king of England, in a bloody battle.

Sabrina was saved by sea nymphs. Her story (with Sabrina often referred to by her Welsh title of Habren) had been retold on many occasions but most significantly in the early seventeenth century by Michael Drayton in his chorographical poetic epic, *Poly-Olbion* (1612, 1622). Sabrina appears on several occasions in Drayton's text, including in Song 7 in the Forest of Dean (referential site, as I will argue in Chapter 2, of much of the *Masque at Ludlow*'s early action) to suppress the lustful satyrs of that domain. It is this Sabrina, emblem of chaste love, the 'gentle nymph' whose 'moist curb sways the smooth Severn stream', to whom Milton assigns the role of guardian angel in the masque, along with the Attendant Spirit who summons her.[77] She appears, apparently from a chariot (effecting an obvious link with the water-based lord mayoral pageants mentioned earlier where Tethys and others appeared in sea-horse drawn carriages) to release the Lady (played by Bridgewater's fifteen-year-old daughter Alice) from the bondage of Comus, himself a version of Drayton's Forest of Dean satyrs.[78] For Schwyzer, Milton's appropriation of the Severn myth of Sabrina is both a harnessing of a centuries-old literary tradition of associating women with rivers (often, as in this instance, a pure woman or virgin who is saved by the waters themselves) and a distinctively English version of this Welsh goddess with all of the national politics that this implies. The invocation of the river is, for me, further evidence that the *Masque* is most clearly comprehensible within the collaborative moment of performance. The spectacular invocation of the Severn in the closing stages of the performance, as with the direct depiction of Ludlow Town and its inhabitants in the final change of 'scene', alludes both to the region and community that surrounded the castle and, by extension, makes visible the cultural geography with which the new president was being required to negotiate.

In the months prior to his death in 1637, Jonson had been effecting his own dramatic engagement with the force and potency, cultural and literal, of a river, this time the River Trent, which flowed so suggestively through

---

[77] The edition of the *Masque at Ludlow* used is the collated version included in Robert Cummings (ed.), *Seventeenth Century Poetry* (Oxford: Blackwell, 2000), l. 825.

[78] Various critics debate the extent to which a real 'chariot' would have been a viable property in a production at the castle (see, for example, William B. Hunter, *Milton's 'Comus': Family Piece* (New York: Whitston Publishing, 1983) and John Demaray, *Milton and the Masque Tradition* (Cambridge, MA: Harvard University Press, 1968), Chapter 5). There are, however, precedents for the use of such machinery in court and provincial entertainments as well as in civic pageantry.

the landscapes and domains of his chief 1630s patron, William Cavendish, the Earl of Newcastle. *The Sad Shepherd*, extant only in fragments, is a tantalizing glimpse of a text that may in practice have born more associations with Milton's 1634 provincial masque than many critics have tended to assume. Certainly, we see in Jonson's version of the Trent a gesture towards the chorographic enterprises of Drayton and to other dramatic precursors such as John Lyly in its regional setting and tone. Whether this was a play intended for a commercial playhouse or for a household entertainment – possibly one that imitated Jonson's earlier 1630s household productions for the Newcastle estates, the *King's Entertainment at Welbeck* in 1633 and *Love's Welcome at Bolsover* in 1634, which had themselves deployed the resonant local and regional myth of Robin Hood and his merry men as part of their aesthetic – its representations of water as a literary, material, and cultural force are striking and resonant. There were clear precedents for Jonson in this: Sampson had made similar links to the River Trent that flowed through the territories of his patron Lord Henry Willoughby in *The Vow-Breaker* just a year previously.

The prologue to *The Sad Shepherd* carefully establishes the very English credentials of this pastoral play: 'it being a fleece, / To match or those of Sicily, or Greece. / His scene is Sherwood' (Prologue, 13–15). The specific resonance of Nottinghamshire's central river to the play is noted by the speaker of this prologue. Eglamour, the eponymous sad shepherd of the title, passes silently over the stage and is described thus to the audience:

> The sad young shepherd, whom we here present,
> [Eglamour,] *the sad shepherd, passeth silently over the stage*
> Like his woe's figure, dark and discontent,
> For his lost love, who in the Trent is said
> To have miscarried. 'Las! What knows the head
> Of a calm river, whom the feet have drowned?
>
> (Prologue, 21–5)

The river is here personified as an elderly storyteller, 'Old Trent' (29), one who can eternally renew his stock (29–30).

In this particular dramatic text, the River Trent is never physically present onstage and yet it is everywhere evoked. It is in the particular plot-line strand of the shepherd Eglamour's grief for his 'lost' love Earine – who, he believes, has been drowned in the high waters of the flooding river – that we receive the most detailed spatial and geographical locations of the play, in a typically brilliant Jonsonian yoking of the pastoral trope of the pathetic fallacy with regional topography:

> Do not I know
> How the vale withered the same day? How Dove,
> Dean, Eye, and Erewash, Idle, Snite, and Soar,
> Each broke his urn, and twenty waters more,
> That swelled proud Trent shrunk themselves dry? That since,
> No sun, or moon, or other cheerful star
> Looked out of heaven;                                   (1.5.51–7)

Jonson's deployment of the regional to deconstruct the tropes or conventions of literary pastoral sits alongside a subtle interrogation of the superstitions surrounding witchcraft. It is equally fascinating how the playwright appropriates the mythical and folkloric elements surrounding a river like the Trent and mixes them up with regional details such as specific tributaries and flooding tendencies.[79] In the midst of his grief, Eglamour offers a remarkable narrative evocation of a flood and its aftermath that he imagines to cause through his weeping, which haunts the imagination, for all that it has to remain resolutely offstage:

> If I could knit whole clouds about my brows,
> And weep like Swithin, or those wat'ry signs,
> The kids that rise then, and drown all the flocks
> Of those rich shepherds dwelling in this vale –
> Those careless shepherds that did let her drown –
> Then I did something; or could make old Trent
> Drunk with my sorrow, to start out in breaches
> To drown their herds, their cattle, and their corn,
> Break down their mills, their dams, o'erturn their weirs,
> And see their houses and whole livelihood,
> Wrought into water with her, all were good:
> I'd kiss the torrent, and those whirls of Trent
> That sucked her in, my sweet Earine.          (1.3.52–64)

Earine apparently drowned while walking near Much the Miller's watermill; at least, that is the narrative spun for Eglamour by the Papplewick witch Maudlin (her clearly asserted Nottinghamshire identity will be revisited in Chapter 2). Asked if they have swept the river for her body, Much gives a strikingly pragmatic answer in which the necessity as well as the cultural symbolism of food is at the centre: 'For fowl and fish we have' (1.3.32). Moments earlier, he has promised a Trent-secured harvest for the feast that Robin Hood is planning: 'all choice that plenty can send in: / Bread, wine,

---

[79] See the contributions by Nicholas Alfrey and Stephen Daniels to the exhibition catalogue to *Trentside*, an exhibition curated at the Djanogly Art Gallery, University of Nottingham by Nicholas Alfrey in 2001.

acates, fowl, feather, fish, or fin, / For which my father's nets have swept the Trent' (1.3.18–20). There is a strong sense, both in Eglamour's evocation of the flood and in these other passing references, of the Trent as a working river, a lived environment and set of spatial practices that encompasses the mills as well as those who glean their living from its waters and shores – that same rich 'margin' on which Eglamour intends to inscribe his grief (1.5.7) – and also the nearby water meadows that create such excellent seasonal grazing lands (Amie, the shepherdess, describes to Marion those times of the year when the 'meadows... [are] grown rough with frost, / The rivers ice-bound, and their currents lost', 2.4.37–8).[80] From this perspective, alongside the 1634 *Masque*, the text with which Jonson's work seems to have the most salient intertextual relationship is *Poly-Olbion* (1612, 1621), the county by county organization of which, and its own awareness of the presiding deities in the localities of the local estate owners, may well have appealed to Jonson's interests. Drayton's two printed parts of *Poly-Olbion* have clear links to the performative aspects of courtly and provincial masques. Many of the rivers, forests, and castles depicted, which were themselves frequently characters who danced and sang in masques, such as Thames and Trent in Samuel Daniel's 1610 *Tethys Festival*, appear in the guise of masque personifications in the woodcut maps that accompanied Drayton's verses in print. These maps are, themselves, like Jonson's play and Milton's provincial masque, a suggestive hybrid of the cartographical, the topographical, and the mythical.

Jonson, like Milton, was deeply aware of the literary precedents for his very English and regional version of stage pastoral. Tracing that literary pastoral inheritance may, in turn, start to make renewed sense of the return to a conscious 'Elizabethanism' for which Anne Barton made such a persuasive case in the 1980s, but also the particular focus on rivers and forests in *The Sad Shepherd*.[81] Drayton is a crucial part of that lineage, but so too was the Elizabethan courtly dramatist, John Lyly. Lyly's *Galatea* is the key text for our purposes. This court drama, written for performance at court before Elizabeth I by the Paul's Boys in 1588, was a decisively and demonstrably English experimentation in the pastoral mode and made its own cultural geographical negotiation with the wetlands landscape of

---

[80] Intriguingly, this is still a working landscape visible in the environs of Belvoir Castle today and as prone to flooding. Bunker, *Making Haste for Babylon* makes intriguing connections between Lincolnshire and Nottinghamshire experiences of this landscape and those who settled and introduced English agricultural practices to the New England saltmarshes in the 1630s (pp. 100, 110–12).

[81] Anne Barton, *Ben Jonson, Dramatist* (Cambridge University Press, 1984), pp. 300–20.

Lincolnshire with which Lyly had direct familial associations. While the playtext's opening scene and lines signal its textual origins in the classical writings of Virgil and Theocritus, in particular, in Virgil's *Eclogues* – the opening line of Virgil's first Eclogue is '*Tityre tu recubans sub legmine fagi* [Tityrus, lying in the shadows of a beech tree]' and this is what we see recreated on stage as *Galatea* commences – the scene tells us we are 'On the banks of the Humber'. This was classical pastoral consciously relocated to Lincolnshire. The unstable Fen-land habitat of the wolds (those same 'drownèd lands of Lincolnshire' referred to by Alken, the witch-hunter, in Jonson's play at 2.8.26) provides Lyly with a perfect English setting for his story of flooded lands and the required ritual sacrifice of a virgin to a monster as a tribute to Neptune. Noticeably, the monster is never seen by the onstage community; are the virgins merely swept away by floods and this has been the explanatory local story woven around such events? Even in his play of gods and goddesses, where Diana, Neptune, Venus, and Cupid all have speaking roles, Lyly retains a sense of geographical realism. In turn, his scepticism towards belief in the power of deities – while the Lincolnshire floods mentioned in the play are associated with gods and monsters, Lyly implies that they have distinctly natural causes – reads very like the dual play of belief and scepticism around witchcraft in Jonson's *The Sad Shepherd* and Milton's *Masque*. Read as an intertextual grouping, these pastoral plays begin to reveal a fascinating blend of the fantastic and the rooted, the literal and the figural. By thinking of Lyly's play as a source text, we begin to confirm the regional embeddedness of both Milton's and Jonson's work as well.

Lincolnshire was certainly a region that Lyly knew first-hand, since his wife had an estate in Mexborough, close by to which the Humber flows. He even incorporated local history and local idiom into the language of his courtly drama. Tityrus talks of the time when the Lincolnshire wolds were under Danelaw (1.1.15–36), and the virgin-stealing monster is called 'the Agar' (see 1.1.53–6), which appears to be a version of the word *eàgor*, a dialect term for the tidal wave on the Humber estuary (again, this telling blend, as in Jonson, of the poeticized and the actual).[82] Crucially, Anne Barton has noted that Lyly's pastoral resurfaced in Caroline culture in printed form in 1632, when Edward Blount assembled six Lyly plays, including *Galatea*, in his folio edition of *Six Court Comedies*.[83] Jonson, an avid reader and open admirer of Lyly (he praises him in the commendatory poem for the 1623

---

[82] The edition used throughout is that edited by G. K. Hunter for the Revels edition of John Lyly, in David Bevington and G. K. Hunter (eds.), *Galatea and Midas* (Manchester University Press, 2000).
[83] Barton and Giddens, *The Sad Shepherd*, *CWBJ*, Introduction, p. 6.

Shakespeare First Folio), was likely to have encountered *Galatea* in this context. Drayton also refers to the same myth in his Lincolnshire 'song' in *Poly-Olbion* (see 18.482–3) and perhaps reading this sent Jonson spinning back to Lyly when creating *The Sad Shepherd* and its resonant imagery of flooding and an unstable watery environment.[84]

We have travelled thus far in this chapter from the wharves and docks of London out through the inland waterways of England, and from the Thames to the Trent, but we have also begun to take on board the complex relationship between the literary understandings of watery environments and the everyday practice and representation of the same. As the second part of this chapter moves out onto the oceans and the high seas, that same complex duality needs to be kept securely in view, as the literary legacy of the sea intersects with the ways in which people interact with and understand their experience of landscapes of water and ice.

PART II: LITTORAL CULTURES AND LITERAL CULTURES: SEAS, SHORELINES, AND THE COASTAL COMMUNITY

*Exploiting the seas*

In *The King's Peace*, C. V. Wedgwood stressed that Charles I's 'dominions were encircled and invaded by the sea. On the western littoral, jagged headlands and rocky cliffs fronted the stormy onslaught of the Atlantic ocean; on the eastern shores the sandy coastline slowly retreated before the pressure of the North Sea'.[85] She went on to note how the sea penetrated

---

[84] We certainly know that Jonson read Drayton's *Poly-Olbion* with some care, since, with typical curtness, he declared its 'failure' as a text in the dialogues with William Drummond of Hawthornden during his 1618–19 sojourn in Scotland – which are recalled in the *Informations* (or *Conversations with Drummond*). In the same passage, Jonson declares that he will try and write his own version of *Poly-Olbion*, proof in itself of an interest in regional matters *c.* 1618–19: 'That Michael Drayton's *Poly-O[l]bion*, if [he] had performed what he promised to write, the deeds of all the worthies, had been excellent' (ll. 18–20); 'That he had an intention to perfect an epic poem, entitled *Heroologia*, of the worthies of his country roused by fame, and was to dedicate it to his country' (ll. 1–3). See Barton on the Drayton–Jonson connections in this respect, *Ben Jonson, Dramatist*, pp. 349–50. In 1620, Jonson's friend and associate, Sir Henry Holland, would publish *Heroologia Anglica*. Following his walk to Scotland, Jonson also explored the possibilities of a 'fisher play' based around Loch Lomond and sent to Drummond for detailed research materials for this purpose (see C. H. Herford and Percy and Evelyn Simpson (eds.), *Ben Jonson*, 11 vols. (Oxford University Press, 1925–52), 1: 208) but this text was either abandoned or lost to the library fire, which destroyed much of Jonson's work in progress in 1623. It is, however, a tantalizing glimpse of Jonson's interests in shoreline or water-based communities in the years leading up to the creation of *The Sad Shepherd*, an interest perhaps reinvigorated by Miltonic versions of something similar in the *Masque at Ludlow*.
[85] Wedgwood, *The King's Peace*, p. 23.

inland via estuaries and waterways; and that the country had areas of bog, marsh, and quicksand where water threatened always to reclaim the land.[86] Like the River Thames, the sea had relevance to domestic and foreign policies. Coastlines and shorelines were, perhaps, the most ambivalent geographical site in this context, performing, as they did, national and local functions, speaking, as they did, to the supposedly firm fact of land – ownable, mappable, definable real estate – and the unpredictable element of water.

Ports such as Yarmouth or Bristol had strong localized cultures, but they also looked seawards towards their trading partners and their communities often had experience or knowledge from others of life away from the terra firma of the nation. They were vulnerable to water-based operatives such as smugglers and pirates, who, as characters, pace the stages of commercial Caroline theatre. The victims of these coastal operatives also figure, albeit in an offstage capacity. One of the spectral geographies of Brome's *The Northern Lass* (1629) is a coastal community in the West Country parish from which Camitha (later Constance) Holdup, the prostitute, has been forced to depart and come to the capital. Justice of the Peace, Sir Paul Squelch, recalls her father, a commissioner of the peace who fell into disgrace:

SQUELCH: Holdup? I have heard of him, and know what 'twas that sunk him. He lived by the seaside; 'twas trading with the pirates, buying their goods, and selling them victals. (4.1.659)

In another of Brome's richly resonant, albeit fleeting, references the cor-poreal figure of Camitha on the stage – doubly vulnerable in view of recently having given birth – conjures up for audience imaginations the black-market economy and nefarious practices of coastal villages in the early seventeenth century.

If there are few extant plays that focused on smugglers and coastal communities *per se*, seafaring dramas clearly had a place on the Caroline stage. The second part of Heywood's *The Fair Maid of the West* is a firmly Caroline play text, performed, apparently to great success, at Whitehall Palace before Charles and Henrietta Maria in 1631, in tandem with the first part, which had first been performed *c*. 1597–1603. Both parts were published together in 1631, indicating a Caroline predilection for their seafaring and romantic content. Many critics have noted the distinctly

---

[86] Wedgwood, *The King's Peace*, p. 23.

different atmosphere of the second part, ascribing to it specifically Caroline cultural values and thereby endorsing claims made elsewhere that Caroline drama can be seen as a distinct genre and even set of practices when compared to its Elizabethan and Jacobean predecessors, for all their implicit intertextuality and intertheatricality.[87] The spatialities of the first part of *Fair Maid* are beyond my remit here, although, with its Plymouth harbourside and tavern scenes, the play confirms a vigorous interest in cultural geography in Heywood's dramatic output.[88] Part 2 picks up the story of Bess, the tavern wench, who has now become a woman performing her cultural role on the open oceans, facing numerous setbacks and adventures in her quest to find a settled love with Spencer (whom for a large part of Part 1 she presumed dead) in Fez, where she is the object of Mullisheg's lustful desire and subject of his wife's jealousy. It is 3.2 which finds us on the ship itself. The wooden stage becomes a ship deck in a striking theatrical trope, which chimes with the claims of many maritime historians that the ship community can be best comprehended in theatrical and performative terms.[89] Clem, climbing the maintop, spies Spencer in a boat rowing towards them (another rich evocation of the ocean as the space just off-stage and out of the spectators' view) and Bess initially thinks that they are saved from Mullisheg's wrath and are ready to set sail for England, only to realize that Spencer's honour forces him to return once again to Fez to pay his due to the noble bashaw who saved his life.[90]

Elsewhere, the text is even more explicit about the need for an early modern (indeed, for any) playhouse-situated theatre audience to imagine the ocean. In 3.4, spectators are instructed quite literally to imagine Bess and Spencer finally under sail, only for news of a French pirate ship to reach them. Spencer and Goodlack gain access to the French ship only for the wind to turn and part the two ships and the two lovers once again:

> at that instant
> The billows swell'd and body use to part
> With no less force these lovers are divided.
> He wafts to her and she makes signs to him.

---

[87] See my *Caroline Drama: The Plays of Massinger, Ford, Shirley and Brome* (Plymouth: Northcote House, 1999).

[88] These ideas are echoed in Richard Rowland's recent monograph *Thomas Heywood's Theatre: Locations, Translations, and Conflict* (Aldershot: Ashgate, 2010).

[89] Edwin Hutchins, *Cognition in the Wild* (Cambridge, MA: MIT Press, 1995).

[90] Lucy Munro also suggests in a private correspondence the relevance of this to the popularity of Shakespeare's *Pericles* in the 1630s, another seabound and ship-based text for large parts of its action.

He calls and she replies. They both grow hoarse
With shrieking out their last farewell.

(3.4.12–17)[91]

The ship and the open ocean are one particular set of spatialities, but the ocean also brings into play (as several scenes in *The Fair Maid of the West* make clear) the liminal space of the shoreline, which both looks inward to its nation-based identity and outwards to the ocean and the further horizon of possibilities.

Shorelines and coastlines are only notionally fixed. As changing maps of the East Anglian coastline indicate, they are permanently evolving boundaries, fluid frontiers, a contact zone between land and water that raises a pertinent set of issues relating to change, mutability, and drift. This liminal space of the shoreline found a particular point of reference in early modern culture in the region of Goodwin sands, as one of those spaces or places where water can make land temporarily disappear. In Brome's *The Demoiselle* (1637), Sir Humphrey Dryground, another of the playwright's 'decayed knights' like Mendicant in *The Court Beggar*, has a project to solve his debts. Vermin, the usurer, speculates (perhaps playing on Dryground's suggestive name) that this must be a drainage scheme. This confirms our earlier supposition that investment in drainage schemes became a stage-shorthand for suggesting get-rich-quick mentalities. To stress the hopelessness of such schemes, Vermin locates this particular one in the treacherous Goodwin sands off the Kentish coastline where loss of life as well as property is distinctly possible: 'Is it not to drain the Goodwins? To be lord / Of all the treasure buried in the sands there?' (1.1.21).

For many, the sea was the ultimate source of investment in this era of exploration, colonization, and emergent imperialism. It certainly had a very practical role in the economy of Charles I's domain: 'At least half the King's subjects derived their living directly from or indirectly from the sea'.[92] The oceans and their counterpart rivers and estuaries were central to the material production of foodstuffs to feed the soaring populations of London and elsewhere, and it is intriguing to note how particular kinds of waters, river, and estuary, are associated with particular kinds of marine produce in early modern drama. Mentions of mussels, cockles, sprats, and eels (and these are surprisingly numerous, a key, in part, to the diet of the early seventeenth century and the importance of fish as a staple foodstuff) can be a guide

---

[91] Thomas Heywood, in Robert K. Turner, Jr (ed.), *The Fair Maid of the West Parts 1 and 2* (London: Edward Arnold, 1968).
[92] Wedgwood, *The King's Peace*, p. 24.

to region and place as much as regional accent on the Caroline stage. For example, the Thames estuary held a 'teeming population' of sprats and eels and this may explain some of their particular resonance for London stage plays. In *The Demoiselle*, the previously cited exchange between Dryground and Vermin on the former's schemes to solve his bankruptcy, his lack of liquidity (and note that bankruptcy is itself a journey into unstable waters, into fluidity or liquidation) includes a striking deployment of metaphors of eel and mud to describe the slippery nature of financial dealings in the city. The world of the Thames estuary is all too vividly evoked in the poetics of this exchange:

VERMIN: You spirited men call money dirt and mud.
    I say it is the eel.
DRYGROUND:           And you the mud
    That foster it.
VERMIN:           It is an eel, I say,
    In such sleek hands as yours; from whence it glides –      (1.1.7–9)

Lampreys were sourced from the Severn estuary; pilchards in Plymouth and Penzance; Berwick was famous for salmon and shellfish; Yarmouth for its herring. Ships also went out for cod, and later for whaling, from the ports of East Anglia – from Lynn, Southwold, Dunwich, and Aldeburgh.[93] Not surprisingly, fishing rights in Scotland were a cause of ongoing grievance throughout this period; and there were regular battles with Dutch rivals, especially around the Orkneys. There was also considerable labour expended in the claiming of supposedly pristine wilderness for English interests.

By the 1630s, remarkably enough, the seemingly remote, largely ice-bound region of Spitsbergen had become the centre of a whaling industry performed by Dutch, Danish, English, and Scottish participants. The Dutch had discovered Spitsbergen in 1596 and by 1607, Henry Hudson had visited on behalf of the London Muscovy Company.[94] By 1636, the industry would be significant enough in terms of profitability for Charles I to declare the 'importation of whale fines, or whale oile, into his Majesties dominions' the monopoly of the company.[95] Veritable 'townships' had sprung up on

[93] Wedgwood, *The King's Peace*, p. 24.
[94] Details derived from Sir W. Martin Conway (ed.), *Early Dutch and English Voyages to Spitsbergen in the Seventeenth Century* (London: Hakluyt Society, 1904). Georgina Harding published a novel *The Solitude of Thomas Cave* (London: Bloomsbury, 2007) that is based on many of these contemporary documents. I am grateful to Georgina for her generosity in sharing research and discussions about her novel.
[95] The proclamation was printed in London in 1636.

the coastal edge of Spitsbergen that not only housed the whalers and their staff of helpers such as cooks, coopers, and so on in wooden huts or 'tents', as they tended to refer to them in logbooks and journals, but also the apparatus for treating the whale carcasses on site, producing the oil, blubber, and whalebone that were such valuable commodities in their home countries. The existence of these communities is remarkable enough – and the considerable hardships that the men endured are testified to in the aforementioned logbooks – but it is the publishing industry that grew up around them at home in London, Amsterdam, and elsewhere that also testifies to deep public interest in the experiences of those who had travelled to the icy northern regions.

There was, of course, high drama in many of those accounts which made it into print. In 1630, for example, an English ship managed to sail away at the end of the whaling season leaving behind a boat and its crew. One of the members of that crew, Edward Pelham, wrote an astonishing account of their experience of overwintering in the Arctic. Published in 1631 – rapidly appearing in print following the return of the sailors, an indication in itself of the level of public interest in these eye-witness accounts – under the title *Gods Power and Providence Shewed, in the Miraculous Preservation and Deliverance of Eight Englishmen, Left by Mischance in Greenland Anno 1630, Nine Moneths and Twelve Dayes*, the document itself is of interest, including, as it does, a map (see Figure 5), again indicating a readership that wished to inform itself about place and landscape as much as to hear the adventures being recounted. It was dedicated to Sir Hugh Hammersly, a London City alderman and governor of the 'Muscovia Merchants' at this time, the sponsors as it were of Pelham's sojourn on the ice. Because the leaving of Pelham and his colleagues had been a mistake, no preparations had been made for their stay and they had only limited provisions to see them through the entire winter they were forced to spend fending for their lives until the whaling ships returned the following spring. Pelham recounts these details with some feeling: 'Bread, Beere, and Wine we had none. As for meate, our greatest and chiefest feeding was the Whale Frittars, and those mouldie too; the loathsomest meate in the worlde'.[96] They hunt for deer and bears, and even seals for sustenance and skins. In fact, it had been while they were on an expedition for deer meat that the weather set in, forcing them further inland than planned and their fellow shipmen to set

---

[96] Edward Pelham, *God's Power and Providence Shewed* ... (London, 1631), sig. A3v. Pelham as author of the document is careful to name his colleagues as William Fakely, Gunner, John Wise and Robert Goodfellow, Sea-men, Thomas Ayers, a whale-cutter, Henry Bett, Cooper, and John Dawes and Richard Kellett, Land-men. Pelham himself was a gunner's mate (sig. A4v).

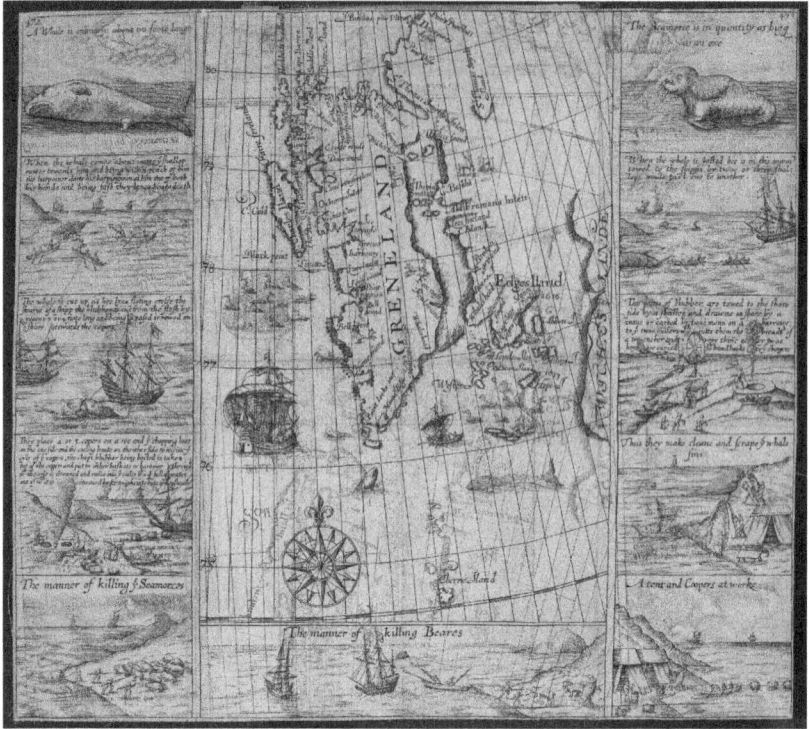

Figure 5: Map from Edward Pelham, *Gods Power and Providence Shewed, in the Miraculous Preservation and Deliverance of Eight Englishmen, left by mischance in Greenland Anno 1630, nine moneths and twelve dayes* (London, 1631).

sail without them or face being trapped there themselves. Initially, Pelham says that they assumed the worst; that they would die there in 'so long, so darksome, and so bitter a winter'.[97]

   One of the striking things about Pelham's document as a response to landscape is how responsive to issues of light and environment it is. Hedged in, as Pelham's discourse is, with the conventional tropes of providential delivery, the literary and sometimes scriptural terms of his narrative are arresting. In one remarkable paragraph, he recounts a moment when the men seem momentarily to pause and look from outside in onto their experience, imagining that they might, like so many other sailors before

---

[97] Pelham, *God's Power*, sig. C1r.

them, end up as meat for the savage bears and arctic foxes that roam the landscape, regarding themselves, as it were, 'like amazed men':

All these fearefull examples presenting themselves before our eyes, at this place of *Bottle Cove* aforesaid, made us, like amazed men, to stand looking one upon another, all of us, as it were beholding in the present, the future calamities both of himselfe and his fellowes. And thus, like men already metamorphosed into the yce of the Countrey, and already past with both our sense and reason; stood wee with the eyes of pittie beholding one another.[98]

I am struck by this almost Ovidian sense of becoming one with the environment in which they find themselves and a cultural or social anthropologist might argue that it was exactly this psychological identification that helped them to survive. By becoming one with the landscape, these men become able to work with its patterns and survive the long winter months.[99] They make a wooden tent to live in of the sails and oars of their now effectively useless boat (the seas are completely iced up within weeks of their being left at Spitsbergen). Pelham provides a detailed account of its construction and how they need to keep two fires burning at all times to prevent their mortar from freezing. They use whalebone needles to sew new clothes and shoes from animal skins. In short, they adapt to their environment in order to survive.[100]

Finally, on 3 February, Pelham records the return of the sun and his more prosaic and practical account suddenly takes on a flight of poesy: 'Aurora with her golden face smiled, once again upon us, at her rising out of bed' and once again it is the return of the light that strikes him most fervently: 'The brightnesse of the Sunne, and the whitenesse of the snow, both together was such, as that it was able to have revived even a dying spirit'.[101] Ships from Hull arrive three months later, presuming that they will find the corpses of the eight men left behind, only instead to be offered

[98] Pelham, *God's Power*, sig. C2r.
[99] By way of comparison, readers might like to compare John Wylie's account of Amundsen's polar expedition as an example of successful embedding in a landscape as opposed to Captain Scott's more aesthetic and detached response to it in 'Becoming-icy: Scott and Amundsen's South Polar voyages, 1910–1913', *Cultural Geographies*, 9 (2002), 249–65. I am indebted to Wylie for the inspiration to look at early modern responses to ice in this way and to David Matless for the original recommendation. See also Barry Lopez, *Arctic Dreams: Imagination and Desire in a Northern Landscape* (London: Harvill, 1986).
[100] The document is also discussed in Ronald Bedford, Lloyd Davis, and Philippa Kelly, *Early Modern English Lives: Autobiography and Self-Representation 1500–1660* (Aldershot: Ashgate, 2007) as an example of how early modern travel writing managed 'encounter'. They note that Pelham's 'representational mode is often dramatic . . . [and that] the relationships are for the most part staged' (p. 65).
[101] Pelham, *God's Power*, sig. E2v.

'the courtesie of the house' when Pelham and the others offer them what remaining victuals they have (I like the sly humour in this moment and the men's reconstruction of English codes of hospitality in this harsh region of ice and polar bears).[102] The narrative ends with a striking account of the journey away from the ice flows and eventually into the River Thames itself as they reach London and home.

Pelham's text and others like it seem to me to constitute some of the most remarkable accounts of and responses to water in its manifold forms to be found in the Caroline period. The effort to locate the impact of narratives like Pelham's on the dramatic imagination are somewhat hampered by the limited survival of evidence (at best, only a list of titles is extant in many instances) of the repertoires of the open-air amphitheatres in the 1620s and 1630s where this kind of geographical material might be expected to make its presence most felt.[103] Kathleen McLuskie has written recently, however, of the ways in which topical issues could and were narrativized into more familiar theatrical tropes in a persuasive account of the ways in which Brome and Heywood's 1632 collaboration *The Late Lancashire Witches* reworked contemporary documentary materials, and it is tempting to think in the light of this that there would have been opportunity to make considerable theatrical impact with material culled from these contemporary arctic whaling narratives.[104] Certainly, whales have a distinct presence in the Caroline cultural imaginary, featuring, as they do, not only in lurid pamphlet accounts of encounters with waterborne and beached individuals, but as pasteboard props in the very particular theatrical spectacle of the Lord Mayor's pageants.[105] Texts like Pelham's operated as easily available aids to boost and inform the cultural imaginary of the ocean, an imaginary on which the playhouses were able to depend and which they were certainly able to mobilize to great effect in a dramatic context.[106]

---

[102] Pelham, *God's Power*, sig. E4v.

[103] I am grateful to Lucy Munro for private correspondence on this topic. For a list of extant titles for the Admiral's Men's productions in the 1620s, see Andrew Gurr, *Shakespeare's Opposites: The Admiral's Company, 1594–1625* (Cambridge University Press, 2009).

[104] Kathleen E. McLuskie, 'Politics and aesthetic pleasure in 1630s theater', in Adam Zucker and Alan B. Farmer (eds.), *Localizing Caroline Drama: Politics and Economics of the Early Modern English Stage, 1625–1642* (London: Palgrave, 2006), pp. 43–68.

[105] Dolphins and cetaceans regularly featured in the iconography of the water-based parts of the shows; see, for example, Heywood's *London's Scaturigo* (1632).

[106] See, e.g., Alexander Frederick Falconer, *Shakespeare and the Sea* (London: Constable, 1964). I am grateful to Dan Brayton for this reference. A significant new edition to the 'new thalassology' as it is sometimes called is Steve Mentz, *At the Bottom of Shakespeare's Ocean* (London and New York: Continuum, 2009).

Piracy, another form of cultural labour performed on water – at its most basic, a means of making a living from the sea – also seems to have captured the theatrical imagination, as the previously discussed example of *The Fair Maid of the West* Part 2 indicates. Another play which broaches related subject matter is Massinger's *The Renegado* (1623–4). His plotline features a renegade pirate, Grimaldi, and several associates who have abducted Paulina and sold her into slavery before the play even begins.[107] Several recent studies have argued the case for piracy, within mainstream society as much as on the stage, as a 'complex and multilayered activity' that needs to be located in the 'context of varied forms, if not traditions'.[108] Coastal raiding was a relatively obvious activity, even a necessity, for those living in coastal areas, and many other locals were either press-ganged into supporting these activities (local inns and alehouses were seen as ripe recruiting grounds in this regard[109]) or tempted into illicit dealings with smugglers and the black market of exchange that defined coastal geographical regions in terms of economic practice and the circulation of goods. Christopher Harding makes the point that 'During the sixteenth century the maritime region of South Devon spawned dozens of English seafarers who made a fair living from commercial voyages. For many of them this was not enough and they turned to piracy for added income'.[110] As well as seeing piracy as a multilayered activity, then, we need to think about the ambiguous spaces of operation of the pirate and the ambiguities of maritime law as a result. Pirates and piracy speak to the environment of the open sea and the complicated legal geography of that space, but also to coastal communities and inland waterways as the smuggled goods themselves make their movements.[111] The Caroline stage's engagement with piracy is complex and varied, as a result. Brome's previously cited example of the prostitute, Holdup, in *The Northern Lass*, forced to sell her

---

[107] For a detailed analysis of the play and its sexual and religious politics, see Claire Jowitt, *Voyage Drama and Gender Politics, 1589–1642* (Manchester University Press), pp. 175–84. See also, Michael Neill's recent edition of the play for the Arden Early Modern Drama series (London: Methuen, 2010).

[108] John C. Appleby, 'The problem of piracy in Ireland, 1570–1630', in Claire Jowitt (ed.), *Pirates?: The Politics of Plunder 1550–1650* (London: Palgrave Macmillan, 2007), pp. 41–55 (43).

[109] Appleby, 'The problem of piracy', p. 51.

[110] Christopher Harding, '"*Hostis Humani Generis*" – The pirate as outlaw in the early modern law of the sea', in Claire Jowitt (ed.), *Pirates?: The Politics of Plunder 1550–1650* (London: Palgrave Macmillan, 2007), pp. 20–38 (26–7).

[111] See Lauren Benton, 'Oceans of Law: The Legal Geography of the Seventeenth-Century Seas', *Proceedings of the Seascapes, Littoral Cultures, and Trans-Oceanic Exchanges Conference, 12–15 February 2003*, Library of Congress, Washington DC, September 2005 www.historycooperative.org/proceedings/seascapes/benton.html [last accessed 29 August 2010].

body in London after her family falls into disgrace following her father's dealings with smugglers, is presented with considerable sympathy to 1629 audiences. Brome, it seems to me, is playing out on the stage through Holdup's dilemma what recent cultural historians have appositely called the 'social roots of piracy'.[112]

Newsletters of the late 1620s are certainly full of references to piracy and attacks on merchant shipping.[113] Pirates haunt the cultural imaginary and, unsurprisingly, that same spectre appears to stalk the early modern stage and alternative modes of literary and cultural output such as ballads and broadsheets. There is an easy typology that links forest outlaws, equally beloved of early modern playwrights, as we shall see in the next chapter, and these Robin Hoods of the open seas.[114] This stage type or trope would surely also have carried very specific contemporary resonances and referents, however embedded these may have appeared in the context of a commercial theatre play. Claire Jowitt has argued that the one-page 1630 broadsheet on the early sixteenth-century pirate Sir Andrew Barton is published at that time because his story spoke in new ways to a Caroline readership. Barton's narrative figures, she suggests, as an analogy for English–Scottish relations more generally, but also as 'a parable of Caroline naval failure'.[115] Charles I's fleet was in poor shape by 1630 after several years of poor maritime performances by the English Navy, including the floundering of the fleet that had set out against Spain at Cadiz in 1625 and the disastrous expedition to relieve the Huguenots at La Rochelle in 1627. Buckingham's port-side assassination in 1628 is similarly linked; he had been held responsible for those policies which had allowed seemingly unlimited reprisals against enemy shipping and which led to 'a revival of

---

[112] Appleby, 'The problem of piracy', p. 54.

[113] For example, Reverend Joseph Mead to Sir Martin Stuteville, Christ College, 9 April 1625 (Birch 1: 6) refers to news that the Dunkirkers have recently taken three merchant ships; see also John Chamberlain to Sir Dudley Carleton, London, 14 May 1626, Birch, *The Court and Times of Charles I*, 1: 22; Mr Beaulieu to Sir Thomas Puckering, Bart, London, 18 March 1629, Birch, *The Court and Times of Charles I*, 1: 68; Reverend Joseph Mead to Sir Martin Stuteville, Christ College, 7 November 1629 (Birch, *The Court and Times of Charles I*, 1: 42): 'The Dunkirkers also then took an English ship that came from the East countries, and two coal-ships', and also Mr Beaulieu to Sir Thomas Puckering, Bart, 18 March 1629 (Birch, *The Court and Times of Charles I*, 1: 68): 'Here are daily complaints made of the continual prizes and wrongs done by the Dunkirkers, not only along the coasts but also within the very rivers of this kingdome, where they have taken divers ships of late.'

[114] Some of these connections have been made in the context of the 'new maritime humanities'. For pioneering work in this field, see Bernhard Klein and Gesa Mackenthun (eds.), *Sea Changes: Historicizing the Ocean* (London: Routledge, 2003).

[115] Claire Jowitt, 'Introduction: pirates?', p. 4. The full title of the pamphlet is Anon., *A True Relation of the Life and Death of Sir Andrew Barton, a Pirate and Rover on the Seas* (London, 1630).

pirating on a large scale'.[116] Some of those invocations of the dangers of the sea by Oceanus in Dekker's 1629 Lord Mayoral pageant *London's Tempe* quoted earlier or the spiritual paranoia of the pamphlet reactions to the storm surges on the Thames, are, then, a direct production of this cultural moment.

### *Estuarine landscapes: the politics of mudflats*

The Thames and other major river networks in the nation were intensely vivid landscapes, material and practical presences in the lives of Charles I's subjects. The world of piracy and sea skirmishes might seem, in the scenic designs of court masques such as *Britannia Triumphans* and *Salmacida Spolia* at least, far removed from the everyday streets and suburbs of London, but in truth that world, too, mapped its presence very directly onto metropolitan topography. Claire Jowitt has outlined what I would describe as the 'geography of execution'; this applied to the sentencing and punishment of convicted pirates and the 'elaborate set of customs' that attached to these highly public rituals. Convicted pirates had 'a gallows for themselves on the mudflats at Wapping'.[117] Mudflats, an essential feature of the estuarine landscapes, were, as Jowitt notes, a very precise place in London cartography, constituting a 'strip of land between the high- and low-water marks [ . . . ] under the jurisdiction of the Lord High Admiral [and] not of the usual criminal courts'. Convicted pirates were taken in a cart accompanied by a chaplain from Marshalsea Prison in Southwark via London Bridge and the Tower of London to Execution Dock. This grim procession, another conscious inversion of the more regal street theatre of entrances and progress, was led by the Admiralty Marshal or his deputy, carrying a silver oar to represent the authority of the Admiralty over those crimes committed at sea, a very public performance of 'legal geography'.[118]

Execution Dock at Wapping is identified in Stow's *Survey* in its 1598 edition. Stow also tells us in his *Annals* that, after hangings, the bodies of pirates and 'sea rovers' were chained to a stake at the low-water mark and made to remain there until three tides had passed over them.[119] The

---

[116] Jowitt, 'Introduction: pirates?', p. 11. N. A. Rodger records that at least 737 English ships, possibly as many as a thousand, were plundered between 1626 and 1630 and that the Isle of Wight had obtained the reputation of being a second Argier; see *The Safeguard of the Sea: A Naval History of Britain, 660–1649* (New York: Norton, 1997), p. 361.

[117] Claire Jowitt, 'Scaffold performances: the politics of pirate execution', in Claire Jowitt (ed.), *Pirates?: The Politics of Plunder 1550–1650*, pp. 151–68 (153).

[118] The phrase derives from Benton's 'Oceans of law'. Jowitt, 'Scaffold performances', p. 153.

[119] Stow, *Annals*, p. 1175.

corpses were then smeared with pitch and hung in gibbets in the Isle of Dogs, Graves Point, or Busby's Reach as warnings to incoming sailors. These semiotics played out over the waters with which these pirates were inextricably associated, in death as in life. We close this chapter, then, with a suitable sense of flow and return, back in the resonant waters of the ever-iconic Thames, looking out to sea. We are left with a potent sense of the symbolic, political, cultural, and practical role that liquid landscapes played for Caroline culture and an understanding that it was inevitable that these uncontainable landscapes had a tangible presence on the commercial stages of London, as well as those of provincial estates and households countrywide. Theatrical artefacts remade the worlds of whaling and piracy as much as early modern households became receptacles for the objects and artefacts of global trade. Water was, it seems, in the 1620s and 1630s, quite literally everywhere.

CHAPTER 2

# Into the woods
## Spatial and social geographies in the forest

There is long literary history of representing woodland and forest geographies as places of escape and exile, of non-normative, and therefore potentially transgressive, practice. In pastoral literary conventions, the forest frequently operates as a space separate from the sites of everyday labour and their attendant rules of behaviour. This particular understanding of the forest is made manifest in Shakespeare's fashioning of Arden in *As You Like It* (*c.* 1599), a play in which we are regularly informed that 'There's no clock in the forest' (3.2.291) and where Arden is a holiday space, a space away from the 'working-day world' and the harsh realities of the court (1.3.12). Yet even in that play the world of real shepherds and tenant farmers living in cottages on the 'skirts of the wood' (3.2.323) is drawn to our attention, revealing in the process the mixed inheritance of understandings of forests and woodlands in the early seventeenth-century cultural and geo-political imagination.[1] As will so often prove to be the case with the focus spaces of this study, the early modern stage proves perfectly able to hold simultaneous literary and material understandings of a site. A mix of the practical and the romantic was identified in the preceding chapter in early modern representations of aquatic landscapes and practices, and the same proves true of the woodland geographies that are the subject here.

It is now well understood in the literature on forests that they were often administrative regions, spaces defined as much by the practices of royal deer parks and hunting regimes as by the fact that they were arboreal landscapes.[2] From 1625 and the accession of Charles I to the English throne, these sites became the focus of renewed governmental attentions

---

[1] Richard Wilson, 'Like the old Robin Hood: *As You Like It* and the enclosure riots', in *Will Power: Essays on Shakespearean Authority* (Detroit: Wayne State University Press, 1992), pp. 66–87.

[2] For wider discussions of the physical geography and cultural history of forests, see Oliver Rackham, *Woodlands* (London: Collins, 2006) and *Trees and Woodlands in the British Landscape*, rev. edn (London: Dent, 1995); and Robert Pogue Harrison, *Forests: The Shadow of Civilization* (University of Chicago Press, 1992).

for a number of reasons. Like his father, Charles was a keen huntsman and therefore continued James VI and I's tendency of combining the practice of royal progress with the performance of hunting rituals. As Daniel Beaver has noted: 'The law code of the Stuart forest regime upheld and protected the environmental demands of the hunt, standing among the highest ritual expressions of royalty and nobility'.[3] Charles also turned his attention to woodlands for financial reasons, as potential sources of revenue for a cash-strapped Treasury. This was especially the case during the years of the so-called 'Personal Rule' (1629–40) when he governed without summoning the parliaments which, in the usual scheme of things, might have been expected to grant him subsidies and prerogative taxations to ease his fiscal difficulties. The 1630s, in particular, therefore, witnessed a revival of interest in and assertion of ancient land-based laws to do with forests, not least the increased sitting and prominence of specific forest courts known as 'eyres', in order to generate income through the levying of fines. These fines were imposed on those who transgressed against codes of practices in the forest, in particular those who protested against the widespread practice of enclosure, which reduced access on the part of those sections of the community who claimed customary gathering rights (so-called 'rights of common') in the royal woodlands. The revived attention to the royal forests in turn empowered representatives of the crown to exploit those same lands, usually for personal gain, through a variety of practices, including disafforestation and the sale of timber as well as the working of mineral resources.

The significance of Charles I's attitude towards and policies regarding the forests and chases of the realm was noted as early as 13 April 1625 by someone (identity unknown) writing to the Reverend Joseph Mead: 'Our sovereign [ . . . ] zealous for Gods truth – frequents and attentively hearkens to prayers and sermons – will pay all his father's, mother's and brother's debts, and that by disparking most of his remote parks and chases.'[4] The suggestion that Charles is paying for the debts of his wider family is perhaps an attempt to avoid making too overt a criticism of the reigning monarch; but the use of the phrase 'dispark' to refer to the conversion of parkland to other (more profitable) designations gives us access to the ways in which the terminology of forest law entered the common lexicon in the key decades of the 1620s and 1630s. 'Disparking' certainly enjoys a sudden flourishing

---

[3] Daniel S. Beaver, *Hunting and the Politics of Violence Before the English Civil War* (Cambridge University Press, 2008), p. 2.
[4] See Birch, *The Court and Times of Charles I*, 1: 10.

of usage in literal and figurative terms in 1630s poetry, including George Herbert's *The Temple* (1633) where, in 'The Forerunners', he asks 'must they dispark / Those sparkling notions'.[5]

Somewhat against the grain of pastoral literary poetics, perhaps, and the self-serving claims of Caroline law, these woodland locales were also very much everyday working spaces and therefore, these attitudes and practices impacted in quite serious ways on the livelihoods of the mixed communities who relied on forest resources – from access to grazing for their animals, to the collection of timber and underwood for the purposes of building repairs and fuel – to supplement their limited income from crafts and trades as varied as felt-making, tanning, weaving, charcoal-burning, cooperage, blacksmithing, and cobbling.[6] Buchanan Sharp's important study of popular protest in these geographical locations notes that a seventeenth-century woodland was anything but a 'wild' space; a visitor to a 1620s woodland would have found hundreds of people living in cottages erected on forest waste or at the side of highways; day labourers, commoners, artisans, and craftspeople.[7] This would have been especially the case in manufacturing areas like the Forest of Dean in Gloucestershire – a focus in later discussion of Milton's Marches-based and Marches-performed *A Masque Presented at Ludlow Castle, 1634* – with its ironworks and mineral mining, or those areas such as East Anglia and Wiltshire which were associated with the cloth-working industries.

The woodlands became in part a spillover site for migrant and mobile workers who did not have established parish identities or dwellings. Many erected temporary housing in woodland areas, often to the chagrin of the local authorities and those locals with whom they were deemed to be in direct competition over common rights. Sharp cites a 1609 report which observes:

At this tyme the waste soyle in all forests is moste extreamly pestered and surcharged with all manner of beastes and cattell as well with sheepe goates and swine beastes not being commonable within a forest by lawe [...] by reason of the daylie increase of new erections of tenements cottages dwellinge houses as well upon the

---

[5] George Herbert, *The English Poems*, ed. C. A. Patrides (London: Everyman, 1974). Although 'disparking' was used in its literal sense from the sixteenth century onwards (witness, for example, Shakespeare's *Richard II*, 3.1.22–3: 'You have . . . / Dispark'd my parks, and felled my forest woods'), the *OED*'s examples of its figurative use are clustered in the 1630s–1650s.

[6] Lists are given of the craft identities of those involved in local protests and rioting for those living in Gillingham Forest in 1629/30 and in the Forest of Dean in 1634 (recorded in the forest eyre that year) in Buchanan Sharp, *In Contempt of All Authority: Rural Artisans and Riot in the West of England, 1586–1660* (Berkeley: University of California Press, 1980), pp. 127–8.

[7] Sharp, *In Contempt of All Authority*, p. 1.

kinges waste soyle as also upon mens owne inclosed landes which new erections
have noe right of common at all within the forest.[8]

He makes the related points that these areas also tended to be involved in,
or highlighted for, their 'riotous activity' or acts of public protest against
the curtailment of common rights and the enclosure or 'imparkment'
of particular areas, not least those rich with natural resources. It is no
coincidence that 1629–31, which was a period of particular hardship and
food shortages in these regions, also witnessed the highest incidence of
protest (in the so-called Western Rising, which included the protests in
the Dean; these continued right up to 1634) and what we receive from this
kind of detail is a far more complicated version of the pastoral cliché of the
'liberties of the forest'. As Patricia Fumerton notes, adapting the theories
of de Certeau and Lefebvre on the cultural and social production of space,
'freedom is more a matter of space than place'.[9] In the plays and masques
which deploy woodland settings that are examined in this chapter, it is
not the forest per se that bestows liberty to its inhabitants, but rather, the
spatial practice of it by particular communities that achieves this condition.
As will so often prove to be the case in this study, space overlaps with
society – and therefore spatial practice with social practice – at all times.

### ROMANCING THE FOREST

'A culture is no better than its woods' (W. H. Auden)

One of the key sets of 'spatial stories' that have mobilized the hybrid
understanding of the forest as site for romance, legend, and myth, but
also as working woodland, is those accruing around the figure of Robin
Hood. These representations of the sometime aristocrat, sometime peasant
woodsman, sometime forest official, who finds himself and his crew of
'merry men' exiled to the space of Sherwood Forest are themselves not
only an interesting blend of generic inheritance (drama, ballad, and song
all figure heavily in Robin's literary portfolio), but also an active blending
of romantic and practical understandings of landscape and dwelling. The
tales of stealing from the rich to give to the poor can very quickly be traced
to roots in issues of customary rights and poaching regimes in royally

---

[8] National Archives Land Revenue 2/194, ff. 267–77, 'a collection of certain great abuses and wronges
done unto his Majestie in his forests', 27 April 1609; cited in Sharp, *In Contempt of All Authority*,
p. 172.
[9] Patricia Fumerton, *Unsettled: The Culture of Mobility and the Working Poor* (University of Chicago
Press, 2006), p. 53.

controlled deer parks.[10] It is therefore not surprising that Shakespeare, too, chose to invoke Robin Hood's name in the context of the Forest of Arden where Rosalind's father, Duke Senior, lives out his woodland exile in ways that mimic the Sherwood literary legacy (1.1.110–11).

We will deal later with a specific late 1630s engagement with the Robin Hood myth that elects not simply to allude to Robin's activities in a woodland space but that actively recreates the paths, walks, and chases of Sherwood Forest on the stage, Jonson's *The Sad Shepherd*. There are a host of other dramatic examples from the Caroline period of plays that evoked the idea of outlaws in the wood for both romance-derived and very contemporary and topical sociopolitical reasons, reasons which, in turn, impact in important ways on contemporary interpretation of woodland space. Massinger's *The Guardian* (*c.* 1633), Brome's *A Jovial Crew* (1641–2), and Shirley's *The Sisters* (1642) all offer significant variations on this theme, depicting, as they do, communities of outlaws or beggars taking up temporary residence within forest spaces and living off their resources.[11] I am interpreting that latter phrase in its broadest sense to refer not only to the foodstuffs and fuel available for 'free' in the woodland, but also to refer to the opportunity to beg from or rob those who pass through this kind of area for a multiplicity of reasons: to carry goods, for the purposes of travel, and sometimes for personal reasons, as in the case of the young lovers Amie and Martin in Brome's play, who have, in classic style, run away to the woods from the tyranny of adults who oppose their relationship. The symbolic significance and potentiality of Brome's mobile community of beggars will be discussed in more detail in Chapter 4, but the terms in which these groups of forest outlaws and 'thieves' are represented on the early modern stage are worth pausing to discuss briefly here.

The so-called 'wastes' of the royal forests were, as noted, a crucial supplement to income for many of those who worked within its environs for

---

[10] Adam Zucker makes excellent related points to Shakespeare's *c.* 1597 play *The Merry Wives of Windsor* in relation to the social and cultural history of Windsor Great Park, part of one of the most high profile of royal forests in the early Stuart period, where, he notes, 'The forest . . . becomes visible as home to a network of everyday relationships that spanned the early modern social spectrum, relationships determined in part by the desire of the crown to regulate the resources of the forest, in part by a desire of local residents to benefit from these resources' (in 'Shakespeare's green materials', Chapter 1, forthcoming in *The Places of Wit* (Cambridge University Press)). I am grateful to Adam for permission to work with this material prior to publication.

[11] Detailed studies of these plays in this context have already been produced by Rosemary Gaby, 'Of vagabonds and commonwealths: *Beggars' Bush*, *A Jovial Crew* and *The Sisters*', *Studies in English Literature 1500–1900*, 34 (1994), 401–24; and Julie Sanders, 'Beggars commonwealths on the pre-civil war stage: Richard Brome's *A Jovial Crew*, John Suckling's *The Goblins*, and James Shirley's *The Sisters*', *Modern Language Review*, 97 (2002), 1–14. See, also, related discussions in Butler, *Theatre and Crisis*, esp. pp. 254–64.

subsistence-level wages. Periods of food shortage often coincided with an increase in the number of attacks on those transporting grain on designated tracks and paths through wooded regions.[12] Woodlands and forests were, then, embodied sites of daily labour and practice, but also spaces through which other people and groupings passed, either for work or recreation, confirming by example Doreen Massey's argument that space is constructed by 'social relations' and sometimes by the breakdown of those relationships.[13] Recurrent scenes in early modern drama which depict the traveller waylaid by thieves are, in part, a dramatic response to this social actuality. In an untitled manuscript drama from the late 1630s that is linked to Nottinghamshire theatrical circles (and which will be examined in greater detail in Chapter 3), two Londoners turned robbers through necessity, Catch and Snap, are witnessed attempting to rob two wealthy young men and their female companion who have got lost on their way through a wood en route to her uncle's estate.[14] In *A Jovial Crew*, we spectate a training session in which novice beggars are instructed how to beg from passers-by; in the process, that play registers the reverse dangers of these activities when female beggars, in particular, prove vulnerable to sexual attack. At 3.1.500, an aristocrat's daughters in disguise, Rachel and Meriel, have to be rescued by the steward Springlove from the unwanted attentions of a high-ranking visitor. Milton's *A Masque* mobilizes similar subtexts when he depicts the virginal Lady proving vulnerable to Comus's attentions and ultimate abduction in the woods. Comus takes her to his palace, where the threat of rape is never far from the surface.

In *The Guardian* a group of forest outlaws – themselves led by an exiled courtier Severino – identify wealthy individuals (who have made their money in morally suspect ways) passing through their wooded territories as part of a long list of those from whom it is ethically acceptable to steal:

> If a Usurer
> Greedy at his own price, to make a purchase,
> Taking advantage upon Bond or Mortgage,
> From a Prodigal pass through our Territories
> I'the way of custom or of tribute to us
> You may ease him of his burthen.
>
> (2.1. p. 32)[15]

[12] See Sharp, *In Contempt of All Authority*, e.g. p. 47.
[13] See Doreen Massey, *Space, Place, and Gender* (Cambridge: Polity Press, 1995), *passim*, but see, e.g., pp. 122, 137.
[14] Osborne MS C132.27, University of Calgary Special Collections. My thanks to the SHRCC funded research team and librarian, Appollonia Steele, for permission to use this manuscript and the collaborative findings of the team as part of my own research.
[15] Philip Massinger, *The Guardian* (London, 1633).

Of even more interest, perhaps, are the indications given in these 'articles', agreed by all new initiates into Severino's company, that other individuals should be left to move safely through their forest dominions. Those exempted from attack include soldiers returning from the wars, 'Rent-rack'd Farmers', 'sweaty' labourers – their perspiration functioning synecdochally here as an indicator of hard work and honestly earned income – as well as 'Carriers that transport / The goods of other men' (2.1. p. 33) and who would presumably suffer potentially ruinous financial losses if they failed to deliver the items entrusted to their care. Severino's respect for the world of necessary labour in these 'articles' is revelatory of the politics of his forest grouping as a whole. He even sees his 'nightwork' as the necessary inverse of the daily labour of those who operate within the woodland's environs:

> Quiet night that brings
> Rest to the labourer is the outlaws day,
> In which he rises to do wrong.
> (2.1. p. 30)

In true Robin Hood style, the outlaws' animosity appears to be focused on those who are clearly identified as exploiters both of other people and of the forest landscape itself, not least: 'Builders of Iron Mills, that grub up Forests, / With Timber Trees for shipping' (2.1. p. 32). Commentators tend to deduce from this play's Neapolitan setting that its depiction of an alternative forest community is only ever a highly abstracted, even idealized, one, but these references to ironworks and deforestation would have had very specific resonances in 1633 when *The Guardian* is believed to have been first performed, probably at the Blackfriars Theatre.

The Great Western Rising, an umbrella name for the series of localized protests that took place in the western counties of England between 1626 and 1634, produced some of its most spectacular 'drama of protest' in the Forest of Dean, where there were a series of well-organized attacks on those seeking to deprive locals of customary rights through acts of enclosure. These enclosures were mostly related to the increased mining of mineral resources in the area and the expansion of the royally controlled ironworks. The Dean protests have been connected, albeit tangentially, to several of the themes and images presented onstage in *A Masque Presented at Ludlow Castle* in 1634 and the above quotation from *The Guardian* would suggest that Massinger was yet another playwright engaged with topical political concerns around forest laws and popular protest.[16] Certainly, in 1625, his *A*

---

[16] See my 'Ecocritical readings and the seventeenth-century woodland: Milton's *Comus* and the Forest of Dean', *English*, 50 (2001), 1–18.

*New Way to Pay Old Debts* had made trenchant attacks on the exploitation
of land and landscape by real-life government agents and monopolists like
Sir Giles Mompesson. Mompesson was an active target of the protestors'
anger in the Dean in the 1630s as well, where he was working in nearby
Mailescott Woods as an agent for the Villiers family, relatives of the late
Duke of Buckingham.[17] The lines of connection that these overlapping
relationships establish, between literary stereotype and material practice,
and between stage representation and actual event, suggest a matrix of
concerns, both local and national, that can be traced in early modern
drama's response to the space and setting of the forest.

Nuanced ideas of woodland geography were being played out on courtly
as well as commercial stages. The 1637 masque *Britannia Trimphans*
includes among its various complex sequences a lengthy 'mock-romanza'
set in a forestscape. This section of the masque involves chivalric literary stereotypes such as a giant, a dwarf, a knight, his squire, and a lady
(whom, we learn, the knight has been romancing by a sunlit hedgerow).
Not for the first time, the considerable influence of Edmund Spenser can
be registered in Stuart masquing culture, but the self-conscious medieval-
ism of this scene – the knight, we are pointedly told, is dressed in 'old
fashioned Armour' (sig. B4v) – masks a more topical set of allusions and
resonances, not least in its geography, that would have struck a chord with
alert spectators.

The giant has been fishing on the seashore, his hook baited with a
dragon's tail in order to catch a whale for his dinner. His angling trip
having proved successful, he is passing back through his forest domains
when he encounters the knight and his lady in the act of embrace. The
lady, or 'Damsel' as the speech prefix in the printed dialogue describes
her, stresses that the couple were in the forest for the innocent purpose
of wild-gathering some hedgerow fruits: 'sloes / And Bullies' (sig. C1v) as
she describes them, evoking the beautiful fruits of the blackthorn and the
wild plum or bullace, popular then, as now, for making winter cordials.
It is this very assertion, however, that provokes, rather than assuages, the
giant's wrath: 'Shall I grow meeke as a Babe when ev'ry Trull is / So bold
to steale my sloes and pluck my bullyes?' (sig. C1v). The giant declares
that the produce of the hedgerow is not 'food for free' to be gathered by
all and sundry, but part of that complex system of customary practice and

---

[17] On Mailescott, see Sharp, *In Contempt of All Authority*, p. 203 and also, National Archives State
Papers Charles I 16/188/20, where the affidavit of Robert Bridges describes how rioters destroyed
hedges and ditches, assaulted Mompesson's agents, filled in pits, and cast timber from the estate into
the River Wye.

common rights which, as we have already noted, governed many woodland communities and their social structures in Stuart England.[18] In turn, the giant intends to enact his own form of rough justice on the knight and his lady in response to their perceived encroachment of his common rights:

> If I but upward heave my oaken Twig,
> Ile teach thee play the Tom-boy, her the Rig
> Within my Forest bounds:  (sig. C1v)

There were different ways of reading this scene available to aristocratic audiences who would have watched the masque in 1637. The giant would have been seen, by some at least, as an encloser, restricting the free access of others to his lands and its riches and natural resources; but it is perhaps more likely that in the Whitehall Palace performance context, if not necessarily the published afterlife of the masque, the brute force of contemporary common rights protesters and anti-enclosure campaigners in disputes in the Forest of Dean, Gillingham Forest, Sherwood Forest, and elsewhere would have been signified.[19] In the latter interpretation, the knight and his lady stand as representatives of elite demands for access to crown-controlled lands.

In a familiar plot trope, the giant intends to abduct the lady to his castle in the 'vast forest', a locale which can frequently be seen in Jones's extant scenery designs for shutters and painted backdrops for use in court masques (see, for example, Figures 6 and 7: scene designs for *Salmacida Spolia* from 1640), and to turn her into his personal cook for the evening, forcing her to prepare and serve his whalemeat along with other locally sourced produce: 'She shall sauce bore, fry tripes, and wild hogs harsnet' (sig. C2r).[20] The knight is appalled by the notion of his lady soiling her fine fingers in a working kitchen, where she will be required to 'stir a seacole fire, or scumme a Cauldron' with hands more used to playing frivolous games in the ashes of a stove lit and maintained by others

---

[18] See Steve Hindle, '"Not by bread only"?: Common right, parish relief and endowed charity in a forest economy, *c.* 1600–1800', in Steve King and Alannah Tomkins (eds.), *The Poor In England, 1700–1850: An Economy of Makeshifts* (Manchester University Press, 2003), pp. 39–75; and David Underdown, *Revel, Riot, and Rebellion: Popular Politics and Culture in England 1603–1660* (Oxford University Press, 1987).

[19] On the complex interpretative afterlife of masques in print, see Lauren Shohet, 'Reading triumphs: localizing Caroline masques', in Alan B. Farmer and Adam Zucker (eds.), *Localizing Caroline Drama: Politics and Economics of the Early Modern English Stage, 1625–1642* (London and New York: Palgrave, 2006), pp. 69–96; and her *Reading Masques: The English Masque and Public Culture in the Seventeenth Century* (Oxford University Press, 2010).

[20] For discussion of Jones's work on stage backdrops in general, see John Peacock in *The Stage Designs of Inigo Jones* (Cambridge University Press, 2006).

Figure 6: Inigo Jones's 1640 design for Scene 1 of the masque *Salmacida Spolia* depicting 'a horrid scene . . . of storm and tempest' in a dark forest. © Devonshire Collection, Chatsworth. Reproduced by permission of Chatsworth Settlement Trustees.

Figure 7: Inigo Jones's 1640 design for Scene 2 of *Salmacida Spolia* 'the sky serene . . . in the landscape were cornfields and pleasant trees'. © Devonshire Collection, Chatsworth. Reproduced by permission of Chatsworth Settlement Trustees.

(sig. C2r). The mention of sea-coal establishes clear status differences between the lady and those who would need to use such a cheap fuel, and it is difficult to know how these demarcations of elite versus labouring class practice would be received in a courtly context. Already, however, what might have seemed a standard romance setting of a giant's property in a forest becomes something more located within the contemporary social and political geographies of Caroline England. By 1637, Charles I's revival of ancient forest laws was a deeply vexed issue, the subject not only of anti-enclosure riots but also of performative incursions by poaching gangs and, consequently, of numerous prosecutions both at the Whitehall court of the Star Chamber and in more localized forest eyre hearings. Even in the performance venue of Whitehall in the late 1630s, when Charles's government seemed increasingly distanced from political and social realities in the wider country, and which might therefore be deemed most likely to invoke escapist and romantic versions of forests, aspects of real woodland practices are visible within the context of Davenant's masque.

What *Britannia Triumphans* engages with at its deepest levels is the question of forest domains as spaces of resource and the attendant battles over those resources that characterized mid-seventeenth-century responses to forests and woodlands as literal and imaginative geographies.[21] Battles over venison and common rights will be seen to lie at the heart of Jonson's *The Sad Shepherd*, but they also propel much of the remarkable dialogue and action of Milton's collaborative 1634 Ludlow masque to which this chapter now turns.

RESOURCE AND RIOT IN MILTON'S LOCALIZED MASQUE

'loose and disorderly persons in the night tyme' (King's Bench 9.797/5)

*A Masque Presented at Ludlow Castle, 1634* and its creation for the purposes of a site-specific performance for the inaugural occasion relating to the Earl of Bridgewater's installation as Lord President of the Council of Wales and the Marches has already been discussed in the previous chapter and the topographical resonances of the text, not least with its themes relating to the local watercourses of the River Severn in its final sections, identified.[22]

---

[21] See Beaver, *Hunting and the Politics of Violence* on the riots in 1641 in Windsor and 1642 in Waltham Forest, in particular, as the 'politics of unmaking the forest' just prior to the civil wars (p. 3).

[22] Milton's *Masque* was not the first theatrical entertainment to be staged as part of the inaugural celebrations. Earlier that summer a masque, presumed to be the work of Sir Thomas Salusbury, was staged at Chirk Castle in North Wales for the Bridgewaters. That it shares themes and characters

The first setting of the masque is not, however, riverine: '*The first scene discovers a wild wood*' (s.d. 0) and much of the action unfolds amid the thickly drawn branches of an English forest.[23]

Henry Lawes, the Caroline court musician, not only wrote the music for this collaborative theatrical production, but also performed the role of Thyrsis, the Attendant Spirit. The Spirit, a kind of genius of the place, has descended to the woods surrounding Ludlow Castle, where his intention is to assist three young adults, two brothers and their sister (referred to in the text as 'Lady'), the 'fair offspring' (34) of the earl, who are trying to make their way through the 'perplexèd paths of this drear wood' (37) to reach their father's castle. The slippage between literary, theatrical, and actual event is immediate; Lawes was the music tutor to the Bridgewater children who themselves took the leading roles in this masque (Lady Alice Egerton taking a major speaking role, the radicalism of which for a 1634 quasi-public dramatic event should not be underestimated). This kind of slippage would, in turn, have encouraged watching audiences to effect a similar movement between the 'wild woods' of the text and the major forested domains in the Earl's new territories in the Marches, the Forest of Dean in Gloucestershire.

These slippages could presumably have been further encouraged in performance by use of a painted backdrop of a forest of the kind we have already observed were commonly used in court masques. There are three key 'scene' changes signalled in the text, from wood to palace to a panorama of Ludlow Town itself, and it has been speculated that these transitions would have been effected via the use of changing backdrops in Ludlow Castle's Great Hall, which is deemed the most likely site for the 1634

such as a Genius of Place with Milton's work suggests a context for production that is collaborative and intertextual, which in many respects makes it much more typical of household and provincial entertainments of this time than it has often been held to be; see Cedric Brown, 'The Chirk Castle entertainment of 1634', *Milton Quarterly*, 11 (1977), 76–85. Brown includes a full transcript of the entertainment from BL Egerton MS 2623 in the article. For a parallel article that argues for Milton's greater embeddedness in 1620s and 1630s theatrical culture than has previously been acknowledged, see Ann Baynes Coiro, 'Anonymous Milton, or "a maske" Masked', *English Literary History*, 71 (2004), 609–29.

[23] The edition of *A Masque Presented at Ludlow Castle* referred to throughout is that contained within Robert Cummings (ed.), *Seventeenth-Century Poetry* (Oxford: Blackwell, 2000). Despite the title of that anthology, this version is admirably alert to the complex textual and performance history of the masque and its existence in variant forms, including the Trinity College manuscript, described here as 'Milton's working copy': the fair copy in the Egerton papers in the British Library, which is held by many to represent the performance text, in view of its notable cuts and redactions, and the 1637 printed edition under the imprimatur of composer and performer (he played the Attendant Spirit) Henry Lawes. See also S. E. Sprott, *John Milton: 'A Maske': The Earlier Versions* (Toronto: University of Toronto Press, 1973) and J. S. Dickhoff (ed.), *A Maske at Ludlow* (University of Ohio Press, 1968).

theatrical happening. However, detailed attention to the text (which is extant in variant manuscript and published forms) as a performance text suggests that a hybrid staging including indoor and outdoor elements, and varying deployments of the audience which was itself a mix of insiders and outsiders to the earl's community, was both more likely and more productive of meaning.[24] In such a staging, the experiential geography of the forest in the early stages of the masque proves crucial to the overall effect and, as part of their experience, the audience was surely being asked to imagine and remember their local knowledges of the nearby Dean.

In terms of seventeenth-century forests, the Dean was an exceptional case, since its resources not only rested in its timber and in introduced species such as deer, but in the mining and metallurgical riches of the site. Many workers and artisans lived within and on the fringes of the woodland because of the labour made possible by the longstanding ironworks and mining operations there. As a result, Sharp and others have identified it as 'a case study of a particularly bitter clash between long-standing custom and unique forest community on the one side and the economic and legal rights of the Crown on the other'.[25] Some of those unique aspects included the free miners of the Dean, who made claim to their own juridical systems and practices.[26] The Earl of Bridgewater, as newly inaugurated President, would be expected to intervene in these 'bitter clashes', which had, in the early 1630s, manifested themselves in physical protest and violence in which fences and palings enclosing the ironworks were destroyed, timber stands burned, and crown agents attacked.[27]

The most obvious way in which the new Lord President would be expected to assert his authority was through the courts. In the case of the law, the forest was once again home to a series of site-specific practices and customs. Forest law was enacted through a tripartite series of courts:

---

[24] This argument is central to collaborative research on the masque by myself and Susan Bennett, presented in 'Rehearsing across space and place: rethinking *A Masque Presented at Ludlow Castle*', forthcoming in Anna Birch and Joanne Tompkins (eds.), *Performing Site-Specific Theatre*. I am indebted to Susan for ideas and inspiration derived from our joint workshopping of this masque and its performative possibilities.

[25] Sharp, *In Contempt of All Authority*, p. 175.

[26] Cf. Sharp, *In Contempt of All Authority*, pp. 176–7 and see also C. E. Hart, *The Free Miners of the Royal Forest of Dean* (Gloucester, 1953), pp. 37–45.

[27] These attacks frequently spilled over into adjacent woodlands, in the early 1630s, as noted earlier, embracing the region of Mailescott Woods, overseen by the Villiers family, close relatives of the late Duke of Buckingham, whose agent was Sir Giles Mompesson, the same rapacious encloser who was the inspiration for Massinger's creation of Sir Giles Overreach in *A New Way to Pay Old Debts* in 1625. In the 1620s, Buckingham was also a Justice of the Eyre and a forest constable for Windsor.

eyres were the biggest and a high representative of the Court – determined by regional geography, since that role was taken in different parts of the country by a Chief Justice in the Forest Eyre south or north of the River Trent – would usually serve; lower down the scale of importance came the swanimote courts, followed by woodmote or verderers courts.[28] All of them had ostensible jurisdiction over 'trespasses against the vert [i.e. the trees and plants] and venison of royal forests', though in a hierarchy of descending importance and national significance.[29] In some regions both forest eyres and swanimote courts had continued as a custom – this certainly appears to have been the case in Sherwood Forest[30] – but by the 1620s the majority had lapsed, only then to be reactivated by Charles I's new interest in forest law. Eyres were first held in their revived form in Windsor in 1632, in the Dean and at Waltham Forest in Essex in 1634, in the New Forest in 1635, and in 1637 at Rockingham.[31] They became part of the social and political theatre of Caroline England and therefore we might expect drama to respond to these occasions in some way, especially theatrical events such as Milton's *Masque* that were designed for performance at a particular place and within a particular locality. The date of the Dean Forest eyre in July 1634 resonates strongly with the Ludlow Castle masque, which was performed on 29 September (Michaelmas Eve) that same year. Sharp notes, however, that this was itself a kind of show trial, intended 'as much to impress the "common sort" and reduce them to some sort of compliance with the Crown's will as it was to make money'; although fines of up to £134,000 were imposed in the Dean Eyre, very little of that sum was actually collected.[32]

With forest eyres recently held in the district, it seems likely that a highly localized understanding of the forest (both in terms of time and space) bled into the performance and the plot line of the masque, not

---

[28] Roger B. Manning in *Hunters and Poachers: A Social and Cultural History of Unlawful Hunting in England, 1485–1640* (Oxford: Clarendon Press, 1993), p. 66. It is worth observing that Henry Rich, Earl of Holland was Chief Justice in the Forest Eyre South of the Trent in the early 1630s; this is the same Henry Holland who was official Keeper of Hyde Park in London and to whom James Shirley dedicated his 1632 play *Hyde Park*, which is itself keen to play on that location's origins as a royal deer park. For a more detailed discussion of this play, see Chapter 4.

[29] Manning, *Hunters and Poachers*, p. 66.

[30] Manning, *Hunters and Poachers*, p. 67. He notes that Nottingham Castle was where the Swanimote Court of Sherwood Forest was held and recounts particular hearings in the 1620s that were part of ongoing disputes between Lord Stanhope and Sir John Byron in Newstead. These were held before Francis Manners, Earl of Rutland, who will resurface in this chapter as one of the real-life figures standing behind Jonson's *The Sad Shepherd* (p. 94). For details of the Stanhope–Byron hearings, see National Archives STAC 8/70/7, 28/10, 259/7.

[31] Beaver, *Hunting and the Politics of Violence*, p. 9.

[32] Sharp, *In Contempt of All Authority*, p. 210.

least in the depiction of Comus and his gang of beast-headed assistants who dwell in the woodlands and lay in wait for wandering travellers, seducing them with exotic liquor (64–5). In a number of ways, Comus represents the transgressive and the non-compliant and this idea would also have had local applications. Compliance with the Crown's will in the Dean region was desirable at this time; many of the artisanal and labouring protesters involved in recent fracas were facing prosecution at the 1634 eyre, including Dean miners, ironworkers and metal-men, carpenters, coopers, and joiners (for whom the trees of the Dean would have been vital raw materials for their trade) as well as shoemakers, glovers, and chandlers (who were dependent on animal products from the woodland).[33] Both the protests and the trials were the culmination of a series of disputes. Tensions existed both between commoners and landowners in relation to crown agents, but also within the woodland community itself, not least because it had been the site of migration by labourers seeking employment in the iron-workings and mines as well as an opportunity to live off the rich resources of this fertile and well-provisioned landscape. A petition said to be from inhabitants of the Dean had been sent to the King sometime between 1626 and 1631 objecting that:

there are a great number of unecessarye cabins and cottages built in the said forest by straungers whoe are people of very lewd lifes and conversations leavinge their owne and other countries and takynge this place for a shelter as a cloake to there villainies. By which unruly crue your Majestys woods and Tymber Trees ar cutt down and imbezeled and your Majesties game, of deere much disquieted and destroyed.[34]

Intriguingly, the vocabulary here resonates sharply with the seemingly magical and supernatural world of Milton's masque. Comus and his 'crew' are incomers to the wood (62–4) who 'all their friends, and native home forget' (77). Even the Attendant Spirit takes on the guise of a local as a 'swain' or tenant farmer from the nearby estate, one 'That to the service of this house belongs' (85). When Comus abducts the Lady, he initially appears to take her to a lowly cottage or cabin of the kind described in the contemporary petition and of the sort Sharp regards as typical in this period: 'The population in such forested and industrial areas consisted largely of

---

[33] For a full breakdown of the protesters' trades, see Sharp, *In Contempt of all Authority*, p. 183. If Comus was, as Brown has speculated, performed by a local actor these resonances could only have been enhanced; see 'Presidential travels', p. 9.

[34] National Archives State Papers Charles I 16/44/45; petition to king from inhabitants of the Dean (cited in Sharp, *In Contempt of All Authority*, p. 188).

cottagers, with no land attached to their dwellings beyond a garden or, at best, an acre or two of pasture. These cottagers supplemented their wages by exploiting the woods and pastures of the royal forests.'[35] Comus offers to show the Lady 'a low / But loyal cottage' (319–20), a supposedly safe place within the forest domains, but his planned exploitation is of a wholly other order. This could locate him in audience minds as a troublesome 'straunger', although in other ways he makes claim to local specialized knowledge of the place, and the Lady certainly takes him for a 'Gentle villager' (304):

> I know each lane, and every alley green
> Dingle or bushy dell of this wild wood
> And every bosky burn from side to side
> My ancient walks and ancient neighbourhoods.
>
>                                        (311–14)

Here, the necromancer invokes and appropriates the more familiar discourse of woodlands farming and husbandry, albeit to sinister and sexualized ends:

> I shall ere long
> Be well stocked with as fair a herd as grazed
> About my mother Circe.          (151–3)

Comus was introduced in the florid opening section to the masque as a son of Circe, so here we have the kind of mythological rooting of characters familiar from Jonsonian court masques, and the hybridized bestial forms of Comus and his 'crew' would appear to continue this theme of exotic strangeness (71–3). There are other ways, however, in which his 'rout' (s.d. 92) might appear all too familiar to the Ludlow citizens whom we know were present on the occasion of the masque's 1634 performance.[36] To understand how this might be so, it is important to address the question of popular protest in Caroline England.

Much has been written about the public theatre of protest at this time and the specific ways in which common rights activists deployed the

---

[35] Sharp, *In Contempt of All Authority*, p. 5.

[36] Entries in the Bailiffs and Chamberlains' Accounts for 1633–4 note payments to 'some officers when we were invited to the maske', Shropshire Record Office LB 8/1/155. f[11v]*; reproduced in Volume 1 of J. Alan B. Somerset (ed.), *REED: Shropshire* (University of Toronto Press, 1994), p. 113. This and related entries are discussed by John Creaser in '"The present aid of this occasion": the setting of *Comus*', in David Lindley (ed.), *The Court Masque* (Manchester University Press, 1984), pp. 111–34. For other ways in which this hybrid audience was in various ways interpolated into the proceedings of the masque, see Bennett and Sanders, 'Rehearsing Across Space and Place'.

language of skimmington and carnival in their actions and appearance. Many anti-enclosure protesters and poaching gangs (and the two group-ings frequently overlapped) wore blackened faces or masks; some even adopted carnivalesque identities such as 'lady Skimmington' and carried domestic utensils as weapons of protest.[37] This accords new meaning and significance to the description of Comus and his night-time followers (admittedly, Comus's own words) as a 'wavering morris' (116) and the Lady's implicit association of them with a slightly threatening form of rural celebration:[38]

> I should be loath
> To meet the rudeness and swilled insolence
> Of such late wassailers.          (177–9)

Ultimately, Comus and the lady will recognize their difference from each other from the distinct sounds their footsteps make. This raises fascinating ideas about the practice of walking a landscape and its link to the perfor-mance of personal identity; but by extension it connects issues of custom, inheritance, labour practice, and social status. This, in turn, sheds new light on Comus's claim to know (i.e. to understand) the 'ancient walks' of the Dean neighbourhood. The description of the noise made by Comus and his crew in terms of wassailing links them directly with the sounds associated with woodland protesters. One account of Dean anti-enclosure protesters in March 1631 claimed that they: 'did with two rummes, two coulers, and one fife in a warlike and outrageous manner assemble them-selves, together armed with gunnes, pykes, halberds and other weapons'.[39] Sharp has written of the 'localization of riot' in areas like the Dean in this period, but it is equally interesting to talk in terms of the ways in which Milton and his performers localized the theme of riot within the masque.[40]

If anti-enclosure riots and the 'theatre' of poaching at this time were closely tied to periods of hardship and want and therefore with particular scrutiny of access to the natural resources of an environment like the Dean, this in turn serves to make sense of the elongated debate over 'Nature's store' that is conducted between Comus and the Lady once he has imprisoned

---

[37] See, for example, Sharp, *In Contempt of All Authority*, p. 223; and Manning, *Hunters and Poachers*, p. 47.
[38] One indictment relating to nearby Mailescott Woods in 1633 notes that recently restored enclosures were destroyed once again 'by loose and disorderly persons in the night tyme'; see National Archives Kings Bench 9/797/5 (cited in Sharp, *In Contempt of All Authority*, p. 96), a wonderfully evocative phrase in lieu of Milton's masque that I have used as the epigraph to this section.
[39] Sharp, *In Contempt of All Authority*, p. 95 (25 March 1631).
[40] Sharp, *In Contempt of All Authority*, p. 2.

her in his 'stately palace' (s.d. 658; the second of the masque's key locations or settings). Earlier in the performance the Lady has spoken of the 'kind hospitable woods' (187) and she became separated from her brothers when they went on a berry-picking expedition (182–7) – an action of wildcrafting which prefigures the spatial tensions of Davenant's *Britannia Triumphans*. For Comus this kind of plenty in the woodlands is there for rapacious rather than measured exploitation:

> Wherefore did Nature pour her bounties forth
> With such a full and unwithdrawing hand,
> Covering the earth with odours, fruits, and flocks
> Thronging the seas with spawn innumerable
> But all to please and sate the curious taste.
>
> (710–14)

If humankind did not consume at will the produce of the natural world, Comus suggests it would be overrun and laid waste by its own fecundity. The Lady counters with a rhetoric of moderation, suggesting that Nature is a 'good cateress' (756), who:

> Means her provision only to the good
> That live according to her sober laws
> And holy dictate of spare temperance:
> If every just man that now pines with want
> Had but a moderate and beseeming share
> Of that which lewdly-pampered luxury
> Now heaps upon some few with vast excess
> Nature's full blessings would be well dispensed
> In unsuperfluous even proportion.    (766–74)

It is interesting to ponder how these lines played out on the occasion of the masque's first performance when presumably there was a genuine risk that Comus's stately palace and banqueting hall, with its glistening glasses of wine, would have directly mirrored the real-life situation in the Great Hall of Ludlow Castle.[41] Yet this is exactly the kind of slippage of space, place, and time that the masque is all the time embarked upon.

That slippage is present in the description of the surrounding landscape offered by the Attendant Spirit at the opening; as early as line 5 he refers to the 'smoke and stir' of the earth, on the surface a generalized description of the world but in a Shropshire and Forest of Dean context this could have had a very precise set of resonances, referring to the open mines and

---

[41] Bennett and Sanders argue that the production would most probably have moved into the hall at this point, presumably with a more select audience (see 'Rehearsal Across Space and Place').

ironworks of the nearby working woodlands in which so much of the action of the masque unfolds. What we witness throughout the performance right up to the remarkable moment when the scene transforms to that of Ludlow itself:

*The scene changes, presenting Ludlow Town and the President's Castle, then come in country dancers, after them the Attendant Spirit, with the two brothers and the lady.* (s.d. 957)

is a complex melding of literary and material landscape, and of the conceptual notion and actual practice of space and place. The Attendant Spirit has, in a sense, prepared the audience for this from the start when he fashions the landscape as a veritable taskscape in which they are active participants as much as the characters on the stage; 'But to my task' (18), he states, going on effectively to limn the physical and cultural geography of the masque setting for spectators.[42]

   In one very obvious way within the plot line, Nature appears to lend its store cupboard of products to the side of the Attendant Spirit, who arms the Brothers against Comus with a plant imbued with magical and healing properties. Referred to within the masque-text as 'haemony' (638), and therefore seeming to contain mythical properties explicitly linked to the plant used to overthrow Circe's powers, this is nevertheless a plant that was given him by someone local to the Dean woodlands, a 'certain shepherd lad' with botanical knowledge of healing herbs and the properties of plants. The plant which we know grows, now as then, in the Gloucestershire and Shropshire woodlands that abutted Ludlow was St John's Wort. Its yellow flowers carpeted the Dean landscape at various times of year. The masque-text tells us that this plant is part of the daily practice of walking this landscape performed by the all-important local labour force who are, in part, its inspiration: 'the dull swain / Treads on it daily with his clouted shoon' (634–5).[43] The swain stands metonymically here for the kind of local people to whom Comus and his type, as exploitative incomers – be they characterized as enclosers and ironworks managers, or as unwelcome migrant workers erecting unofficial dwellings at the woodland edge – offered a direct threat and whom Bridgewater and his new policies were promising to counteract and control.

---

[42] These ideas are very much ones produced in collaboration with Susan Bennett during research on the masque.

[43] The 'clouted shoon' is an indicator of the peasant labour force who work this landscape and who required heavily soled shoes held on with iron nails or 'clouts' for the purpose; compare with references to the 'hobnailed commonwealth' in Brome's *The Queen and Concubine*, 5.3.1288.

The containment of threat in the masque remains only a promise for the future, not a performed fact, since, much to the Attendant Spirit's annoyance, the necromancer and his supporters escape back out into the protective cover of the Dean. There was, however, a very immediate after-life to this production when, just two years later, at Skipton Castle in Yorkshire, there appears to have taken place a provincial performance of a 'Mask' that required 'a paire of shoes for Genius loci' and 'gold tinsell for Comus & his Company'.[44] We cannot be absolutely sure that this was Milton's text reconfigured for a Yorkshire performance as part of a series of theatricals commissioned by the Clifford family at their Skipton residence that year, although we do know that the masque had a rich post-production history with Lawes requested on several occasions to produce fair transcript copies of it.[45] Nevertheless, what we hear sounded in the archive in these references is the possibility that the woodland geography explored in this masque, for all its topographical exactitude at the time of its initial performance, found a new occasion and relevance, a new space and place, in the context of Yorkshire theatrical culture in 1636.

### HUNTING AND HOSPITALITY: FOREST LAW IN JONSON'S *THE SAD SHEPHERD*

'Never inquire whence venison comes' (Proverb, *c.* 1630)[46]

*The Sad Shepherd* has already been invoked as a play deeply engaged with the regional particularities of the Midlands in both its settings and themes (see

---

[44] The references are from Chatsworth, Bolton MS. 175, fol. 182v, as transcribed and analysed in Martin Butler's 'A Provincial Masque of *Comus* in 1636', *Renaissance Drama*, 17 (1986), 163–8.

[45] The point about the requests for copies of the masque is made by Lawes in the 1637 print edition. For the full details of the Skipton Castle season, which included performances of *The Knight of the Burning Pestle* and *A New Way to Pay Old Debts*, see Butler, 'A Provincial Masque', p. 153. Both these plays use woodland space in interesting ways and the latter has specific links to contemporary grievances over enclosure and rapacious land-grabs by incomers that may suggest some themed rationale for Sir Henry Clifford's selection of texts for performance, though Butler's general point about the performance of his status in the local community at a time when he was threatened by personal financial indebtedness is also significant (p. 152). Clifford was an avid collector of masque texts in the 1630s and is also linked to the playwright Thomas Nabbes. Butler speculates that Nabbes's *The Spring's Glory*, a household entertainment from *c.* 1638 (it was published that year), may well have its provenance in the Skipton context (pp. 161–2).

[46] This suggestive proverb is cited by Manning in *Hunters and Poachers*, p. 153; from M. P. Tilley, *A Collection of the Proverbs of England in the Sixteenth and Seventeenth Centuries* (Ann Arbor, Mich.: University of Michigan Press, 1950; repr. 1966), p. 696. It might be added, however, that in the end *The Sad Shepherd* turns out to be all about the provenance and sociopolitics of venison rather than turning a moral blind eye.

Chapter 1). Understanding the play in this way renders its representations of Robin Hood, Maid Marion, and the band of merry men resident in Sherwood Forest less a depoliticized invocation of romance and legend by an ageing playwright, than a careful analysis of the operations of woodland communities at the time of composition. As with Milton's *Masque*, the ways in which this aspect of the drama would or could have played in a provincial performance context gains depth from these suggestions. In their recent edition, Anne Barton and Eugene Giddens reflect on the significance of the carefully delineated setting for the action provided in the play's printed version:

The Scene is Sherwood: consisting of a landscape of forest, hills, valleys, cottages, a castle, a river, pastures, herds, flocks, all full of country simplicity. Robin Hood's bower; his well; the witch's dimble; the swinherd's oak; the hermit's cell. (Persons of the Play, 28–31)

Barton and Giddens note that 'All the action of the play occurs in the forest, or at Lorel's house and grounds on its outskirts, but Jonson wanted to locate Sherwood against a visual panorama of the surrounding countryside'.[47] I would want to add that there is also a clear politics in depicting the cottagers and commoners within the landscape in this fashion, but what Barton and Giddens rightly extract from this initial scene heading is the idea that the setting was to have a degree of 'visual realism'. The term 'landscape' had a precise theatrical connotation at this time and its use here could imply that Jonson envisaged for productions of this play those same perspectival shutters or painted backdrops mentioned earlier and that Jones and John Webb had pioneered in masque performances in the 1630s, not least in the production of Jonson's *Chloridia* in 1631.[48] This, in turn, raises questions about the performance context(s) Jonson envisaged for his pastoral drama. Barton and Giddens admit that if the play did require perspectival shutters, this made a staging in the mainstream commercial theatres unlikely: 'This was not to be a play for Blackfriars, let alone the Globe';[49] they further speculate that it could have been intended for the Cockpit in the Court, or perhaps the Salisbury Court Theatre – where perspectival staging may have been used for a performance of Nabbes's *Microcosmus* that same

---

[47] This point is made in the note to lines 28–31 of Barton and Giddens's edition of the play for *CWBJ*.
[48] For examples of perspectival scenery from the period, see Stephen Orgel and Roy Strong (eds.), *Inigo Jones: The Theatre of the Stuart Court*, 2 vols. (London: Arts Council of Britain, 1973); and for a wider discussion of landscape in Jones's and Webb's work, see Peacock, *The Stage Designs of Inigo Jones*, pp. 158–69. My thanks also to Barbara Ravelhofer for discussions on this topic.
[49] Barton and Giddens, 'Introduction', *CWBJ*, p. 6.

year[50] – but Jonson's relationship to the Caroline court by 1637 was so estranged that a court commission at least seems unlikely. The regional embeddedness as well as the material conditions of performance suggested by the extant script would, for me, place it more convincingly in a semi-amateur Midlands theatrical context of private household performances. Although Barton and Giddens rightly distinguish this text from Jonson's (presumed lost) pastoral drama *The May Lord*, the way in which they categorize that entertainment (extrapolating from references to it embedded in the *Informations*, the 'record' of Jonson's exchanges with Drummond of Hawthornden during his 1618–19 sojourn in Scotland) as possessing 'very much the look of an in-group private theatrical, half-masque, half-play . . .' would seem equally applicable to the design and make-up of *The Sad Shepherd*.[51]

   The specifics of the Midlands theatrical culture at this time will be the focus of more detailed discussions in the next chapter, but it is worthwhile noting here the ways in which *The Sad Shepherd*, with its themes of local politics, hunting, and gift-giving cultures, and its engagement with the vexed issue of the performance of hospitality within a community, seems to ally itself creatively with other household drama. Certainly, the 'Persons of the Play' is a useful key to the creation of Robin's 'family' (3), or household in the woods, as one directly mirroring provincial rural estates. Robin himself is 'chief woodman' and 'master of the feast' (2), the term 'woodman' acting in this context less as a signifier of the outlaw of romance and legend than a formal forest official working for the Crown within a defined geographic and administrative domain.[52] As Barton and Giddens have demonstrated, the vocabulary of forest 'walks' in the play has a very precise set of connotations. A forest walk is not just a path but an administrative unit overseen by a woodsman or gamekeeper like Robin. In 1.4 we witness Robin greeting guests 'to the jolly bower / Of Robin Hood and to the greenwood walks'; later, Clarion describes how Robin and Marion are 'the sum and talk / Of all that breathe here in the greenwood walk'

---

[50] From 1637 onwards, Salisbury Court became very interested in courtier dramatists and court drama, so it is not unlikely that it began experimenting with court-influenced perspectival staging at the same time; see Martin Butler, 'Exeunt fighting: poets, players, and impresarios at the Caroline Hall Theaters', in Adam Zucker and Alan B. Farmer (eds.), *Localizing Caroline Drama: Politics and Economics of the Early Modern English Stage* (New York: Palgrave Macmillan, 2006), pp. 97–128. My thanks to Lucy Munro for discussion of this topic.

[51] Barton and Giddens, 'Introduction' to their edition (henceforth 'Introduction'), p. 4. Interestingly, the only seventeenth-century record of a performance of this play appears to be for a Restoration household performance (BL Sloane MS 1009); see 'Introduction', p. 6.

[52] Barton and Giddens stress that there is no indication in the play that Robin is an outlaw 'any more than there is that the stag killed in Sherwood has been illegally poached' ('Introduction', p. 4).

(1.5.106–7). The deictic references throughout to walks and chases and, indeed, to parallel sites such as Lorel the swineherd's woodland edge cottage offer a precise representation of the particular spatialities of the seventeenth-century forest that we have already been tracing in the *Masque Presented at Ludlow Castle*. This kind of spatiality connects *The Sad Shepherd* to other plays from the period that feature the daily practices of parks and keepers, for example the Keeper and his assistant Slip doing the morning rounds of Marylebone Park in Nabbes's *Tottenham Court*.[53]

In *The Sad Shepherd* we also hear the particularized and localized language of those from the rural and craft industries, not least the woollen industry, with its seasonal shearings and washing of sheep. These are the individuals with whom a forest official such as Robin would have had to have regular dealings and negotiate over shared practice of the forest space, not least the wastes and spoils on which such workers often depended for supplements to regular income.[54] The lambing season, a pivotal moment in the lives of those in the woollen trade, is the ostensible reason for Robin's feast, which seeks to celebrate the skills of the shepherd who delivers the first lamb of the year with a flower garland.

While the idea of crowning a festival king or queen has a long history in pastoral literature, what we observe in *The Sad Shepherd* is not just the idealized trope of pastoral; in the same breath as he describes the important arts of lambing, Robin will acknowledge the existence of the 'sourer sort of shepherds' in the Vale, puritanical opponents to festivities such as theirs. This, of course, mirrored events in the provinces when

---

[53] One playwright who was particularly renowned for forest settings in his plays was the courtier-playwright Lodowick Carlell, some of whose plays transferred to a commercial context (*The Deserving Favourite* was performed at Blackfriars in the late 1620s). He was appointed one of the two keepers of Richmond Park in 1637 and was resident in a keeper's lodge there for several years after (see Julie Sanders, 'Carlell, Lodowick (1601/2–1675)', *DNB Online*). The prologue to *The Passionate Lovers* makes direct reference to this fact ('This author hunts and hawks and feeds his Deer / Not some, but most fair days, throughout the year') and Carlell's oeuvre therefore provides us with a wonderful example of slippage between actual practice and pastoral convention.

[54] Manning reflects on the potentially lucrative nature of forest offices granted by the Crown; roles as forest and game officials were especially desirable as they came with an allowance of venison as well as good fiscal rewards, so-called 'fee-deer' (*Hunters and Poachers*, p. 28). As well as lodgings, in 1633 a lord warden or lord lieutenant of a forest could be paid as much as £6,642. There was also the widespread assumption that keepers benefited from trading venison and game on the black market: 'royal game officers had to pay the wages of servants but some of them also profited from illegal trafficking in venison which clearly exceeded the amounts which they were allowed in fee-deer' (Manning, *Hunters and Poachers*, p. 28). An earlier drama, the anonymous *The Merry Devil of Edmonton* (1608), depicts the keeper of Enfield Chase reprimanding a knight for 'spoiling of the king's deer by darkness' (cited in Manning, p. 28). This was a highly topical point to be making at the time; the black market in venison and game was particularly prominent in this area owing to its proximity to the London markets.

Jonson was writing, but the same passage of dialogue also invokes a more rapacious form of competition in the shape of greedy rival farmers who appropriate neighbours' livestock or deliberately 'worry' their sheep with the scent of foxes (the 'tod' of the following quotation) or a troublesome dog (under the false guise of scaring badgers or 'brocks' from the land, which, then as now, were presumed with little evidence to be a danger to farming livestock) and even create pits for the cattle to injure themselves in:[55]

> to their store
> They add the poor man's eanling [lamb] and dare sell
> Both fleece and carcass, not gi'ing him the fell [skin or hide],
> When to one goat they reach that prickly weed
> Which maketh all the rest forbear to feed
> Or strew tod's hairs or with their tails do sweep
> The dewy grass, to doff the simpler sheep
> Or dig deep pits, their neighbours' neat to vex,
> To drown the calves and crack the heifers' necks,
> Or, with pretence of chasing thence the brock
> Send in a cur to worry the whole flock.              (1.4.23–33)

This is a very embedded picture of rural practices and of the mixed economy of forests and woodlands, but it also brings back into view the vexed issue of enclosures and the hostile activities of rival landowners that Milton's *Masque* and, indeed, Massinger's *A New Way to Pay Old Debts* had evoked.

Elsewhere in *The Sad Shepherd* the pragmatics of woodland farming appear to be at the forefront of several characters' thoughts. When Amie the shepherdess seems depressed – a situation caused by her love melancholy for Karolin – Marion assumes that her mood has a very practical line of causation:

> Hath any vermin broke into your fold,
> Or any rot seized on your flock, or cold?
> Or hath your fighting ram burst his hard horn,
> Or any ewe her fleece or bag hath torn,
> My gentle Amie?                          (2.4.9–13)

Amie can seemingly only respond in the restricted and conventional oxymorons of Petrarchan love poetry, but even then her poetics are noticeably located in a forest milieu: 'I burn, though all the forest lend a shade, /

---

[55] On rising opposition by Puritans to rural sports and festivities and its impact upon the literature of the period, see Leah Marcus, *The Politics of Mirth: Jonson, Herick, Milton, Marvell and the Politics of Old Holiday Pastimes* (University of Chicago Press, 1986).

And freeze, though the whole wood one fire were made' (19–20). What we gain here is the idea of the forest as a provider of timber, not least for purposes of fuel; the world of common rights and usage that we identified in Milton's *Masque* is implicit in Amie's language. My point is that Amie, like this play as a whole, remains rooted in a forest setting even when her familiar domain might appear to have lost all the reassuring familiarity of the seasonal cycle under the pressure of extreme passion (2.4.36–45). The magic and romance of *The Sad Shepherd* needs always to be understood in tandem with the practical and pragmatic world of woodland dwelling.

Since a woodsman's or forester's post was an official role that was usually accompanied by the provision of housing, a keeper's lodge, this also seems to tally, as Barton and Giddens observe, with the ways in which Robin's household is established as being a well-provisioned one with a full kitchen (including chimney nook) and, indeed, a cook.[56] Friar Tuck is not only the 'chaplain' but also 'steward' to this household (4), seen in 1.3 preparing the bower for the day's feast. Little John is a 'bow-bearer', which could suggest another formal forest official's role;[57] Scarlet and Scathlock represent different generations of huntsmen; George a Green is employed as an usher; and Much, the local miller's son, is employed as 'Robin Hood's baliff, or acater', which is to say that he purchases or provides provisions other than brewed or baked goods for the household.[58] There is an interesting implication at 1.3.20 that his own father fishes in the Trent for some of these provisions – 'for which my father's nets have swept the Trent' (1.3.20) – which in turn suggests a degree of nepotism in these financial and purchasing networks as well as giving us a glimpse, as elsewhere in the play, into the sideline earnings and cottage industries of rural inhabitants.

In the same way, we get a glimpse of the working world of woodland pastoralists; Lorel is a swineherd living, presumably, on the woodland edges and in the wooing scene with Earine at 2.2, he reveals to us the size of his holdings in livestock and land as well as the range of produce for which he is responsible:

[56] Barton and Giddens, 'Introduction', p. 5.

[57] Manning notes: 'The head keepers of royal forests and parks, perhaps bearing the title of lieutenant or bow-bearer or master of the game, were peers or gentlemen, usually held other offices in the royal household as well and would not have spent all their time in the country' (*Hunters and Poachers*, p. 28). Compare Wye Saltonstall's character of a keeper in his *Picturae Loquentes*: 'a fellow in greene, that's led about by a dog in a line [ . . . ] warden of the wild woods [ . . . ] His lodge is a lone house, often fayn'd in histories to give entertainment to wandring strangers' (sigs. F2v–3r).

[58] The River Trent was dotted with watermills at this time. Millers frequently made side-earnings through catching eels, etc. in traps by their properties. Much's father's offstage role is therefore further indication of the play's interest in the multitasking of subsistence-living rural inhabitants.

An hundred udders for the pail I have
That gi' me milk and curds, that make me cheese
To cloy the mercats; twenty swarm of bees,
Whilk all the summer hum about the hive
And bring me wax and honey in.     (2.2.15–19)

The mention of rents by Lorel – 'what rents I have / Large herds and pastures, swine and kye, mine own?' (2.2.5–6) – suggests, however, that he is no poor swineherd but a landowner with tenants, and this reveals a degree of contradiction in his status in the play. There is also an interesting political undertow to all this; Lorel's emphasis is very much on the fact that he is 'a good man that lives o' my awn gear' (11). Part of Charles I's dissolution of Parliament in 1629, a move that inaugurated the 'Personal Rule', was its expressed desire for the monarch to live more 'of his own' and depend less on subsidies. By contrast, Lorel stresses: 'This house, these grounds, this stock is all mine' (12). We also see in the characterization of Lorel and his family – his mother is Maudlin, the 'witch' of the nearby village of Papplewick, whose disruptive activities lie at the heart of the drama – something of the contemporary anxieties registered in the *Masque at Ludlow Castle* about the ad hoc communities growing up on the edge of and within the formal boundaries of royal forest domains.

*The Sad Shepherd*'s literal geography ranges wider than the domains of Sherwood Forest alone. As the previously cited printed scene heading indicated, the setting is also the proximate space of the Vale of Belvoir, which had its own castle to rival that of nearby Nottingham's (which was the domain of William Cavendish, one of Jonson's key patrons at this stage of his career). Belvoir Castle was inhabited by the Manners family, the earls of Rutland, with whom Jonson also enjoyed close relations.[59] Barton and Giddens note Robin's ability to move between these different domains and spaces as proof that he does not have 'outlaw' status in this play; in fact, the only person to use that term against him is Maudlin herself at 3.4.46 and again at 3.5.3, 'The strong thief, Robin outlaw'. Robin's feast, the details of which are carefully elaborated in the play, can be understood in this context, then, as a performance of his official power within this community.

As noted, in 1.3, Tuck informs us that he has stayed behind to prepare the bower (1–3) and to organize the entertainments that will accompany

---

[59] The Belvoir estate was the subject of a land rights claim by the Duchess of Buckingham in the 1630s; see Birch, *The Court and Times of Charles I*, 2: 223–4 for details.

the feast: 'the fine devices' (4). This makes this high-profile event seem even more comparable to the kind of private (or, indeed, semi-public) household theatricals that will be the focus of more sustained discussion in Chapter 3. Interestingly, one of the things Tuck is organizing is the digging or cutting of a green table – that is to say, a grass table and seating created from stacking cut turf. George a Green says:

> at your commands I am
> To cut the table out o' the greensward
> [ . . . ]
> To carve the guests large seats, and these laid in,
> With turf as soft and smooth as the mole's skin.
>                                    (1.3.8–11)

Jonson evokes a pastoral convention here which has medieval provenance, but one which is equally suggestive of the outdoor performances that characterized the entertainments that accrued around royal progresses in the Tudor and Stuart periods. Cavendish's own 1634 Bolsover entertainment, authored by Jonson and staged in Derbyshire close by the featured localities of this play, deployed the estate's gardens as a conscious performance space and there are numerous comparable references in other contemporary household performances from the region.[60] Similarly, Much the acater's provisions for the feast are suggestive of exactly this kind of grander estate event, that aforementioned list of 'Bread, wine, acates, fowl, feather, fish or fin' (2.3.19). An extravagant list of fish and fowl consumed at Bolsover in 1634 has been identified among the papers of another Midlands magnate thought to be the author of manuscript drama in this decade, John Newdigate III, and this contributes further to a notion of the early modern cultural networking being reconfigured in *The Sad Shepherd*: of people in a locality receiving each other's hospitality, watching each other's entertainments and seeking to emulate and even outdo them. That, in turn, gives a competitive edge to the preparations for Robin's feasting of his 'friends' in this play.[61]

In a household within a woodland geography, the deep significance of hunting (and its social flip side of poaching) to the lexicon and performance of the feast is perhaps inevitable and may itself involve a degree of imitative

---

[60] See Osborne MS C132.27.
[61] Lucy Worsley includes the document in her English Heritage Guide to Bolsover Castle. The specific association with the Newdigate papers is the research finding of Kirsten Inglis, who is a research student on the University of Calgary Osborne MS project and I am grateful to Kirsten and the team for their generous sharing of work.

theatre.[62] As already noted, under James and Charles, royal progresses became intimately related to hunting parties and, in turn, the royal hunt accrued an air of theatricality, becoming 'a kind of masque performed out of doors, [which] dramatized the power and mystique of monarchy'.[63] *The Sad Shepherd* is certainly permeated by the discourse of the hunt. Early on, Tuck says to Marian: 'Here's Little John hath harboured you a deer, / I see by his tackling' (1.2.10); 'tackling' refers to the tools of his trade that John carries, possibly a huntsman's horns, possibly a bow; the 'harbouring' action referred to is the process 'whereby the lair of the largest stag . . . is ascertained, so that he and no other stag may be hunted' (1.2.9n). In his stead, John describes how he has identified the largest stag in the red deer herd:

> For by his slot, his entries and his port,
> His frayings, fumets, he doth promise sport
> And standing 'fore the dogs.        (1.2.12–14)

The 'slot' is the hoofprint or track that the stag leaves in the ground; 'frayings' refers to the marks left on trees by antlers as the deer scratch off old velvet and 'fumets' refers to the heavily scented dung of the stag. Through this kind of density of linguistic reference, the excitement but also the carefully codified ritual practice of the hunt is beautifully conveyed.

Scathlock and Scarlet have gone ahead to rouse the deer and later we will have the description of the 'sports': the five hours it took to wear down the noble stag, and then the butchering of the carcass, as well as the tradition whereby he/she who killed it (and the gender equality of the hunting in this play is another striking aspect of Jonson's creation) makes the 'assay' or first cut (1.6.37) and the casting of the gristly bone on the brisket to the crows or ravens which tended to follow the hunt in hope of obtaining leftover carrion.[64] In this story, of course, the raven is thought to have actually been Maudlin in one of her metamorphic disguises, since she is later witnessed by Alken gnawing on the same bone in a corner of Robin's kitchen (1.6.66). This image of Maudlin and the bone conjures up for audience imaginations a conventional association between witchcraft and the disruption of practices to do with food production and food security

---

[62] An invaluable resource on the cultural significance of this lexicon and the range of practices attached to it is Manning's *Hunters and Poachers*; and Beaver, *Hunting and the Politics of Violence.*

[63] Manning, *Hunters and Poachers*, p. 6.

[64] On the significance of the raven in hunting ritual and practice, see also Susan Whyman, *Sociability and Power in Late Stuart England: The Cultural Worlds of the Verneys, 1660–1720* (Oxford University Press, 2002 [1999]), p. 30.

in vulnerable agricultural communities;[65] this is further emphasized when Alken describes her tendency to steal forth into the Lincolnshire wolds to wreak havoc on the farming and domestic economies based there:

> in the fogs
> And rotten mists, upon the fens and bogs
> Down to the drownèd lands of Lincolnshire.
> To make ewes cast their lambs, swine eat their farrow
> The housewife's tun [brewing vat] not work, nor the milk churn.
>                                                               (2.8.23–7)

The 'raven's bone' narrative also alerts spectators to the significant production in their own minds of the off-stage space of the kitchen with its all-important dresser. This will be the site for the storage and later preparation of the stag's carcass, as well as being the location of the turning spit watched over by the cook that both become a focus of Maudlin's aggrieved curses when she loses a battle of wills with Robin and Marion over the venison hunted for the feast. Maudlin makes the spit cease to turn and therefore causes the meat to burn, and she afflicts the cook with a kind of advanced arthritis (2.7.1–5).

In a separate plot line, Maudlin dispatches her daughter Douce, in the guise of the abducted shepherdess Earine and wearing the magic girdle given Maudlin by 'A Gypsan lady, and a right beldam' (2.3.39) on the night of her own mother's funeral, to Robin's household. The passage relating to the girdle enables an invocation of the pagan customs and folkloric beliefs associated with woodland communities almost as much as witches (Milton's *Masque* played on similar associations). What we are offered in the process is a spatial reinterpretation of village topography during the night-time funeral of Maudlin's mother:

> that very night
> We earthed her in the shades, when our dame Hecate
> Made it her gaing-night over the kirkyard,
> With all the barkand parish tykes set at her. (2.3.41–4)

---

[65] Obvious comparisons would be with the cauldron as a grotesque cooking pot in Shakespeare and Middleton's versions of *Macbeth* and the disruption of the wedding feast in Brome and Heywood's 1634 play *The Late Lancashire Witches*, which shares several kinships with *The Sad Shepherd* in its interest in localized and customary practices, dialect, and issues of female agency. On witchcraft and food, see Diane Purkiss, *The Witch in History: Early Modern and Twentieth-Century Representations* (London: Routledge, 1996). For a more detailed analysis of Jonson's remarkable handling of the witchcraft theme in this play, see my 'Jonson, *The Sad Shepherd* and the north Midlands', *Ben Jonson Journal*, 6 (1999), 49–68.

This striking image of the nocturnal appropriation of the churchyard and the howling of the village dogs is a memorable evocation of the repurposing of local spaces and places common to accounts of supernatural activity; as is the idea of the spinning women placed during this same ceremony at significant crossing points in the village, such as the town turnpikes (48). Spinning and witchcraft were commonly linked – witness Maudlin's later circular dancing in 2.6 – but this scene also enacts witchcraft's supposed capacity to reinscribe everyday spaces of business and travel, such as the turnpikes, which were symbolic of the emergent road and communications networks of Stuart England.[66]

The careful limning of the architectural layout of Robin Hood's woodland residence further connects *The Sad Shepherd* to the domestic realms invoked and deployed in other household and provincial estate performances, where the central drivers of household space – the kitchen and the buttery – were frequently and self-consciously alluded to and often included within the frame of the action.[67] Furthermore, what we observe in practice as the drama unfolds are the intrinsic connections between spaces – domestic and civic, inside and outside, forested and domestic interiors, game park and kitchen, landed estate and tenant cottages – in the careful realization of the overlapping communities and social and moral geographies of this play. However, it is the complicated plot line that accrues around the venison for the feast, and what Roger Manning has termed the 'complex deer-hunting culture' of Stuart England that best embodies *The Sad Shepherd*'s careful evocations of the practices and social implications of forest space.[68] Marion, having brought back the venison for the feast, is impersonated by Maudlin, who not only seizes the opportunity to put strain on the romantic relationship between Robin and Marion (enacted in deeply physical terms in earlier scenes), but also orders Scathlock to take the venison to Mother Maudlin's property – that is to say, her own house – where it will be better valued (1.7.4–11). Issues of social valuation, not only of people's roles but also of the resources available to them are in this way made paramount in the play.[69]

---

[66] See Chapter 4 on the specific mobility paradigms mobilized by these kinds of setting in other early modern plays such as Brome's *A Jovial Crew* or Jonson's *The New Inn*.

[67] See Alison Findlay's *Playing Spaces in Early Women's Drama* (Cambridge University Press, 2006).

[68] Manning, *Hunters and Poachers*, p. 5.

[69] On the significance of venison as social status symbol and relationship lubricant in the later seventeenth century, see Whyman, *Sociability and Power in Late Stuart England*, pp. 17–34. Much of the superb work she does there in tracing the economic and social impact of venison and its distribution among social networks can be applied to Jonson's 1637 play. I am grateful to Adam Zucker for this reference.

The terms in which Maudlin (as Marion) rejects Robin's romantic advances are telling: '[*Robin touches her.*] / Hand off, rude ranger' (1.7.3–4). A 'ranger' was also a forest official and gamekeeper, so this label would seem to confirm the earlier suggestion that Robin holds an official forest position.[70] There is, as Barton and Giddens's edition notes in the commentary, a sexual undertow here; 'ranger' connotes a sense of Robin as aggressively physical, a ranger over women's bodies as well as over royal lands. Maudlin will build on this negative and suspicious attitude towards Robin's official role, depicting him as a kind of government agent not to be trusted, when she accuses him of being an official surveillant, monitoring her behaviour in the forest walks in order to check and maintain the deer stocks. She calls him a 'spy':

> that watch upon my walks
> To inform what deer I kill or give away;
> Where, when, to whom. But spy your worst, good spy.
> I will dispose of this where least you like.     (1.7.20–3)

The 'this' to which she refers is the highly symbolic as well as practically nutritious venison. It is in 2.6 that we see these issues played out to the full. Maudlin, this time as herself, arrives before a confused Robin and Marion to give thanks for the gift of venison she has been sent. She dances with joy at the social inversions the action appears to signify:

> Send me a stag,
> A whole stag, madam! And so fat a deer,
> So fairly hunted [i.e. not poached], and at such a time, too,
> When all your friends were here!     (2.6.5–8)

Maudlin has returned this apparent kindness by bringing a gift apposite to her own life in the woods and presented it to Much the acater for the purposes of the feast. It is a local contribution, a 'pot of strawberries gathered i' the wood' (24) which Lorel's pigs might otherwise have rooted up or trod upon (25), as well as crab-apples, 'wildings' to serve 'scalded' (heated) with cream (26–7). Marion is unimpressed with this return gesture, stressing that the venison is a crucial element of the feast day: 'Red deer is head still of the forest feast' (35).[71]

Maudlin's significant, though not wholly accurate, claim is that she has shared the venison out among her neighbours, a telling attack on the

---

[70] Roger Manning has noted that it was not only the discourse of hunting but also that of forest law that the Robin Hood ballads and narratives mobilized (*Hunters and Poachers*, p. 17).

[71] On venison on the table as a marker of high status, see Manning, *Hunters and Poachers*, p. 110.

exclusivity of Robin's feast as well as the life of luxury in which a small minority live in the forest domains:

> But I knaw ye, a right free-hearted lady,
> Can spare it out of superfluity.
> I have departit it 'mong my good neighbours
> To speak your largesse.                    (2.6.36–9)

The use of a term like *largesse*, so key to the accepted discourse of aristocratic hospitality, is loaded in this context, let alone Maudlin's inference in a phrase like 'superfluity' that Marion and her ilk have not just enough but too much of the forest's resources.[72] Even so, the somewhat imperious Marion feels that this is a transgression against social codes and decorum:

> I not gave it, mother.
> You have done wrong, then. I know how to place
> My gifts and where, and when to find my seasons
> To give, not throw away my courtesies.
>
>                                   (2.6.39–42)

Marion manages in the process not only to sound haughty but to render the act of gift-giving an almost mercenary enterprise. This may well hit on a truth of the operations of early modern honour cultures.

Marion effectively accuses Maudlin of poaching the venison: 'What's ravished from me / I count it worse: as stol'n' (43–4). Poaching and social protest have been identified by social historians as being intrinsically linked and Maudlin is effectively associated with both in this drama.[73] While the magical aspects to Maudlin's storyline and the later entry of the figure of Puck-Hairy might seem to extract her actions from this kind of socio-political context, the play elsewhere appears to insist on these connections.

Admittedly, Maudlin's claims to any kind of proto-socialist sense of the good of the many is undermined by Scathlock's return with the carcass intact, requisitioned at Marion's instructions from the witch's property. Maudlin never did intend to distribute it among the needy, it seems, and yet, by raising the issue of appropriate treatment of the poor by rich

---

[72] Cf. Manning, *Hunters and Poachers*: 'It was an indispensable part of hospitality in the great household, and gifts of venison and invitations to the hunt bestowed upon guests, neighbours and friends allowed a magnate to display his power and largesse' (p. 5). Cf. Alison Scott, *Selfish Gifts: The Politics of Exchange and English Courtly Literature, 1580–1628* (Madison, NJ: Fairleigh Dickinson University Press, 2006); and Felicity Heal, *Hospitality in Early Modern England* (Oxford University Press, 1990). Superfluity would also seem to resonate with the Lady's desire for 'unsuperfluous even proportion' in human interactions with the natural landscape in Milton's *Masque* (l. 774).

[73] See, for example, Manning, *Hunters and Poachers*.

members of forest communities, she has created an intriguing spin on the Robin Hood story. This corresponds, I think, with nuanced representations of witchcraft in this play, both as part of a complex belief structure on the part of this community but also a belief under pressure from more pragmatic community members. When the witch-hunt is instigated later in the play by Alken (2.7.15–16) – the slippage between stag and hag in the terminology of the hunt is deeply unsettling (2.7.19–21) – George reflects with bell-like clarity on the issues involved in the social hounding of difficult neighbours or simply those different from others:

> I thought a witch's banks
> Had enclosed nothing but the merry pranks
> Of some old woman.        (2.8.36–8)[74]

There are other significant ways in which Maudlin's difference is marked in the play, not least through her use of a northern dialect form of speech, especially in her exchanges with her children.[75] In Act 2, Maudlin describes her previous act's activities to her daughter, Douce:

> The jolly Robin, who hath bid this feast
> And made this solemn invitation,
> I ha' possessed so with sic dislikes
> Of his own Marian that, albe' he knows her
> As doth the vaulting hart his venting hind,
> He ne'er fra hence sall nese her i'the wind
> To his first liking.        (2.1.9–15)

The reduction of Marion and Robin's romantic relationship to the base level of animal sexuality is equally striking. Maudlin invokes the lexicon of the rut; the vaulting hart is the mounting stag of the hunt that smells the female or hind in season. What we are witnessing in the scenes involving Maudlin and her family, then, is a linguistic representation of landscape dwelling: forest discourse in operation, performed at the level of dialect, accent, and metaphor.

---

[74] Cf. Sanders, 'Jonson, *The Sad Shepherd* and the north Midlands'.

[75] The northern forms accorded Maudlin and her children are akin to several linguistic markers used by Richard Brome in plays from this period that engage with ideas of northernness and, indeed, otherness; see, in particular, his 1629 *The Northern Lass* (Jonson wrote a dedicatory poem for that play's 1631 quarto publication) and his collaborative drama, coauthored with Thomas Heywood in 1634: *The Late Lancashire Witches*. On Brome and Jonson's engagement with northern dialectic forms, see Katie Wales, *Northern English: A Social and Cultural History* (Cambridge University Press, 2006); and Paula Blank, *Broken English: Dialects and Politics of Language in Renaissance English* (London: Routledge, 1996).

In 2.1 we see Maudlin with her daughter Douce – who, to confuse matters further, is attired as Eglamour's lost lover, the shepherdess Earine, who has been abducted and imprisoned in an oak tree by Maudlin – and her swineherd son who comes, much to his mother's scorn, 'new claithèd like a prince / Of swineherds' to woo Earine.[76] Lorel temporarily frees Earine from her arboreal prison to woo her, but most striking are the terms in which he woos, since these bring most overtly into the play, alongside the hunting and poaching storylines, the vexed issue of forest resources. Lorel offers the reluctant Earine his lifestyle, in the process invoking the raw materials and products of a forest community: small mammals, roots and fruits, and dairy produce:

> Ye kind to others, but ye coy to me,
> Deft mistress, whiter than the cheese new pressed
> Smoother than cream, and softer than the curds:
> (2.2.1–3)[77]

Lorel's performance, which constitutes a customized, localized form of the aristocratic gift-giving familiar from provincial drama and the practices of royal progress, is a source of some gentle humour. The scene would, I believe, have played with particular resonance and genuine impact in the contexts of an actual household performance:

> Why scorn you me?
> Because I am a herdsman and feed swine?
> *He draws out other presents.*
> I am a lord of other gear, this fine
> Smooth bauson's cub, the young grice of a grey.
> Twa tiny urchins, and this ferret gay.
> (2.2.36–40)

'Bauson' and 'grice' are dialect terms for a badger; the 'tiny urchins' are hedgehogs. Barton and Giddens have suggested that Earine is bound as a

---

[76] The play appears to endorse a very practical kind of magic compared to Shakespeare's *The Tempest*; the large oak in which Earine is imprisoned apparently has a door by which Lorel temporarily releases the shepherdess for the purpose of (unsuccessfully) wooing her; presumably, this suggests the empty trunk of a large oak which would be able to hold a person as well as suggesting a tree of symbolic power such as the Major Oak in Sherwood Forest that is such a source of Robin Hood-related tourism today.
[77] NB: 'deft' meaning 'pretty' is a phrase also used in Brome's *The Northern Lass*; Jonson and Brome appear very much allied in the Caroline period in terms of approaches and interests, and, most probably, regional networks. The specific Midlands significance of these networks to both writers is discussed in greater detail in Chapter 3.

working shepherdess to flinch from the offer of badgers, since these animals were held to be a threat to herds, not least to cattle. As editors, therefore, they defend Earine's cold-hearted response to Lorel's courtship offers, but there is at least as much room to see her scorn as a quasi-aristocratic contempt for the life of those who make their living from the woodlands. The grounds on which Earine rejects the gifted creatures is, after all, that they make her clothes smell and that the hedgehogs' prickles threaten damage to their fine materials: 'they fewmand all the claithes / And prick my coats' (2.2.43–4). She is similarly dismissive of the lower-status Lorel, calling him a 'limmer lown' (a worthless loon or fool). He returns her to the tree, wracked by disappointments only to face the further scorn of his unsympathetic mother (the 'my mistress' is an indicator of the issues of social scale at play in this exchange): 'Thou woo thy love, my mistress, with twa hedgehogs, / A stinkand brock, a polecat' (2.3.6–7). The focus in *The Sad Shepherd* on the resources of Sherwood Forest and the adjacent Vale of Belvoir proves to be fairly typical of 1630s depictions of a forest landscape and environment. Lorel's courtship practices, but also the battles over the venison for the feast between Maudlin and Marion, invite audiences to think about the issues of commoning and natural resources that we also saw played out in the masquing contexts of *A Masque Presented at Ludlow Castle* and *Britannia Triumphans* and in the more glancing but nevertheless freighted allusions of plays such as *The Guardian*. These representations raise for consideration the social and environmental impact of activities such as hunting and poaching in Caroline culture.

The dramatic texts examined here limn for us the cultural geography of individual seventeenth-century woodland pastoral communities, such as those of the Dean and Sherwood, in ways that afford us considerable insight into topical concerns centring on land use, royal prerogative, social mobility, resources, and food security.[78] Forests emerge in these plays, masques, and household entertainments, as well as within wider Caroline culture, as 'dynamic political arenas', spaces constantly coming into being, both actively made and unmade by those who try to live within, in, and off the landscape.[79] What remains key, however, to the ways in which these

---

[78] Cf. Beaver, *Hunting and the Politics of Violence*, p. 8, where he notes that: 'forest politics . . . involved a negotiation between royal claims to the forest as a hunting preserve and the legitimate rights of the commons to fuel, pasture, and other forest resources'.

[79] Beaver, *Hunting and the Politics of Violence*, p. 8; cf. also Massey, *For Space*, p. 95. Zucker makes a wonderful parallel point in his discussion of Windsor Forest in Shakespeare when he invokes de Certeau on the idea of space being brought into being through the 'ensemble of movements'

spaces operate on the stage is the subtle way in which early modern drama invites its audiences to retain simultaneously a sense of the literary and the material semiotics of woodlands space.

deployed within it (see *The Practice of Everyday Life*, p. 117). I agree with Zucker that 'we must look in part to men like park keeper and dog-owners to understand the local history of a forest' (*The Places of Wit*, Chapter 1).

# CHAPTER 3

# 'Hospitable fabrics'
## Thinking through the early modern household

In thinking through the particular geographies of domestic space in the mid seventeenth century, it is important to pose the question as to what exactly constituted a household. Often, when we speak of the early modern 'household', it is the larger country estates that spring most readily to mind; the regional power bases of eminent families such as the Cavendishes or the Newdigates in the Midlands counties of Nottinghamshire, Leicestershire, and Derbyshire; the Stanleys in Lancashire and on the Isle of Man; and the Fanes in Northamptonshire – all of whom are touched on in the discussion here. These were families who held power in the provinces as well as having influence at court and in the capital. It is the intimate connection between these zones of influence that has a major bearing on the idea of the household as a fluid and dynamic space, material and conceptual, that this chapter presents. No house or household, whether it was located in central London, in the suburbs, or in a particular region or province of the country, was a discrete entity; their interactions with other spaces and ideas, local and national, are key to a fuller understanding of their operations.

## THE COUNTRY ESTATE: A CASE STUDY OF BOLSOVER CASTLE

The large country estates of major political and landholding families are a useful starting point for any examination of the spatial dynamics and cultural geography of the early modern household. Alison Findlay and Richard Dutton have described these households as communities in their own right, often possessing their own 'playing spaces and micropolitics'.[1] The Cavendish estates are a fine example of this potent combination. William Cavendish, Earl, and later Duke, of Newcastle, and his brother

---

[1] Richard Dutton and Alison Findlay, 'Introduction' to Richard Dutton, Alison Findlay, and Richard Wilson (eds.), *Lancastrian Shakespeare: Region, Religion and Patronage* (Manchester University Press, 2004), pp. 1–31 (3).

Charles oversaw impressive households in the 1620s–1650s, at Welbeck Abbey – the family's main residence – and, additionally, at nearby Bolsover Castle and Worksop Manor.[2] These sites were renowned as places of architectural, scientific, philosophical, and artistic pursuit. William and Charles were active patrons of, and participants in, the major theatrical, artistic, and scientific research of the day; Charles was deeply engaged in questions of mathematics and architecture; William wrote poetry and plays, as well as encouraging and commissioning the work of Jonson, Brome, Shirley, John Ford, and others.

The architectural expansion of the Bolsover site under the aegis of John Smythson, heir to the architectural practice of his father, Robert – who had himself designed and built several of the most significant Elizabethan and Jacobean prodigy houses, including Hardwick Hall in Derbyshire, part of the wider Cavendish–Talbot family estates, and Wollaton Hall in Nottingham – was at its peak in the 1620s and 1630s. This coincided with a major site-specific theatrical commission to be performed there: Jonson's *Love's Welcome at Bolsover*, which was staged before Charles I and Henrietta Maria in July 1634. Commentators on the design of the Little Castle in particular, which sits at the heart of the Bolsover complex, suggest that it was a consciously theatrical statement made within the surrounding landscape, Mark Girouard suggesting that it functioned as a veritable play-castle.[3] Little Castle is a perfect example of the agency of theatrical and masquing culture at a material level in early modern society; if Bolsover was a gesture towards the fantastic and the theatrical, it was directly informed by the particular aesthetic form of the early Stuart court masque and its acute sense of the 'poetics of space'.[4] Already, the deep imbrications of ideas of theatre and theatrical practice within the literal spaces and geographies of this particular Cavendish household become visible.

When thinking about the Bolsover Castle estate, we are working with four major zones within the complex: the Terrace Range, the Riding School, the gardens, and the Little Castle itself. The theatrical experience of the

---

[2] Helpfully, there are surviving estate surveys of Welbeck dating from 1629 revealing to us the exact ground plan of the house in the context of the surrounding gardens and landscaped areas. These were undertaken by William Senior. See a brief discussion of these in Henderson, *The Tudor House and Garden*, p. 129.

[3] Mark Girouard, *Robert Smythson and the Elizabethan Country House* (New Haven and London: Yale University Press, 1983), p. 19. See also Lisa Hopkins, 'Play Houses: Drama at Welbeck and Bolsover', *Early Theatre*, 2 (1999), 25–44.

[4] The link is made by Martin Butler, *The Stuart Court Masque and Political Culture* (Cambridge University Press, 2009), p. 12, with reference to the scholarship of Stephen Orgel. Butler is himself alluding to Gaston Bachelard's *The Poetics of Space*, trans. Maria Jolas (Boston: Beacon Press, 1994).

Figure 8: View of the approach to Bolsover Castle, Derbyshire. Photo: Mimi Yiu.

household and its grounds for visitors to the site occurred in several, related stages. There was a slow approach, by means of a carefully located coaching route through the landscape, itself a performance of the Cavendish family's holdings in lead-mining and the mineral deposits of the surrounding hill-sides, and into the main castle complex, positioned in true fairytale style atop a commanding promontory with astounding views (see Figure 8).[5] On arrival, visitors succumbed to a careful orchestration of their movements, especially once inside the Little Castle. Timothy Raylor's pioneering work has made clear the sensory engagements that the castle encouraged as visitors traversed its lower and upper storeys, taking in its highly stylized walls and ceilings and the carefully themed paintings located within each room.[6]

Bolsover is an extant site, so we can put into practice the methods of the new archaeology promulgated by Tilley and others, that stresses the importance of walking sites and considering their materiality and

[5] Cf. Henderson, *The Tudor House and Garden*, on the 'drama of the approach', p. 1.
[6] Timothy Raylor, '"Pleasure reconciled to virtue": William Cavendish, Ben Jonson, and the decorative scheme of Bolsover Castle', *Renaissance Quarterly*, 52 (1999), 402–39.

specific effects.[7] What Raylor's article encourages us to do is to read the 'iconography' of the painted interiors of the Little Castle in a dynamic fashion, reading them textually, but also spatially. If we start on the ground floor, where, as Raylor points out, we are in the realm of the earthly and elemental, the rooms depict the humours and the labours of Hercules.[8] This suggests Cavendish's personal battles to overcome the earthier aspects of his own personality and temperament. From here, we ascend to the more spiritual and celestial space of the Star Chamber and the Heaven room, although, as Timothy Mowl has observed, the tensions remain, even in the upper echelons of the Little Castle, since the Heaven room with its biblical allusive framework still vies with the more Ovidian and classical paganism of the Elysium room: 'Sir William could choose between sacred and profane love merely by opening one door or another'.[9] Here, then, spatial practice also becomes active choice or statement.[10] This is an observable example of Lefebvre's 'lived space'.[11] It is as far as possible from being an 'everyday' space, in the sense that it is a theatricalized, performative site of display, and yet it is an integral part of the conceptual framework and practices by which the Cavendish family conducted themselves, on their own estates, in their region of the North Midlands, and in the context of the wider gaze of the Jacobean and Caroline courts.

The most overt textual and theatrical embodiment of that 'lived theatricality' at Bolsover Castle was *Love's Welcome at Bolsover*, the provincial masque that William commissioned from Ben Jonson to entertain the royal couple in 1634. The commission followed hard on the heels of the entertainment that Cavendish had staged for Charles I on his 1633 progress

[7] See Tilley, *The Materiality of Stone* and *A Phenomenology of Landscape*. For a useful overview of landscape theories, see also John Wylie, *Landscape* (London: Routledge, 2007).

[8] Raylor, 'Pleasure reconciled to virtue', pp. 404–5.

[9] Timothy Mowl, *Elizabethan and Jacobean Style* (London: Phaidon, 1993), pp. 120–1. Also cited in Raylor, 'Pleasure reconciled to virtue', p. 425.

[10] Compare this with Alison Findlay's analysis of the Fane estate at Apethorpe in Northamptonshire: 'The ideological power of Fane's pastoral is increased when we consider her entertainments in spatial terms in the context of the Long Gallery at Apethorpe where they were probably performed. This room, 100 feet long, 15 feet high, and just over 20 feet wide runs the whole length of the eastern facade of the courtyard, and is perfectly symmetrical with nine bays letting in extensive light. Long galleries like this gave what Timothy Mowl calls "an almost external dimension to the house". At Apethorpe, spectators could easily descend to the loggia and gravel garden immediately below the Gallery, or go up to the roof walk before, during, or after the performance. From these positions, the garden constituted a threshold between the aristocratic household and the surrounding rural landscape and community'; *Playing Spaces* (Cambridge University Press, 2006), p. 97.

[11] See Lefebvre, *The Production of Space*, pp. 33, 38–9. For a useful survey article on these ideas, see Zhongyuan Zhang, 'What is Lived Space?' Review article, *Ephemera*, 6 (2006), 219–23.

to Scotland for his belated coronation. The *King's Entertainment at Welbeck*, also authored by Jonson, was performed, as its title suggests, at the main Cavendish residence just over the border from Bolsover in Nottinghamshire. That entertainment can certainly be interpreted in terms of its local and regional inflections, but *Love's Welcome at Bolsover* is a rather different text in tone and timbre, partly because, alert to the additional audience member of Henrietta Maria in 1634, it experiments with Neoplatonic constructions and ideas.

The structure of Jonson's masque deliberately brings into play all the significant 'zones' of the Bolsover site, as well as enacting the dominant spatial practices of the early modern estate, and the provincial masque genre, such as dancing, feasting, and debate.[12] Performed on 30 July 1634, *Love's Welcome* began with a banquet, probably held somewhere in the Terrace Range. The company then 'retired' to the garden, where the royal couple was entertained by the anti-masque section of the performance. Cedric Brown has described the garden as another theatricalized space within the Bolsover complex, occupying the site of, and thereby drawing attention to, the medieval historical traces on the estate, and thereby contributing to the contemporary vogue for nostalgic chivalry hinted at in the architectural references of the Little Castle.[13] Intriguingly, the anti-masque drew attention to the architectural scheme of the event, featuring, as it did, a thinly veiled parody of Inigo Jones (Jonson could never resist the opportunity for a gibe against his former collaborator). Jones appears translated into the figure of Colonel Iniquo Vitruvius who, along with a group of mechanics, represents the workmen who were in the process of bringing Bolsover's theatricalized fantasy to life in bricks and mortar. The building was incomplete at the time of the 1634 royal visit.

From this outdoors experience, the guests moved on to a second banquet indoors and, ultimately, to the masque proper: a Neoplatonic debate between Eros and Anteros, the content of which has been related by several interpreters to the literal statuary and architecture of the Bolsover estate,

---

[12] On the provincial masque form, see Martin Butler, 'Private and occasional drama', in A. R. Braunmuller and Michael Hattaway (eds.), *The Cambridge Companion to English Renaissance Drama* (Cambridge University Press, 1990), pp. 127–59; and Karen Britland, 'Masques, courtly and provincial', in Julie Sanders (ed.), *Ben Jonson in Context*, (Cambridge University Press, 2010), pp. 153–61.

[13] Cedric C. Brown, 'Courtesies of place and arts of diplomacy in Ben Jonson's last two entertainments for royalty', *The Seventeenth Century*, 9 (1994), 147–71. This idea is explored as a specifically Caroline set of reconfigurations of the tropes of chivalry by J. S. Adamson in his article 'Chivalry and political culture in Caroline England', in Kevin Sharpe and Peter Lake's ever-seminal collection *Culture and Politics in Early Stuart England* (Basingstoke: Macmillan, 1995), pp. 161–98.

in particular the Venus fountain.[14] The fountain was built with Derbyshire stone, a further material 'performance' of localism and regionalism that connects to Jonson's poetic description of another Stuart estate, Penshurst Place in Kent, belonging to the Sidney family, which he described as being constructed with the local stone and by local hands: 'though thy walls be of the country stone, / They're reared with no man's ruin, no man's groan' ('To Penshurst', ll. 45–6).[15] Discussing various intertexts for the Little Castle, Raylor invokes the contemporary Jonsonian drama, *The New Inn* (1629). This play – with its lengthy expositions on love and valour and its carefully inflected account of Neoplatonism – has been linked to the ethical values and stances of William Cavendish, who was Jonson's chief patron at this time. For some critics, the play brings Cavendish directly onstage in the shape of the melancholic courtier, Lord Lovel.[16] Raylor's reading is more subtle: he points out that the central debate or combat in *The New Inn* is between Neoplatonism and Ovidianism, thereby bringing onto the stages of commercial London theatres, such as the Blackfriars where this play received its first controversial performance, the intellectual conflict being played out in the architecture and interior design of Bolsover.[17]

Neoplatonism, like theatrical innovation, staged its debates on an architectural platform as well as on the boards of the commercial playhouse; it impacted upon cultural output to the point where it is difficult to see where one set of practices or beliefs begins and another ends. Jones's symbiotic career as architect and masque-maker may be instructive, indicating as it does the inextricable relationship between the architectural and the literary or textual at this time; between the built environment and imaginative practices; and between the spatial and the performative.

[14] Cf. Henderson, *The Tudor House and Garden*, p. 169. Lucy Worsley has made the striking suggestion that the iconography of the fountain 'becomes more explicable if its audience is thought of as the quarrelsome Cavendish household itself, not just visiting courtiers, or William's socially educated equals', which suggests additional audiences at play in the self-conscious theatricalism of this estate; see her 'The "artisan mannerist" style in British sculpture: a bawdy fountain at Bolsover Castle', *Renaissance Studies*, 19: 1 (2005), 83–108. In the same article, Worsley makes the persuasive case that the raised wall walk that connected the Little Castle and the Terrace Range, both prime locations in the 1634 masque, can be best understood as an externalized long gallery.

[15] *CWBJ*, Forest 2. See also Don Wayne, *Penshurst: The Semiotics of Place and the Poetics of History* (London: Methuen, 1984).

[16] Raylor, 'Pleasure reconciled to virtue', p. 435. The article that delineates the links between Cavendish and *The New Inn* in detail is Nick Rowe, '"My best patron": William Cavendish and Jonson's Caroline drama', *The Seventeenth Century*, 9 (1994), 197–212.

[17] Raylor, 'Pleasure reconciled', pp. 435–6; and see, for example, *The New Inn*, 3.2.119–25. *The New Inn* was apparently hissed from the stage by its first Blackfriars audiences, though the reasons for this remain clouded in obscurity; for a detailed discussion of this, see my introduction to the edition of the play in *CWBJ*. *The New Inn* is, incidentally, a play much interested in the spatial possibilities of the inn-house, not least as site for theatre; this will be explored further in Chapter 4.

Masques were often highly occasional, site-specific happenings, but so in a sense was every performance, daily and 'extra-daily', at a locale such as Bolsover.[18] We need to read the built environment in this period, urban and provincial, as a dynamic, kinaesthetic space if we are begin to reconstruct both the everyday practices and conceptualizations in which its inhabitants were engaged. In doing so, we need to think in terms of the cultural geography of a house as being more than simply the footprint of its physical fabric; houses, especially a prestigious regional estate like Bolsover or Welbeck, stood metonymically within early modern culture for the wider operations of their owners: in the local community; in the larger space of the 'region'; through the circles and networks of acquaintances he or she moved within and often actively patronized; and in the national landscape.

PROVINCIAL NETWORKS AND MASQUING CULTURES

Brome's 1641–2 play, *A Jovial Crew*, conjures for its audiences a vivid image and idea of Squire Oldrents's Nottinghamshire estate from its opening scene. Oldrents's friend Hearty declares his envy of the idyllic estate over which Oldrents presides:

> Did ever any
> Servant, or hireling, neighbour, kindred, curse you.
> Or wish one minute shortened of your life?
> Have you one grudging tenant?    (1.1.12)

In this exchange, we receive the idea of the 'household' or 'estate' as a concept far exceeding a physical floor plan. The 'household' is a social concept of community; a 'good ruler', such as Oldrents, maintains family, servants, tenants, and the wider neighbourhood in a happy equilibrium through a combination of his hospitality and benevolence. Heavy stress is placed throughout the play on Oldrents's kindness to the poor and to those lower in the social hierarchy.[19]

---

[18] The phrase 'extra-daily' was coined by performance practitioner Eugenio Barba and refers to the power of performance 'to conjure images and transport the spectator from their everyday existence to an extra-daily dimension' (Jane Turner, *Eugenio Barba* [London: Routledge, 2004], p. 9). Barba outlines his theories in *The Paper Canoe: A Guide to Theatre Anthropology* (London: Routledge, 1995), pp. 15–16.

[19] A comparable household is nostalgically recalled by Lord Bornwell's steward in Shirley's *The Lady of Pleasure*:

> The case is altered since we lived i' th' country:
> We do not invite the poor o'the parish
> To dinner, keep a table for the tenants,
>     (2.1.121–3)

The larger subject of vagrancy and begging will be examined in Chapter 4.

In this same scene, we witness the practical aspects of estate management laid bare for us in the auditory account books produced by Oldrents's restless steward Springlove:

> You may then be pleased
> To take here [*Showing him the pages*] a survey of all your rents
> Received, and all such other payments as
> Came to my hands since my last audit for
> Cattle, wool, corn, all fruits of husbandry.          (1.1.30)

As well as listing these incoming profits – Hearty has already suggested that the estate brings in over £4,000 a year (12) – Springlove reveals the regular outgoings of a household of this stature, on items such as 'housekeeping, buildings, and repairs' (30) and on 'Journeys, apparel, coaches, gifts, and all / Expenses for your personal necessaries' (30).[20] What Brome gives us in the striking verbal detail of this scene is a means of imagining the daily rituals of this household, as well as the physical fabric of its buildings and grounds. When Springlove announces his wish to retire from his post and go wandering in the countryside with beggars and vagrants, Oldrents is shocked by the choice his steward appears to be making between a life of physical comfort and organized and controlled space and the unpredictable world of nature and the hedgerows and byways of the open road. In the process of delineating his shock, however, Oldrents paints for us a vivid picture of his Midlands estate:

> Does not the sun as comfortably shine
> Upon my gardens as the opener fields?
> Or on my fields as others far remote?
> Are not my walks and greens as delectable
> As the highways and commons? Are the shades
> Of sycamore and bowers of eglantine
> Less pleasing than of bramble or thorn hedges?
> Or of my groves and thickets than wild woods?
> Are not my fountain waters fresher than
> The troubled streams, where every beast does drink?
>                                      (1.1.47)

The reasons why Brome might want us to imagine in such detail this estate – its manicured gardens, the arbours of trees, the fountains, all feature elements in a property open to the public gaze, as we saw in the

---

[20] For some instructive real-life parallels, see the account books of John, 1st Viscount Scudamore, from the 1630s which are in Hereford Cathedral Library, MS 6417. The details of these account books, including coaching trips to and from the capital, are explored in more detail in Chapter 4.

real life example of Bolsover Castle – are worth pondering. This play was written and performed as late as 1642, when the commercial theatres were clearly suffering from the troubled political climate, as the country slid into civil war. Oldrents's well-managed estate could be seen as a romantic and nostalgic throwback to better times. There may, however, be a more precise set of referents at work in Brome's setting for this play and his careful imagining of its landscapes. In 1635, he had dedicated his city comedy *The Sparagus Garden* to William Cavendish and, like his mentor Jonson, in the later 1630s Brome appears to have nurtured links and associations to a Nottinghamshire network of patrons and artists. In 1637, as we have seen, Jonson located *The Sad Shepherd* in the Vale of Belvoir and its surrounding villages, that is to say, in the landed estates of Cavendish and his near neighbour and rival, Francis Manners, the earl of Rutland.[21]

Randall informs us late on in *A Jovial Crew* that Oldrents's property is in Nottinghamshire (5.1.904), a precise piece of internal mapping which begs further explanation. A simple response would be that Brome was appealing to the sensitivities of his powerful patron, the support of whom would appear to be all the more pressing as the theatres came under threat during the social and civic upheavals of the early 1640s. The King and the Court had already decamped to Oxford in what was perceived as a significant, proto-exilic move. This meant that many of the regular patrons of the commercial theatres were absent from their seats; Brome might understandably feel the need of powerful friends at this time. However Brome was also a playwright acutely conscious of place and the connotations of particular sites and spaces.[22] When he asks the audience to conjure a North Midlands setting for his 1642 play, there must be an ulterior motive other than mere financial gain.

Recent research into provincial drama in the Midlands area in the 1630s suggests that Brome, like Jonson, had extensive links to the networks in that region, and not just those involving Cavendish himself. One of the dedicatory verse writers for the quarto publication of *A Jovial Crew* in 1652 was John Tatham. Tatham went on to have significant connections with the city of London, authoring several lord mayoral shows and civic pageants in the 1650s, but in the 1630s he was a schoolmaster in Bingham in the Midlands. While resident there, he authored a pastoral drama, *Love Crown[e]s the End*, which, as its printed title-page informs us (it was

---

[21] Rutland's base was Belvoir Castle, a site which, along with Welbeck and Bolsover, Jonson had visited in person on his 1618 foot-voyage to Scotland.

[22] See, for example, Steggle, *Richard Brome*.

published along with Tatham's poetry under the title *The Fancies Theater* in 1640), was performed by 'the schollees of Bingham in the county of *Notingham* in the yeare 1632'.

*Love Crowns the End* opens in a grove and exhibits throughout an awareness of the classical and literary aesthetics of pastoral. We have the familiar domains of valleys, groves, thickets, and woods as the sites for romantic play and love melancholy, and even madness when Gloriana suspects that her lover Lysander has been brutally murdered. Yet it is precisely in one of Gloriana's set-piece conventional speeches of mental distress that an intriguing and momentary shift from the classical forest domain takes place. Spying Cliton in the disguise of a hermit, she declares: 'Ha, ha, what, are you *Lysander*? What, with that beard, there's a great bear beard indeed: heark you Fryer *Tuck*, doe you see yon handsome shepherd *Lysander*?' (sig. K7v). That reference to Friar Tuck suddenly brings into the frame of the performance an all-too-real forest locale close to Bingham (which remains today a small market town to the east of the city of Nottingham): Sherwood Forest. There is, of course, in this citation of a well-known landmark, a simple appeal to a locally drawn audience. However, just one year after the Bingham school performance, Jonson would author the first of his Nottinghamshire-specific masque commissions, the *King's Entertainment at Welbeck*, which included extensive Robin Hood elements. Cavendish was then Sheriff of Sherwood Forest. That Jonson would go on to write *The Sad Shepherd* with a Sherwood Forest setting and a Robin Hood theme suggests that the significance of a Nottinghamshire locale in the 1630s was far from happenstance.

Another pairing of manuscripts that indicate a Midlands provenance, and in the case of one of the manuscripts a Nottinghamshire one, relates to the play that is often referred to by the title of *The Humorous Magistrate*.[23] The play exists in two substantively different forms: one is a heavily worked manuscript that is part of a collection of plays in the Arbury Hall papers of the Newdigate family, currently on deposit in the Warwickshire record office; a further manuscript is located in the University of Calgary and this has come to be known as the 'Osborne manuscript' (after Edward Osborne, who purchased the text in a sale at Watnall Hall in Nottinghamshire in the 1940s). Margaret Jane Kidnie argues that the Arbury Hall manuscript suggests a play in progress and that the Osborne version represents a

---

[23] The title was accorded by T. H. Howard-Hill as part of his early research on the Arbury Hall manuscript version of the play ('Boccaccio, *Ghismonda*, and its foul papers, *Glausamond*', *Renaissance Papers* (1980), 19–28).

'more polished' later version.[24] While that genealogy is attractive in many regards, it does not fully account for the substantial textual differences that exist between the two versions. In thinking about them in a 'site-specific' context, a concept upon which the next section will attempt to elaborate, perhaps what we have are two different performative versions of the play, subtly adapted and inflected for different Midlands household contexts.

The identity of the playwright has not been established, though possible candidates for the role have been advanced, including Tatham (there are some internal linguistic similarities with his work) and property holder John Newdigate III, who, in the 1630s, was an avid theatregoer and patron of the arts, and who, from the evidence of his commonplace book and one published poem, was a writer.[25] Virginia Larminie notes that in the 1630s Newdigate made frequent visits to London for the purposes of bowls, cards, visiting Hyde Park, and attending various pageants, masques, and theatre.[26] In the process, he patronized a variety of playhouses, including the Blackfriars, the Cockpit, and the Red Bull, even visiting backstage at the Cockpit, so he was clearly immersed in theatrical practice.[27] That image of a theatrically literate man, who, in his regional home, was part of an equally vibrant literary and theatrical network, is further strengthened by knowledge of Newdigate's literary acquisitions at this time. In the 1630s, although by now resident mostly at a farmstead in Croydon (he leased out Arbury Hall after 1637), he was an avid collector of artwork and literature including poetry, notably the work of John Donne and George Herbert, masques, and plays. The play texts he purchased for household consumption (and possibly exchange between the families in this richly literate Midlands grouping), include Jonson's *The New Inn*, Fletcher's *The Scornful Lady* and *The Loyal Subject*, and Ford's *The Lover's Melancholy*. Newdigate was clearly well

[24] M. J. Kidnie, 'Near neighbours: another early seventeenth-century manuscript of *The Humorous Magistrate*', *English Manuscript Studies* (2007) 187–211 (196).
[25] See T. H. Howard-Hill, 'Another Warwickshire playwright: John Newdigate of Arbury', *Renaissance Papers* (1988), 51–62. The Tatham possibility is explored, though largely rejected, by Jean-Sébastien Windle's unpublished Masters thesis at the University of Calgary, 'Dating Osborne MS C132.27', September 2006. Many thanks to Jean-Sébastien and the Osborne MS team at the University of Calgary for permission to use this research in my work, and for their generosity, and that of the Social Sciences and Humanities Research Council of Canada, in supporting two research visits between 2008 and 2010. In 2010, findings from the project presented at the New Directions in Medieval and Renaissance Drama workshop suggested that the manuscript may well be authored by Newdigate. The full findings are forthcoming in a Malone Society edition of the play edited by Jacqueline Jenkins and Mary Polito.
[26] Virginia Larminie, *Wealth, Kinship and Culture: The Seventeenth-Century Newdigates of Arbury and their World* (Woodbridge: Boydell & Brewer, 1995), p. 169.
[27] Larimie, *Wealth, Kinship and Culture*, p. 170.

read in Caroline culture, having also received newsletters throughout the 1620s. Newsletters were, of course, purveyors of theatrical news from London as well as details of political events. According to Larminie, Newdigate appears to have obtained texts of masques that he and his wife had attended, including one in 1634; this would have been either Shirley's *The Triumph of Peace* or Thomas Carew's *Coelum Britannicum*.[28] In 1632 he purchased a copy of Aurelian Townshend's *Albion's Triumph* and Jonson's *Chloridia*. He bought Davenant's *The Temple of Love* in 1635, and either *Britannia Triumphans* or *Luminalia* in 1636. We can therefore state with some certainty that he was actively engaged with Stuart masquing culture at the prime moment of influence for the kinds of household theatrical represented by the Arbury Hall and Osborne manuscripts.[29] Whether Newdigate was the actual playwright is still contested, but unpacking the cultural geography of his particular circumstances in the 1620s and 1630s when these manuscripts appear to have been produced (handwriting evidence and internal references within the Osborne manuscript have led to a persuasive dating in the late 1630s) helps us to see the kind of embedded and site-specific household theatre that this chapter has hitherto been describing in operation.[30]

The Newdigates were based at Arbury Hall in Warwickshire, but through manuscript communities and literary circles, not least those patronized by Lady Jane Burdett in nearby Derbyshire, the family had close links to both the Nottinghamshire and Derbyshire branches of the Willoughbys. One of the Willoughbys' chief residences, already mentioned in the context of the Smythson family's pioneering Midlands architecture in the late sixteenth and early seventeenth centuries, was Wollaton Hall. Wollaton was renowned as a hub for literary and artistic pursuits, not least musical, and stood, in geographical terms, close by Watnall Hall, home of the Rollestons, the same family which, centuries later, oversaw the household sale in which Edgar Osborne purchased his manuscript version of our household play in 1947.[31] What begins to emerge from this kind of social mapping exercise is the ways in which families with acknowledged literary and theatrical

---

[28] Larminie, *Wealth, Kinship and Culture*, p. 170.

[29] It is interesting that the play contains a scene about the patronage of travelling players and singers. This constitutes a further interesting overlap with *A Jovial Crew* (which features an inset amateur performance). For details on touring theatre at this time, see Keenan, *Travelling Players*.

[30] Mary Polito and Jean-Sébastien Windle, '"You see the times are dangerous": the political and theatrical situation of *The Humorous Magistrate* (1637)', *Early Theatre*, 12: 1 (2009), 93–118.

[31] Alice Friedman, *House and Household in Elizabethan England: Wollaton Hall and the Willoughby Family* (University of Chicago Press, 1989); see also Windle, 'Dating Osborne MS C132.27'.

traditions overlapped and interacted in the period in question. Kidnie cautions that we only have 'circumstantial evidence of their possible inter-action', but it remains a tempting possibility that we might begin to see the complex social networks of regional and provincial England becoming visible through these manuscript traces.[32]

Although the manuscript play in both its manifestations is set in an unnamed county shire, there do at least appear to be gestures towards a Midlands context. When Constance runs away from her controlling father, the corrupt Justice Thrifty, she goes in search of a benevolent relative, Master Wellcom of Wellcom Hall. The theme of hospitality was commonplace throughout the period, but the aural links between Wellcom, Wollaton, and Watnall are, at the least, suggestive. Mary Polito and Jean-Sébastien Windle have helpfully drawn our attention to the links between the Arbury/Osborne play and *A Jovial Crew*.[33] There are shared themes of hospitality, household playing, escaped daughters, and forest-dwelling alternative communities, which, while not uncommon to Caroline drama, also suggest more precise kinships as in the portrayals of Thrifty and Clack, the corrupt justices in each play. These kinships encourage further speculatation as to whether Brome had access to a manuscript of, or even witnessed a household production of, the play and whether this, in turn, influenced the content, tone, and tenor of *A Jovial Crew*. If we accept the suggested dating of these plays, the direction of influence has to take place in this order and this is helpful in challenging the usual critical hierarchy whereby the metropolitan author is always deemed to have shaped the provincial experience rather than vice versa. Newdigate was Sheriff of Warwickshire from 1625 onwards and a commissioner of the peace from 1630; William Cavendish's comparable role as Sheriff of Nottingham is surely part of the fun of the cultural landscape presented in Jonson's *The Sad Shepherd*; fun that would have only been enhanced if the play did envisage an afterlife in the context of Midlands household performance as outlined here. As well as Jonson, then, we might start to establish for Brome a series of sustained connections to Nottinghamshire circles and networks in the later 1630s and to the theatrical and masquing cultures in which they clearly participated; and, therefore, to imagine the possible

---

[32] Kidnie, 'Near neighbours' makes the point that the Newdigates, Rollestons, Willoughbys, and Burdetts 'shared not only a network of friends and acquaintances but also geographical proximity that could well have facilitated the passing of manuscript drama between their houses' (p. 207). Kidnie further notes that Newdigate House, in the centre of Nottingham itself, was not completed until later in the seventeenth century, but would have facilitated ongoing transmission of texts between these families (p. 207).

[33] Polito and Windle, 'You see the times are dangerous', *passim*.

influences and effects that they might have had on the geography, actual and conceptual, of *A Jovial Crew*.

Up until the fourth act of the Osborne manuscript version, events appear to take place in interior spaces, ostensibly Thrifty's household and its various rooms, both public and familial, since, as a JP, he has receiving rooms where he hears specific charges laid by the local constable or the petitions of local people, as in Act 5 (we might compare a similar mixed use of his residence by Justice Squelch in *The Northern Lass*). Then we find ourselves outside in a pastoral scene involving the King of Shepherds and a feast-day event. The 'King' is only monarch for the day, so this alternative government, like so many in early modern drama, is a holiday occurrence, hence the discussion by the shepherds of the comparative injustices of real-life landlords: 'I am of that mind too, but I dare not say so, for feare of displeaseing my landlord; for he saies, his worship, being a Justice, keeps the beggars in a more formall subiection then the king of the shepheards his vnder dealers' (fol. 18r). The forest locale bears obvious comparison with plays such as Massinger's *The Guardian*, but it is the exterior spatial setting of this scene of alternative government that concerns us here. It is interesting that in the King of Shepherds scene, according to the stage directions the shepherds 'dig a table' (fol. 18r). How much more effective might this have been if the moment was staged outside? In that context the fourth-act transition would be not simply dramaturgic or architectural, but actual, material, and sensory. In this respect, it would compare directly to the shift to garden scenes in masques and entertainments written for the layouts of specific household estates, including, as we have seen, *Love's Welcome at Bolsover*.

There is comparable slippage between play-setting and the actual estate context in the next major stage direction in the Osborne manuscript: 'Enter 6 country wenches with provisions' (fol. 18r). This again seems strikingly similar to extant household entertainments from this period; for example, Lady Rachael Fane's Christmas entertainments at Apethorpe Hall in Northamptonshire in the late 1620s, with their heavy emphasis on food and gift giving. The consumption of food often punctuated performances.[34] Specific rooms within households regularly used for the purpose of amateur and professional performances, such as the great hall, often stood in proximity to the working areas of the property, such as kitchens and butteries. A number of texts therefore evoke these resonant rooms and

---

[34] On the significance of foodstuffs in Cavendish family theatricals, see Findlay, *Playing Spaces*, p. 48.

their related crafts and activities.[35] Observations of this nature suggest a need to reread *The Sad Shepherd*, with its themes of alfresco banqueting and appropriated venison, in the context of household entertainments, not least those recently performed in the localities of Jonson's Nottinghamshire patron, Cavendish. This notion gains strength when looking in detail at 2.2 of that play, in which a cook is punished with pricking and itching by the curses of Maudlin, the local village witch. Placed alongside the fifth act inbuilt theatricals at Justice Clack's residence in *A Jovial Crew* and the King of Shepherd's banquet in the Arbury/Osborne play, any clear distinction between real and 'staged' households is necessarily blurred.

The Osborne manuscript play enjoys exploiting these selfsame blurrings and slippages by bringing the world of the London commercial playhouses into its scenes, via the characterization of the forest thieves, Catch and Snap. This dubious pair waylay Spruce and Constance in the woods and attempt to rob them, albeit with only partial success (they themselves then fall prey to a far more hardcore gang of robbers). Catch and Snap also serve to usher in an active memory of the offstage locale of the capital in their recallings of a former life: 'O that it were as it had bene, that I had such a little duck as this, to vsher to a play, or wait vpon to the stillyard [ . . . ]' (fol. 16r). Theatre-literate audiences in a Midlands context might share some of these memories, as well as a vaguer knowledge of the world of prostitutes and sexual escorts that is conjured by the specific reference to the 'stillyard' or Steelyard tavern, which was located on the north bank of the Thames. Some audience members watching *A Jovial Crew* in 1642, which includes its own counterpart scenes of the rather more gentrified footpads, Vincent and Hilliard, recent runaways to the countryside, attempting to rob two gentlemen who are somewhat surprised by the gentility of their manner ('Here's a new way of begging!', says the first, 3.1.446), might have remembered Catch and Snap from this earlier Midlands drama.[36]

A further play text which potentially overlaps with the Midlands grouping detailed here is Sampson's *The Vow-Breaker, or The Fair Maid of Clifton* introduced in Chapter 1 in relation to the topos of river navigation. The place name in the subtitle of the play refers to a village that lay just outside Nottingham in the early seventeenth century (now an outlying part

---

[35] Findlay notes that Apethorpe Hall's Great Hall, one of the posited performance spaces for the Fane family theatricals in the 1620s–1640s, was situated close to kitchen and store rooms; *Playing Spaces*, p. 41.

[36] More violent versions of highway robbery are kept to the imaginative sidelines of Brome's stage, with Oliver's account of the 'counterfeit lame rogue' who threatened him with a cudgel (3.1.454).

of the city) and the title page to the printed version of Sampson's text is potentially revealing in terms of this Nottinghamshire connection. The play is described thus: 'In Notinghamshire as it hath beene diuers time feted by severall Companies with great applause'. The syntax is ambiguous and 'In Notinghamshire' could simply be explaining the geographical location of Clifton, much as I have sought to do, but, alternatively, it could imply that this play had been performed several times in the county during the Caroline period.[37] The use of the term 'Companies' suggests that these performances may not have been amateur ones by family or household members, but more probably a commissioned performance by a travelling company of professional players.[38] Family account books and records indicate that the Willoughbys of Wollaton Hall, rather than retaining a household troupe like some other aristocratic estates, tended to employ professional travelling companies to perform at that property and their Warwickshire base at Middleton Hall.[39] The mention in addition that Sampson's play has been enjoyed by audiences 'diuers times' adds weight to suppositions made above in relation to the Osborne and Arbury manuscript play versions that these texts may have enjoyed a peripatetic existence travelling between different, even neighbouring, households in a single locality; this idea of plays being passed around and possibly altered to suit each specific occasion is parallel to the ways in which we understand manuscript poetry to have circulated and evolved within provincial and urban communities.[40] A far more secure idea of early modern Nottinghamshire's theatrical culture begins to emerge from studying this series of seemingly disparate texts alongside each other, and in turn makes it more

[37] The ambiguities are discussed by the *DNB Online* entry on Sampson, but the Nottinghamshire connections detailed there – as well as being patronized by the Willoughby family, he co-published with significant local figure, Sir Gervase Markham – do lend credence to suggestions that this was a provincially performed drama; see David Kathman, 'Sampson, William (b. 1599/1600, d. in or after 1655)'. This is certainly the reading adopted by Ian Lancashire in his researches in the Nottinghamshire archives for the *REED* project; see his 'Records of drama and minstrelsy in Nottinghamshire to 1642', *Early Theatre* (University of Toronto Press, 1977), pp. 15–28. Lucy Munro, in personal correspondence, makes the suggestive link to Brome's *The Lovesick Maid*, which is also presumed to have had a provincial existence, at least prior to its commercial theatre life.

[38] Cf. Keenan, *Travelling Players*.

[39] The account books are part of the Middleton Papers in the Department of Manuscripts at the University of Nottingham. See also Alice Friedman's published research in *House and Household in Elizabethan England*.

[40] See Arthur Marotti, *Manuscript, Print and the English Renaissance Lyric* (Ithaca: Cornell University Press, 1995); and Arthur Marotti and Michael Bristol (eds.), *Print, Manuscript and Performance* (Ohio State University Press, 2000).

likely that engaged commercial playwrights such as Jonson and Brome, who already had links to the area through the patronage of Cavendish, were part of the circulating community.[41]

When we turn from the suggestive title page to the print edition of *The Vow Breaker*, the facilitating example of the Willoughby family theatricals at Wollaton and Middleton Hall accrues genuine relevance to the argument. Sampson dedicates his play to 'Mistris Anne Willoughby', the daughter of Henry, head of the Derbyshire branch of the family, who had their chief residence at Risley in that county. A recent manuscript discovery relating to Jonson's 1618 walk to Scotland confirms that Henry was one of the significant Midlands individuals whom Jonson met and received hospitality from en route to Edinburgh (at the same time as he spent a week in the Cavendish household at Welbeck).[42] Sampson, too, was clearly intimate with the family, enjoying Henry's patronage, as this dedicatory letter makes clear. Deploying the familiar trope of text as child, he describes the play in the following terms:

This infant received breath, and being under your noble Fathers roofe (my ever honored Master) and therefore as an Aire-lover belonging to that Hospitable Fabricke, it properly prostrates it selfe to you for a patronesse. (sig. A3r)

A phrase such as 'hospitable fabric' proves telling in this context. Sampson materializes the physical fact of the Willoughby property into a form of synecdoche for the household's wider operations in the community, both local and geographical, as well as in the more abstract artistic sense as a commissioning house.

The locally embedded aspects of *The Vow Breaker* are considerable and sustained, rather than constituting mere token references or allusions to local landmarks. As the title suggests, the play is partly located in Clifton, telling the story of a group of Nottinghamshire soldiers (or 'lads' as they are tellingly described at one point), who find themselves far from home at war with the French in the northern reaches of the nation: 'Making for Edenborough to the Queene' (sig. C1r). We witness a neighbourhood being dispatched to war. The poignancy of this in the context of a local performance, where there could have been comparable figures to characters

[41] We can add Shirley to this list, since he is an identifiable presence in Cavendish's personal manuscripts (held in the Portland Papers at the University of Nottingham) having assisted him with the creation of plays such as *The Variety* in the late 1630s.

[42] The manuscript is currently the subject of a joint research project with James Loxley.

such as Miles the miller of the nearby village of Ruddington in the real-life audience, is striking.

The play is unusual in some respects, since it is clearly located in Elizabethan times, going so far as to name specific courtiers such as William Cecil, and the tense relationship with Mary Queen of Scots, as well as directly portraying the Queen in the fifth act.[43] This more nationalistic-minded material, a version of the history play that might be placed alongside other 1630s experimentation in this form such as Ford's *Perkin Warbeck* (c. 1633), hedges around the melodramatic and ill-fated love story of Anne Boot and young Bateman.[44] Anne swears loyalty to Bateman as he departs for the wars, but her head is soon turned by another man. She is encouraged in this switch of affection by her father, who opposes the match to the lowly Bateman. The upshot of Anne's decision to marry her new partner, Jermane, is that Bateman returns from the war a hero, only to be rendered so distraught by his lover's betrayal that he hangs himself. The onstage enactment of his suicide, and its immediate aftermath in which the audience endures the sight of Bateman's elderly father's grief on finding the corpse hanging from a plum tree – the site of previous love trysts between Bateman and Anne – mobilizes direct intertheatrical echoes of Thomas Kyd's *The Spanish Tragedy*, the archetypal revenge drama. Not only is the complex relationship of Sampson's play with the revenge drama tradition signalled by this intertextual allusion, but the literary knowingness of the play indicates that, as a writer, he expected Midlands audiences to be theatrically literate.

The geospecificity of the fifth act of *The Vow-Breaker* has already been noted; in that act, the soldiers' leader, Clifton, is made Deputy Lieutenant and Lord Warden of Nottingham Castle.[45] The play text has earlier invoked the local landmark of the Trent, when Anne, pursued both in her mind and physically onstage by young Bateman's ghost, describes a dream in which she imagined herself walking by the riverside:

---

[43] Precedent for the Elizabethan setting could have been found in Jonson's 1633 play, *A Tale of a Tub*, which Chapter 5 will argue is deeply invested in the topic of parish politics.

[44] On the concern with national identity in plays of this decade, specifically in 1633, not least issues circulating around the union of the kingdoms on which *The Vow Breaker* might also seem to touch, see Lisa Hopkins, 'We were the Trojans: British National Identities in 1633', *Renaissance Studies*, 16 (2002), 36–51.

[45] There is possibly an in-built panegyric here to the character's local Nottinghamshire namesake, Sir Gervase Clifton of Clifton Hall. In the 1630s he was associated with military endeavour to the extent that he had a remarkable closet room decorated with images of military choreography (still extant).

Me thought I walk'd a long the verdant banks
Of fertill Trent, at an un-usuall time,
The winter quarter; when herbs and flowers
Nature's choicest braveries are dead.
[ . . . ]
Yet, then, though contrary to nature
Upon those banks where foaming surges beat
I gathered flowers, pansies, pinks and gentle daffodils.

(sig. H1v)

The Ophelia-esque connotations are quite deliberate and in themselves affirm an interest in *Hamlet* as a specific theatrical intertext in a number of the Nottinghamshire-connected playtexts from the period.[46] They also prepare a knowledgeable member of the audience for Anne's demise, not literally in the flooded waters of the river as in this flower-gathering dream, but later in the play when she dies of hypothermia following her ghost-driven escape into the snowy landscape surrounding her father's house. The midwives describe tracking her footsteps in the snow like a hare, but can, in the end, only return her limp corpse to her father's household. The Trent then reappears in the formal and civic context of the final act exchanges between the Mayor and the Queen, when the Mayor seizes the opportunity of having the monarch's ear to lodge his petition for the river's increased navigability. The Queen grants his 'former motion' to have the river made 'navigable'.[47] Here, we are witnessing the ways in which house-hold or provincial drama could use the performance script as a form of local wish-fulfilment, since it is not clear whether full navigability of the kind envisaged by the Mayor in his motion had been achieved by the time this play was performed. Sampson's rarely discussed play gives us potential access not only to evidence of a vibrant early modern Nottinghamshire the-atrical network, but also insight into the way in which these site-particular moments of theatre might both be performed and understood by the local community.[48]

---

[46] The Osborne play manuscript, for example, contains extended allusions to *Hamlet* and, in particular, to the figure of the melancholic prince; see Windle, 'Dating Osborne MS C132.27' and the notes and commentary accompanying Windle's working transcript of the manuscript.

[47] Thomas S. Willan, *River Navigation in England, 1600–1750* (London: Routledge, 1964).

[48] Shirley also appears to have had Nottinghamshire connections, not only to Cavendish, with whom he collaborated on theatre in the late 1630s, but with Edward Golding, a Colston Bassett man to whom he dedicated *A Contention for Honour and Riches* in 1633, a dramatic interlude that may also have had household performance connections.

SITE-SPECIFIC PERFORMANCES

each line of it
Betray's the Time and Place wherein t'was writ.
(Abraham Cowley, *Love's Riddle*, printed 1638)

In her important study of domestic life in relation to the domestic tragedy produced and performed during the early modern period, Catherine Richardson emphasizes the 'close relationship between the spatial and the interpersonal which characterizes domestic space'.[49] Arguing that we need to bring to bear an awareness of the early modern spatial imagination in our reconstructions and recuperations of these households and their theatrical and theatricalized cultures, Richardson invites us to imagine ourselves in the rooms and passages of the early modern household, to think about its particular intimacies, pressures, and tensions, about what is visible and also what is not visible, and how these spaces might correspond to and correlate with the active spatial imaginations required of audiences for early modern drama. This is important and pioneering research, but there are examples of theatre that were produced for and within household spaces that give us more direct, albeit necessarily partial, access to the ways in which the inhabitants and occupants of those spaces understood and imagined them. There has been major scholarly effort invested in recent years in the drama written for, read by, and often staged within early modern households; the so-called amateur or 'household' theatre that both distinguished itself from those plays written by professional playwrights for the commercial stages of London and was influenced by them, that imbibed energies and practices from the masquing and theatrical cultures prevalent at the court and yet that were simultaneously resolutely local and 'site-specific' in their concerns and their production conditions and conventions.

The study of 'site-specific' art and performance has tended towards a focus on the contemporary, on productions that can be clearly documented and archived by the performance studies researcher in the current moment.[50] Yet, there seems to be considerable intellectual mileage in the application of the terms and tenets of site-specific theory to the particular subgenre of household theatre in the seventeenth century. These productions could themselves be quite varied in type. Sometimes created and

---

[49] Richardson, *Domestic Life*, p. 9.
[50] See Nick Kaye (ed.), *Site-specific Art: Performance, Place, and Documentation* (London: Routledge, 2000).

performed by members of the household (for example, the Fane family productions in Apethorpe, Northamptonshire), in other instances, as we have seen with Cavendish and Jonson's Bolsover masque, these texts were commissioned by the owner of the household with an eye to a larger national context, and yet, in most instances, it would seem that they were composed and created with an active idea of their performance taking place in the particular rooms and gardens of the commissioning residence. In several instances, the extant manuscript copies we have of these plays – themselves a rich mixture of masque, entertainment, and full-blown five-act dramas – suggest that they were performed by and for local audiences, or at least, as in the case of *Love's Welcome at Bolsover* or *A Masque Presented at Ludlow Castle*, for a mixed audience of local people, family members, and household servants, as well as dignitaries and visitors to the region. Such performances then, and the Bolsover and Ludlow masques are both instructive examples, required of their audiences an intensely active mode of engagement that saw them at various times in the production melting in and out of a specific awareness of their surroundings and the sociopolitical and cultural symbolism of the site in which the theatrical happening was taking place. There was often inbuilt within the plotlines or actions, and sometimes embedded within the characterizations themselves, a very 'local' aspect to the narratives.[51]

Household theatre as a genre encourages the making of connections between personal and staged events. This might function at the level of the shared jest or in-joke; the fun of seeing a familiar figure from the household – the cook or the butler, for example – involved in comic or apposite experiences in the context of the drama. There is an important parallel to be drawn in this respect with the school drama of the kind Tatham was producing at Bingham in 1632 or, indeed, William Hawkins's *Apollo Shroving* performed by Suffolk schoolboys at the Hadleigh free grammar school in 1627. *Apollo Shroving* was a Shrove Tuesday pastoral drama which, while adhering to pastoral conventions in the main, has significant instances of this kind of 'local' referencing. In an appeal to the boy performers, and presumably to the audience, who would most likely have known intimately or at least recognized the actors, the script provides a range of boy's roles which latch on to the distractions of childhood. The bored Ludio knocks down fences as he tries to find someone to play with him on the Shrove Tuesday holiday, and Slug, who cannot get out of bed, arrives belatedly for everything, including the play's ending. We can

---

[51] Richardson, *Domestic Life*, p. 14.

only begin to imagine the real-life traits of the performers to whom these presumably alluded and the laughter they occasioned.[52]

We must practise considerable caution against offering homogenizing accounts of the experience of this kind of localized amateur drama;[53] there would have been a series of very different responses on behalf of different members of these schools and households, be they, for example, masters, servants, women, schoolboys, or neighbourhood tenants. Nevertheless, the application of site-specific theory to these texts is a potentially revealing method. While in modern performance theory, 'site specificity' more usually refers to work produced in non-traditional venues which take the site and space as the subject matter of the performance, in an early modern context it might be more helpful to think in terms of Mike Pearson's working definition:

Site specific performance is the latest occupation of a location where other occupations are still apparent and cognitively active. It is conceived for, and conditioned by, the particulars of such spaces: it then recontextualizes them.[54]

Provincial masques and entertainments commissioned for specific spaces and places in our focus period benefit from this kind of analysis. Many of the mythical and classical themes they perform rely on the audience's cognitive blending of these with other local and specific knowledges of the place where the performance is occurring, including the landscape, the daily uses of the building(s), the real-life personae of the sometimes amateur performers, and other kinds of local history and memory. These productions are, in Pearson's terms, conditioned by the sites in which they take place, but are also active in the recontextualization and reconfiguration of the understanding and practices of those places.

The Chirk castle entertainment that was staged in the Welsh countryside in 1634 for the Earl of Bridgewater, the same year that Milton and Lawes coproduced the Ludlow masque for him, certainly has a pronounced sense of place. It commences with the *genius loci*, the Genius of the place, 'wrapt in

---

[52] Important evidence of schools drama at this time is also provided in the commonplace books of the Reverend William Williams, National Library of Wales MS 15, 140A, ff. 54–5*, 116–17v*, 68–9v*, and transcribed in the Beaumaris entries in David N. Klausner (ed.), *RE[E]D: Wales* (University of Toronto Press, 2005), pp. 42–5.

[53] Richardson, *Domestic Life*, p. 7.

[54] Mike Pearson, cited in Gay McAuley, *Space in Performance: Making Meaning in the Theatre* (Ann Arbor: University of Michigan Press, 1999), p. 602. See also Mike Pearson, *'In Comes I': Performance, Memory, and Landscape* (University of Exeter Press, 2006). I am indebted to Susan Bennett for discussion of this material; see her unpublished seminar paper 'Performing environments' for the Shakespeare Association of America seminar on 'Sites of memory/sites of performance', Washington DC, April 2009.

amazement, at some happy changes hee observes in his Soyle, & Climate'.[55]
The sense of ownership of this land by the host family, the Myddeltons, is
openly asserted by Genius:

> See how the heauns smile on *our* land,
> & plenty stretch her opened hand,
> enritching us with hearts content,
> civility, & governement.
>
> Wee in our Country, that in us
> both happy are, & prosperous,
> & of our youth noe more made poore
> shall find ye Court eu'n at our dore.[56]

This developed sense of the local soil and climate, its visual splendour
(there are several references to the 'neighbouring Mountaines' that in a
very real sense provided the background to the performance[57]), but also
its productivity in agricultural and therefore in sociocultural terms – those
same mountains we are informed 'yeald / us goats, & in ye next adjoining
fields / pasture our muttons'[58] – is pursued throughout the masque as
the seasons are ushered in by Orpheus and lay stress on the foodstuffs
that the estate has provided for the feast that is an essential part of the
entertainment.

The masque libretto for the Chirk entertainment may have been the
work of a local man, Thomas Salusbury, whose reoccurrence in 1641 as
author of a wedding masque at Chirk Castle indicates an extended interest
in performance not only within the Myddelton family, originally from
Herefordshire, but also in the household(s) of the Salusburys of Lleweni.
There are records of Christmas masques at the Salusbury residence throughout the 1580s and 1590s and Thomas clearly inherited the family interest
in household theatre as a form.[59] The 1641 Chirk masque, for which only
a fragment is extant, was for a wedding in the Myddelton family, between
Sir Thomas Myddelton's daughter, Elizabeth and a Cheshire gentleman,
George Warburton of Atley.

Thomas Salusbury was actively involved in local politics in Denbigh
in Wales in the 1630s and wrote poetry and plays as well as provincial

---

[55] The edition referred to in parentheses is 'A Chirk Castle masque', transcript of BL: Egerton MS 2623,
art. 13 ff [1–3], provided in David N. Klausner (ed.), *RE[E]Drama: Wales* (University of Toronto
Press, 2005), pp. 141, 18–19.

[56] 'A Chirk Castle masque', p. 142, 15–23.      [57] 'A Chirk Castle masque', p. 143, 1.

[58] 'A Chirk Castle masque', p. 143, 1–3.

[59] Findlay suggests that while the textual traces may not always be extant, these 'supportive family
contexts' are likely to have been common in certain social circles (*Playing Spaces*, p. 42).

masques.[60] Unlike the masques, there is no clearly traceable performance history for his formal dramas, but their existence clearly establishes Salusbury as a significant player in the dramatic history of the provinces in this period. A fact which further strengthens those links is that the Salusburys were connected by marriage to the Stanley family, the earls of Derby, who, both at their residences in Knowsley in Lancashire and at Castle Rushen on the Isle of Man, were active proponents of theatrical activity in the 1630s and 1640s. Findlay and Dutton have stressed the significance of households 'such as those of the Earls of Derby [that] were networks of power, patronage and culture which rivalled those of the capital'.[61] Though we have only one extant Twelfth Night masque from Knowsley House dating from 1640/1, other evidence suggests that these events were a reasonably regular occurrence in the Stanley household, perhaps even taking place on an annual basis. Similar Twelfth Night masques are known to have been performed in the early 1640s at Castle Rushen after most of the family retreated there following the collapse of the Caroline government and the Parliamentary takeover of London. Extant songs composed by the family chaplain and a prologue as well as episcopal announcements of Twelfth Night masques in 1643 and 1644 suggest that these performance events took place.[62]

The Knowsley masque would have had a running time of about an hour and appears to have been composed fairly rapidly by Salusbury; the manuscript claims that it was 'Designed & written in six howres space'.[63] While it is not so easy to unpack specific uses of the architectural surroundings of Knowsley from the manuscript, the entertainment's invocation of the locality through its resident population is more than clear. The Prologue to the production was spoken by the household apothecary, Abraham L'Anglois, in his apparently 'broken English'; he is later given a gift of 'English hony' to aid and 'annoynt' his tongue in the speaking of this foreign language.[64] This alone makes for interesting connections to depictions of larger household establishments in contemporary commercial plays, such as Jonson's *The Magnetic Lady*, performed at the Blackfriars Theatre in 1632, and which features among the retinue to Lady Loadstone's household a doctor, Rut, and his apothecary Tim Item. Jonson's less

---

[60] See, for example, National Library of Wales MS 5390D.

[61] Dutton and Findlay, 'Introduction', p. 3.

[62] A transcript of the Knowsley House masque and the extant sections of the Castle Rushen entertainments is provided in David George (ed.), *REED: Lancashire* (University of Toronto Press, 1991), Appendices 4 and 5.

[63] 'A masque at Knowsley House', *REED: Lancashire*, p. 255 (10).

[64] 'A masque at Knowsley House', p. 255, 15; p. 261, 18.

than salutary version of household medicine will be the subject of detailed discussion in Chapter 5, but this kind of linkage again suggests that the worlds of household drama and commercial playwriting may not have been as distinct from one another as they have sometimes been held to be.

Other household employees who make an appearance in the Knowsley House masque include the cook, Peter, who in the gift-giving sequence later in the script is handed three pounds of Fullers' Earth to aid his and others' complexion, perhaps suggesting an in-joke about the condition of his skin (he may well have suffered from eczema or psoriasis, for which Fullers' Earth is still prescribed today).[65] Andrew Broome, the 'Clarke of the kitchin', is mentioned early on by the character of Christmas and later appears in the role of 'November' in the sequence of the months;[66] the chaplain (it could have been one of three men – Humphrey Baguley, John Lake, or Samuel Rutter, although Rutter's known participation in the Castle Rushen masques, he composed songs which are preserved in manuscript in the Manx Museum library, might encourage us to lean towards identifying him as the performer at Knowsley[67]) and other senior household servants, including the steward and the marshal, play roles in this entertainment which ran to seventeen speaking parts in total. There is benefit in conducting an active comparison between this example and the presence of household servants in the Fane family entertainments, as well as aforementioned scenes in commercial drama that involve household and, specifically, kitchen servants, such as *The Sad Shepherd*.[68]

As the mention of the presence of Christmas as a character in the Knowsley House masque suggests, the topic of that particular household entertainment is the familiar, but also very current, one in 1640/1 of Puritan objections to Christmas festivities.[69] Early on in the script, Christmas is subjected to the appearance of lean, ghost-like figures representing the fasting days of which he stands in contravention: 'thin gutt fridayes / sent to distroy thee' as Dr Almanac puts it; in 1640 and 1641 Christmas

---

[65] 'A masque at Knowsley House', p. 260, 13–15.

[66] 'A Masque at Knowsley House', p. 259, 20, 22.

[67] Roger Dickinson, 'Musical and dramatic entertainment in the Isle of Man', in David George (ed.), *REED: Lancashire* (University of Toronto Press, 1991), pp. 267–70 (268–9).

[68] There remains, of course, the working possibility that Jonson's play was written for a specific household performance (perhaps in Nottinghamshire, as previously speculated) or that the playwright had an eye to a possible afterlife in this kind of performative context. This afterlife would clearly have been highly viable in the Nottinghamshire cultural context, not least among the Cavendish family circles to which Jonson's play was so closely allied in theme and setting.

[69] Compare the allusions in Sampson's *The Vow-Breaker*, where there is a subplot involving the Puritan soldier Joshua, who attempts to hang his cat for killing a mouse on the Sabbath (3.1. sig. F2v).

fell on the traditional fasting day of a Friday.[70] The lengthy gift-giving sequence is fairly typical of household drama of this kind, which tended to fall between the festive dates of Christmas and New Year; it is also suggestive, in its active demonstration of Stanley family hospitality, of the kinds of older rural values that Oldrents is intended to signify in Brome's *A Jovial Crew* (and to which Justice Clack's mean-spirited household in the fifth act provides the counterpoint: 'I love a miser's feast dearly. To see how thin and scattering the dishes stood, as if they feared quarrelling', 5.1.963). The Knowsley House masque also mobilizes another trope familiar from other household entertainments, which is the casting of household servants and neighbours. All of these echoes and chimes, linguistic and performative, suggest the fertile interplay of ideas and content between these family and household entertainments, and therefore more widely between different provincial theatrical households. That Salusbury himself has links to household productions in Wales, Lancashire, and the Isle of Man suggests a greater degree of mobility and exchange, physical and intellectual, between these types of entertainment and theatrical event than is usually inferred from these 'unique' manuscript vestiges of performance.

The 1641 Chirk Castle fragment by Salusbury is a blend of Christmas entertainment and wedding masque, since the wedding in question took place on 30 December 1641 during the height of the Christmas masquing season. There are extant speeches which refer to the arrival of a troupe of gypsies at the house, presumably the anti-masque section of the entertainment. This was a familiar trope in itself from Jonson's household masque *The Gypsies Metamorphosed* (1621), which had enjoyed sponsored performances in several different household venues of varying significance, including the Duke of Buckingham's residence in Leicestershire and Windsor Castle itself (manuscript variants suggest that it was subtly altered on each occasion, confirming that texts were, indeed, thought of as 'site-specific' in the ways I am implying here). The gypsies' appearance in the Chirk Castle masque might also relate to a more contemporary drama, itself responsive to Jonson's Jacobean masque in both theme and character, Brome's *A Jovial Crew*.[71] We begin to unpack, then, in this series of connections and overlapping interests, a far more fluid interplay of texts and practices, not only between different manifestations of amateur or household theatre both within and outwith specific regions, but also between

---

[70] 'A masque at Knowsley House', p. 256, ll. 35–6.
[71] Once again, my thanks are due to James Knowles for sharing preliminary thinking on this masque; his full research will be published as part of his forthcoming edition of *The Gypsies Metamorphosed* for *CWBJ*.

commercial and amateur theatre, and therefore, by extension, between amateur and metropolitan sites of performance.

In the 1641 Chirk Castle masque, there are speeches by various wedding guests, including Sir Thomas Myddelton and his wife and various members of the Myddelton and Warburton families. In this almost round-robin performance of set speeches by specific family members, representing the generations as well as the genders, the masque recalls other Caroline household performances, around which there has recently been much interesting scholarship, in particular the dramatic juvenilia of Lady Rachael Fane at Apethorpe. She authored a series of masques and entertainments in the late 1620s in her teenage years, and those plays written and staged (often with elaborate scenery and stage mechanics and huge casts – all belying easy assumptions about the stripped-back nature of household performances) in the years subsequent by her brother Mildmay.[72] In her Christmas entertainment of *c.* 1626–8, Fane composes and directs the 'symbolic gift-giving typical of pastoral and private entertainments to reiterate the message of harmonious community at Apethorpe'.[73] In the sequence, members of the family are given gifts befitting their everyday roles and status – a young male scholar in the group is presented with a book, for example – but the gifts also reflect the physical and material fabric of the rooms in which the performance was intended to be executed. The natural emblems of birds, beasts, and flowers from the garlanded jester's emblem book draw into the body of the performance images that would have been present on the walls and fixed furniture of the house, as well as on hangings and tapestries.[74] The audience is being invited, as in previously cited examples at Bolsover, Ludlow, or Chirk, to melt in and out of the performance, and to remain constantly aware of the real-life setting and context in which events are taking place. Fane's self-conscious puns on household names also echo the architectural embedding of this kind of playful internal referencing in architectural splendours such as the Smythson-designed Hardwick Hall, where the initials of commissioning spirit Bess of Hardwick ('ES' for Elizabeth of Shrewsbury), as well as family mottoes and emblems, thread in and out of the designs. In this way, then, these household theatricals deploy the physical fabric of their setting as much more than just a venue. The

[72] For Rachael's work, see Kent Archives Office, Sackville MSS U269 F 38/3; Mildmay Fane's work is in the Egerton MSS collection in the British Library, and includes several sketches of theatre designs.

[73] Findlay, *Playing Spaces*, p. 100. Cf. Scott, *Selfish Gifts*.

[74] Surviving Jacobean and Caroline fireplaces at Bolsover's Little Castle and at Stokesay Castle in Herefordshire, for example, include coats of arms and natural emblems of this kind. On tapestries and hangings specifically, see Findlay, *Playing Spaces*, p. 94.

performance embodies the space and the building itself carries over the embodiment of the performance into everyday understandings of its spatial operations and significances. The everyday is theatricalized as much by these entertainments as the scripts gesture towards the everyday operations of the household through performative reiteration.

Alison Findlay has speculated at length on the possible areas of Apethorpe Hall in which Lady Rachael's masques and entertainments would have taken place, and for which they would presumably have been written.[75] Ruminating, in particular, on the play fragment and the way that it is 'exploiting the physical domestic space at Apethorpe Hall as part of its gender politics', Findlay suggests that it could have been performed either in the Long Gallery or in the Great Hall.[76] With reference to the entertainments' interest in foodstuffs and domestic production, she notes the proximity of the Great Hall to the kitchens and store rooms. Audiences were, in a sense, being invited to bring an active awareness of those 'off-stage' spaces into play when thinking about the themes of housekeeping and estate management that Findlay so astutely tracks in the Fane manuscripts. The in-jokes about Peter the cook and Andrew Broome the clerk of the kitchen in the Knowsley House masque inhabit a similar space of awareness and allow us to ponder an analogous location for that entertainment in the Stanley family's Lancashire property. Once again, these observations and analogies draw into the frame those scenes in Jonson's *The Sad Shepherd* involving the cook and the off-stage kitchen space (2.2). That play's themes, as we saw in Chapter 2, are closely bound up with notions of estate management, the functioning of hospitality within a rural community, and the inversion of decorum and social practice with regard to the provision of food. Maudlin the witch not only inverts everyday kitchen practice by stealing the venison intended for Robin Hood's banquet, but also by subjecting the offstage cook to all manner of cramps. As already noted, it has tended to be the assumption of Jonson scholars that this play was intended for commercial theatre performance, but that has never quite explained its deep imbrication in a North Midlands landscape, literal and political.[77] Perhaps these specific scenes, which demonstrate kinship with the Caroline household theatricals being explored here, indicate, at the very least, a dual purpose intended for this text – an initial London commercial theatre staging, perhaps, but also an afterlife in the rich Midlands amateur theatrical and household culture we have been unpacking. As with *The Gypsies*

---

[75] Findlay, *Playing Spaces*, p. 41.   [76] Findlay, *Playing Spaces*, p. 41.
[77] Eugene Giddens and Anne Barton argue as much in their forthcoming edition for *CWBJ*.

*Metamorphosed* in the early 1620s, there is a strong case for recognizing 'site-specificity' in the text, but also inbuilt adaptability to other future places and spaces.

Speculation as to the particular rooms in the house in which the Fane family entertainments were performed and other proximate spaces and practices that they might have evoked brings home the developed spatial awareness exhibited by the surviving family manuscripts. As Findlay notes, 'What kind of a stage the Long Gallery provided at the time of Rach[a]el's manuscripts is not clear, although the plays written by her brother Mildmay and performed at Apethorpe in the 1640s detail three separate doors, three flat revolving wings on each side of the stage, and a curtained area at the rear'.[78] Rachael may not have left the kind of detailed stage designs that are a feature of her brother's dramatic manuscripts, but her writings nevertheless include detailed stage directions that suggest a clear conceptualization of where and how these entertainments would take place, as well as the ways in which she envisaged adapting them, depending on the number of actors available to her.[79] Examining Rachael's account books from later decades, Findlay notes her close interest in household and estate management, suggesting that this rivalled that of her husband's stewards.[80] She goes on to suggest that Fane's masques and entertainments, with their dominant sense of the household, are proleptic of those later concerns.[81] This daughter of an aristocratic estate turns out to have more in common, in some ways, with Springlove the steward and his carefully kept account books in *A Jovial Crew* than with the restrictions endured on her father's estate by her literal namesake in that play.

We might also compare Brome's fictional estate daughters with the daughters of his patron and mentor, William Cavendish. Jane and Elizabeth Cavendish (later, Lady Jane Brackley and the Countess of Bridgewater, respectively) authored impressively conceptualized plays and pastorals, presumably for site-specific performance at the Welbeck estate where they were predominantly resident. It is noticeable how the two sections and sites of their 1644–5 drama *The Concealed Fancies*, for example, map onto the chief family properties of Welbeck Abbey and Bolsover Castle.[82] That play, and its companion piece *A Pastoral*, are also

---

[78] Findlay, *Playing Spaces*, pp. 97–9.    [79] Findlay, *Playing Spaces*, p. 41.

[80] Findlay, *Playing Spaces*, p. 42. On the importance of these account books for understanding Rachael's personality, see Smyth, *Autobiography in Early Modern England*, pp. 15–56.

[81] Findlay's source for these findings are the Todd Gray (ed.), *Devon Household Accounts Part II: Henry, Fifth Earl of Bath and Rachel, Countess of Bath, Tavistock and London 1637–1655* (Exeter: Devon and Cornwall Record Society, 1996). Rachael's account book appears on pp. 169–295.

[82] See Findlay, *Playing Spaces* esp. pp. 44–5.

intriguingly bound up with the everyday household practices of food production and storage as well as the creation and curation of household
'receipts' (recipes), both culinary and medicinal. Once again, the space of
the drama can be seen to embed and reconfigure the everyday lived practices of the household for which it was written. The influence of Jonson
on the aesthetic style and generic practice of Jane and Elizabeth's writing is
clear – *A Pastorall* involved an anti-masque of witches which owes much
to Jonson's version of the same in earlier Jacobean court masques such as
*A Masque of Queens* (1609) – and in this we can begin to measure the
impact of their exposure as relatively young women to the splendour and
excitement of the masques commissioned by their father and performed at
and with reference to the family properties in 1633 and 1634. The Welbeck
and Bolsover masques become a register in this way of the rich interplay
between courtly and metropolitan culture and the theatrical identity of
the provinces, not least in the Midlands, or, as the Welbeck entertainment
puts it so strikingly, 'here in the edge of Derbyshire (the region of ale)'
(132–2). While it would be wrong to elide the cultures of distinct regions
and sites, it is an equally false dichotomy to sever London performances
entirely from those in the provinces. It is more a case of mutual influence
for which we need to account.

The London notebooks of Robert Smythson, architect of Hardwick Hall
and father of John, who, as noted, presided over the Bolsover development
in the 1620s and 1630s, are a visual reminder of how trips to the capital
could inform provincial architecture in very real ways. Smythson Senior
was much influenced by some of Inigo Jones's continental innovations,
not least in terms of the grammar of domestic buildings. Jones's interest in
symmetry and light, which might from another angle be viewed as being
deeply informed by his involvement in theatrical experimentation in collaboration with Jonson in the Stuart court masques, fed into the Smythson
designs for the Cavendish family and therefore directly into the spaces
and frameworks with which the daughters, as well as Jonson, worked for
the production of their theatrical ventures. Similarly, the Fane family had
London connections and the experimentations with scenography in which
Rachael's brother Mildmay indulged at Apethorpe were an attempt to
realize, albeit within limits, Jones's theatrical and scenographic techniques
within a household context. All of the families discussed in this chapter
had London residences for at least part of the year;[83] on sojourns in the

---

[83] The Newcastle London house was in Clerkenwell; the Stanleys were based at Lathom House.

capital they regularly viewed or participated in court masques; they would certainly have had access to contemporary drama in the professional playhouses; they also purchased material artefacts, commodities, and furniture, which they transported back to their country estates. As Alice Friedman has shown, 'the apparently straightforward term "country house" obscures the multiple functions of the architectural type and oversimplifies the image of the highly complex culture it embraces'.[84] The journey of products could, of course, be from, as well as to, the provinces. For example, Joan Thirsk details the vogue for rush matting in grand houses both in the regions and in the capital, that boosted the indigenous craft industry in the East Anglian Fen lands.[85] Why, we are compelled to ask, should the traffic in goods and commodities not also include the drama in which provincial households were clearly engaged at this time? Undoubtedly, commercial theatre had its impact upon this drama; visitors to the capital both saw and purchased print editions of the latest plays and masques; but, in turn, we need to allow for the conceptual space in which the bolder experiments and themes of provincial drama might have wrought influence upon commercial playwrights such as Jonson and Brome.[86]

What I am invoking here yet again is the geographical model of flow. We can interpret this as a flow of bodies and experiences as well as of tangible material goods, and also, therefore, of ideas, of texts, and of theatrical practices. As we saw in the example of John Newdigate III, books are just one of the significant artefacts that made the journey to the provinces at this time, along with newsletters containing accounts of London theatre and court masques. One striking moment in the aforementioned Suffolk school drama by Hawkins, *Apollo Shroving*, involves a fascinating exchange where the writings and feats of John Taylor, the water poet, and his wherry adventures are mentioned. This example alone suggests far more cultural interpenetration between London and county cultures than is always acknowledged. It would be equally wrong to assume that the cultural and intellectual traffic was all one way: Jonson's and Brome's

---

[84] Alice Friedman, 'Inside/out: women, domesticity and the pleasures of the city', in Lena Cowen Orlin (ed.), *Material London, ca. 1600* (Philadelphia: University of Pennsylvania Pres, 2000), pp. 232–50.

[85] Joan Thirsk, 'England's provinces: did they serve or drive material London?', in Lena Cowen Orlin (ed.), *Material London. ca. 1600* (Philadelphia: University of Pennsylvania Press, 2000), pp. 97–108 (104).

[86] The working relationship that existed between William Cavendish and James Shirley is, as noted, a further case in point. See Barbara Ravelhofer, 'Non-verbal meaning in Caroline private theatre: William Cavendish's and James Shirley's *The Varietie* (c. 1641)', *The Seventeenth Century*, 21 (2006), 195–214.

involvement in identifiable Nottinghamshire networks in the 1630s suggests that they would, or could, have had exposure to the household theatricals being indulged in within those same spaces and places. Is Brome's *A Jovial Crew* and its explorations of ideas of good government on a country estate and the possibility of localized performances (witness the all-too-relevant household drama performed by the players arrested by Justice Clack at his property for the entertainment of his houseguests in the fifth act of that play) a direct response to the kinds of theatre he experienced in Midlands locales? If the Brome connections remain for the moment hypothetical, what is surely without doubt is the fact that there were rich, ongoing, multidirectional exchanges of goods, people, and ideas between the provinces and the capital throughout our focus period and that drama provided one of the main vehicles for this cultural and social traffic.

CHAPTER 4

# Moving through the landscape
## Mobility and sites of social circulation

In 1628, William Harvey, member of the Royal College of Physicians and later to become chief physician to the court of Charles I, published *Exercitatio Anatomica de Motu Cordis et Sanguinis in Animalibus*, translated as *An Anatomical Study of the Movement of the Heart and of the Blood in Living Beings*, in which he set out his revolutionary theories of the flow of blood through the body.[1] Harvey's theories of circulation, a product of anatomical experimentation, have been cited by sociologists, including Richard Sennett, as having transformed disciplines other than the purely medical; ideas of flow and circulation fed into urban planning and architectural theory from the eighteenth century onwards.[2] Ideas of mobility, circulation, and flow, however, are not merely post-Enlightenment phenomena and in this chapter, I explore the ways in which dramatists working during Harvey's lifetime were also thinking through these practices and modes of being in the world. This will be achieved by means of a diverse investigation into the social, cultural, and practical effects of mobility across a range of plays.[3]

Mobility studies have been a focus of considerable cross-disciplinary interest in recent years, establishing, as Tim Cresswell terms it, the 'new

[1] Harvey became 'Physician in Ordinary' to Charles I from 1630 onwards. See Geoffrey Keynes, *The Life of William Harvey* (Oxford University Press, 1966).
[2] See Richard Sennett, *Flesh and Stone: The Body and the City in Western Civilization* (New York: Norton, 1994), p. 256. Cf. Tim Cresswell's related discussions of the impact of Harvey on modern concepts of mobility in *On the Move: Mobility in the Modern Western World* (London: Routledge, 2006), pp. 6, 14. Cresswell makes the crucial point that to understand modern concepts of mobility, a historical knowledge is required ('Mobilities need to be understood in relation to each other', p. 9). On the impact of Harvey's theories in the early modern period, see Jonathan Sawday, *The Body Emblazoned: Dissection and the Human Body in Renaissance Culture* (London: Routledge, 1995), p. 23; and Jerome J. Bylebyl (ed.), *William Harvey and his Age: The Professional and Social Context of the Discovery of the Circulation* (Baltimore, MD: Johns Hopkins University Press, 1979).
[3] McRae has written in *Literature and Domestic Travel* of 'early modern struggles to make sense of mobility' (p. 7). My own thoughts on mobility owe much to years of productive intellectual exchanges with Andrew on this subject and I am grateful to him for sharing work and ideas.

mobilities paradigm'.[4] Social mobility, the movement of people both within and across cultures, has been one major wing of analysis and will underscore much of the discussion here. In addition, as well as examining particular spaces and environments as part of the so-called 'spatial turn', there has been new emphasis on thinking about the social production and agency of movement of various kinds, from transportation and new technologies to journeys on foot, from networks of communication to dance. The implication of the body, of the corporeal, in all these considerations proves central and, in that way, drama becomes an obvious artistic and aesthetic genre through which to explore mobility in both its literal embodiments and its figurative representations.

Bodies loom large in this chapter as we consider cultural types, such as the beggar and the gypsy and, indeed, the city stroller, as they were both realized and actively promulgated on the early modern stage in plays such as Brome's *A Jovial Crew* and his earlier city comedy *The Sparagus Garden*. Alongside bodies, sites and spaces can be re-examined from the vantage point of mobility studies. As Cresswell notes, 'Mobility is just as spatial . . . as place'.[5] Particular kinds of building allow for or foster particular kinds of relationship; they also facilitate particular kinds of movement. Inns, alehouses, and ordinaries will be a focus of discussion, in this regard, representing, as they do, crucial nodal points in national networks of circulation – of people, post, and ideas. Inns and alehouses were also social spaces that produced a significant set of meanings for early modern audiences; Jonson's 1629 *The New Inn* and its engagement with all these topics will enable a detailed case study of these ideas.

An analogous site to inns, in terms of providing a space of transition and encounter, can be identified in the parks and green spaces both within and on the edge of London, which became a focus of urban leisure activities between the 1620s and the 1650s. Our focus period witnessed the new predominance of pleasure gardens as a key aspect of urban experience and intra-urban mobility. One of the primary texts looked at in this chapter, Shirley's *Hyde Park* (1632), was a rapid response in dramatic terms to this shift in social and spatial practice. Nabbes's *Tottenham Court*, performed the following year, was another play that embraced spatial environments such as parks, as well as facilitating an exploration of urban walking as a specific cultural and geographical phenomenon in the 1630s.

This chapter, then, witnesses mobility operating on different levels and scales within early modern society. We commence out on the open road,

---

⁴ Cresswell, *On the Move*, pp. ix–x.    ⁵ Cresswell, *On the Move*, p. 3.

invoking wider ideas of community, nationhood, and national travel. A discussion of itinerant workforces and vagrancy is offered, but this, in turn, invokes the seeming polar opposite of those groupings that is the mobile aristocratic community of royal progresses. From this counterpointing, we move steadily 'inside' to explore inns and ordinaries as crucial signifying vectors on the cultural and imaginative map of mobility. This chapter's own trajectory of movement is quite deliberately, from the provinces and hinterlands of England towards the cultural and political centre of London, a movement that in some ways mirrors the geographical structuring of this volume. The by now familiar arguments about flow and scale pertain here also, as we examine London as one point in a complex matrix of national communication networks and as a space into which people enter or arrive; but the city also functions as a site from which people seek, albeit temporarily, to escape into locations for refuge and pleasure. The creation of spaces of 'resort' was dependent on new technologies of transport and movement, and the history of public transportation proves a central element in any account of these forms of social transition. I focus, in particular, in this chapter on the phenomenon of coach travel both as it impacted upon Caroline society and as it affected the plot lines of Caroline drama.

If the figure of the wandering or walking beggar is our opening image, we end with a rather different kind of walker, the purposeful city stroller whose movements and bodily choreography can tell us much about the new urban society of the 1620s and 1630s. I am interested in the ways in which those walkers practised, and, indeed, created the practice of, certain spaces and places. All of these examples serve to identify the ways in which early modern drama sought to engage with mobility in many guises and on all levels and scales, from the national to the local, from the public to the personal, from the bodily to the spatial. The plays invoked as examples give literal body and material shape to the definition and claim that: 'mobility is practiced, it is experienced, it is embodied. Mobility is a way of being in the world'.[6]

WANDERING AND MAKING PROGRESS ON THE ROAD

Roads constitute a chief facilitating locus in this chapter and will be considered in their rural and urban manifestations. The ways in which roads connected or fragmented communities, but also the ways in which people

---

[6] Cresswell, *On the Move*, p. 3.

travelled on and along them, prove central to any attempt to chart the social transitions that were taking place in the 1620s–1650s. My focus dramatists sought to respond to emergent road networks partly in their self-assigned roles as documenters of the social scene, but also with a developed sense of the agency and potential impact of their representations.

Perambulation of various kinds will be considered in this chapter, culminating in the urban and urbane context. The first form of walking roads and highways that I want to examine, however, brings into view the world of the itinerant poor and suggests the anxieties that were associated with roadways and mobility in the early modern mindset. Patricia Fumerton's enlightening study of socially marginal groups, which she clusters under the generic title of the 'unsettled', has been instrumental in drawing our attention to those sectors of society who were 'place-less', literally home-less, in this period.[7] She examines the 'itinerant poor, who were frequently subject to arrest as they moved geographically along various lines of gainful employment'; individuals such as chapmen, peddlers, carriers, entertainers, wire-drawers (button-makers), seasonal harvest workers, and wage labourers, whom she describes as 'itinerant and multitasked workers'.[8] Fumerton's point is that their voices are harder to locate in archives that have an elite or governmental provenance, and are sometimes therefore lost to scholarship. These are the same itinerant communities that David Rollinson has argued must provide the key to a new, more dynamic form of social history, one based less on fixed patterns of settlement in which landscape is invoked as 'passive backdrop' and more on an understanding of the operation of 'networks in space', be these networks of kinship or employment.[9] These kinds of social grouping and their movements are available to us in part in those archival documents that Rollinson suggests we must read 'through' as 'a source of evidence . . . to physical spaces', but also, I would argue, through their representation in the drama of the day.[10]

---

[7] Patricia Fumerton, *Unsettled: The Culture of Mobility and the Working Poor* (University of Chicago Press, 2006), p. xi.

[8] Fumerton, *Unsettled*, p. xii. See also A. L. Beier, *Masterless Men: The Vagrancy Problem in England, 1560–1640* (London: Methuen, 1985), pp. 70–1; and Paul Slack, *Poverty and Policy in Tudor and Stuart England* (London: Longman, 1988).

[9] David Rollinson, 'Exploding England: the dialectics of mobility and settlement in early modern England', *Social History*, 24 (1999), 1–16 (13).

[10] Rollinson, 'Exploding England', p. 15; although it should be noted that Fumerton dismisses the potential of Brome's *A Jovial Crew* and other early modern beggar plays as a social document or source in this regard (*Unsettled*, p. 45) I think that there is considerable mileage in the application of her findings to Brome's treatment of the themes of vagrancy and begging in his 1642 play.

Nabbes's probable provincial household entertainment of 1638, *The Spring's Glory*, includes towards its close a change of scene that reveals the following dynamic: 'Here the Scene suddenly changeth into a Prospect, with trees, budded, the earth somewhat greene and at one side an old Barne, out of which issues a company of beggars, with a Bag-pipe.'[11] The swift scene change is an indication that audiences were expected to compute its meaning fairly rapidly. The sheltering of the homeless in barns on their estates over the winter (also those months when short-term employment in an agricultural context was least likely to be available) was an expected act of kindness on the part of good aristocratic landlords, and Nabbes, by implication, praises his household patrons – if this text is, as Martin Butler has persuasively argued, most likely a 1630s household entertainment[12] – as an example of this form of good practice. This is also the beneficent behaviour demonstrated by Oldrents, the aristocratic landlord in Brome's *A Jovial Crew*, which, as was argued in Chapter 3, has strong compositional and thematic links to a range of household dramas and entertainments from this period. Over the winter months, Oldrents has been sheltering and offering provisions to a community of beggars in the large barn on his estate, as well as housing a closer companion, Hearty, in his own property.

Randall, Oldrents's elderly house-servant, makes this practice of hospitality both visible and tangible to the audience in 1.1 when he appears onstage with fellow servants carrying a kettle (cauldron), jacks (large leather jugs for carrying beer), and an empty bread-basket (1.1. s.d. 58). The beggars, we are informed, have consumed the contents with gratitude: 'they have all prayed for you' (1.1.59). Randall may have some stated reservations about whether this is the most advantageous way for Oldrents to perform acts of charity in the community, wondering if it 'might be better [ . . . ] to help breed up poor men's children, or decayed labourers past their work or travel, or towards the setting up of poor young married couples' (1.1.65), but he is clearly drawn to the sense of fellowship represented by the beggars

---

McRae's *Literature and Domestic Travel*, heavily influenced in its turn by Fumerton's research, is similarly hesitant about the potential of drama to realize or represent the road as a space. He reflects that, by comparison with rivers, roads are not usually seen as poetic and suggests that 'They have little place on the stage either', although his own complementary study of inns in that same book and my corresponding introduction to my edition of *The New Inn* in *CWBJ* go some way to suggesting how plays can engage with the road network in suggestive and potentially transformative ways ('inns and alehouses [ . . . ] provide opportunities for authors to interrogate the emergent economy of mobility' (McRae, *Literature and Domestic Travel*, p. 69). See also my 'Domestic travel and social mobility'.

[11] Thomas Nabbes, *The Spring's Glorie* (London, 1638), sig. C2r.
[12] Butler, 'A provincial masque', pp. 161–2.

and, not least, their association with music and merriment. The presence of the beggars in Oldrents's barn is a striking example of what Fumerton has, in other contexts, described as 'the porous nature of the house or private sphere in this period, as well as the extent to which the idea of "household" itself was unsettled, multiple, mobile'.[13] Oldrents's hospitable management of his estate, much admired within the play, clearly extends to all sections of society. In the process, Brome's play, like Nabbes's entertainment, reflects what would have been genuine experiences in contemporary rural communities; social historian Paul Slack has pointed out that many vagrants would have found 'familiar haunts in a local ale-house, [or] an isolated barn'.[14] What Brome limns with impressive dramatic economy is the world of informal poor relief on which so many early modern communities were dependent.[15]

Despite these obvious links to a specific country residence and its expected codes of social practice, *A Jovial Crew* is, as Garrett A. Sullivan Jr observed in his influential reading of this play, essentially a drama of roadways and highways and therefore one in which the beggars' community that constitutes the 'jovial crew' of the title is directly linked to the newly visible world of itinerant labourers in the 1630s.[16] The drama begins on Oldrents's protected Nottinghamshire estate, but events soon transport several of the main characters, as well as the audience, out onto the common highway, as well as into, through, and over the surrounding hedgerows. Now that the first signs of spring are appearing in the landscape, Oldrents's steward Springlove is restless to hit the road once again, despite the protestations of his patron and mentor who rescued him from a previous existence as an itinerant beggar: 'Can there no means be found to preserve life / In thee but wandering like a vagabond?' (1.1.47). It is striking just how dense a vocabulary Brome finds in this play to describe the act of walking or traversing the common highways and their adjacent

---

[13] Fumerton, *Unsettled*, p. xviii.

[14] Paul Slack, 'Vagrants and vagrancy in England, 1598–1664', *Economic History Review*, 2nd series 27 (1974), 360–80 (365). Also cited in Fumerton, *Unsettled*, p. 7.

[15] For a detailed analysis of the operations of poor relief, see Steve Hindle, *On the Parish?: The Micropolitics of Poor Relief in Rural England, c. 1550–1750* (Oxford: Clarendon Press, 2004). Sullivan, in his excellent discussion of this play in Chapter 5 of *The Drama of Landscape*, argues that the fifth act resolutions of the play seem particularly heartless in that they sentence the beggars to a 'free pass', which means not as it might appear on the surface a granting of liberty but a formal return of each individual to their home parish, thereby demanding of their parish that they take responsibility for the relief of their poor (p. 191). The sentence is passed by J. P. Clack, who is throughout the play the antithesis of Oldrents's benevolent hospitality.

[16] Sullivan, *The Drama of Landscape*, p. 176.

fields: 'gadding', 'vagaries', 'pilgrimages', 'wandering', 'journey', 'stroll-the-land-over', 'motion', 'ramble', 'progress', 'tramplings', 'survey', 'hoofing'.[17] There are also notions of moral and ethical 'wandering' in cognate phrases such as 'errancy'; we have entered into the realm of what Cresswell has termed 'moral geographies'.[18]

On the surface, Springlove would appear to be rejecting a responsible professional position, as household steward, in favour of a life of idleness. John Taylor in his 1621 rumination on beggars would assert that they performed no labour other than begging to survive – 'A begger doth not dig, delue, plow, or sow / He neither harrowes, plants, lops, fels, nor rakes' – but Springlove's nomenclature and his decision to join an age-old spring migration mirrors the mobility patterns of the itinerant early seventeenth-century workforce that would shelter over winter on welcoming estates and then head out to seek employment in the fields when the agricultural season recommenced.[19] Similarly, Oldrents resists Springlove's efforts to compare his particular desire to be on the move to a 'pilgrimage', stressing that his seasonal wanderings are to no 'holy ends' (1.1.51). Elsewhere in the play, journeys to sacred sites do appear to have been reduced to a kind of religious tourism: Vincent and Hilliard, suitors to Oldrents's daughters, having failed with their initial proposal to whisk the restless young women off to London to enjoy pleasure gardens and playhouses (2.1.139), propose instead rural escapades to see the Cotswold games or to visit shrines at St Winifred's Well or Nantwich.

In other ways, Springlove's decision to reject the fixed life of the country household is evoked in terms of social experimentation and the new professions and sciences of geometry and cartography. When Randall has to inform his master that the steward has left on his summer travels, he does so in terms provided by Springlove himself: 'he is gone, he says, a journey to survey and measure lands abroad about the counties' (2.2.268). Once again, Oldrents rejects the terms in which his steward's movement is being described – 'I know his measuring of land. He's gone his old way. And let him go' (2.2.269) – but the relationship between Springlove's curious and questioning mind, one that is not satisfied with the status quo, has nevertheless been linked to those professions involved in suggesting new ways of

---

[17] See, for example, 1.1.45, 50, 65, 72, 106; 2.1.197, 248; 2.2.268; 3.1.380.
[18] See Cresswell, *On the Move*, p. 26. In deploying the term, Cresswell is examining the binary between sedentarist and nomadic notions of mobility in a range of disciplines, including literary criticism, citing the examples of T. S. Eliot, Raymond Williams, and Richard Hoggart as profoundly sedentary in their politics.
[19] John Taylor, 'The praise, antiquity, and commodity of beggery, beggers, and begging' (London, 1621), sig. D3r; Sullivan, *The Drama of Landscape*, p. 174.

describing, understanding, interpreting, and, by extension, practising the landscape. He has already in this scene described his keeping of detailed accounts and inventories for the estate in terms of a 'survey' of all the rents and income available to his master (1.1.30). Sullivan compares the 'purposive measuring' of the land undertaken by surveyors and suggests that, by implication, Springlove's own 'wanderings' are made to seem experimental and even vocational, rather than merely escapist.[20]

Through this kind of carefully achieved linguistic texture, Brome creates a nuanced sense of motion and mobility throughout the play, not just in the literal scenes of highway travel and encounter, but through these evocations of a world of restless movement and transition (echoing, possibly deliberately, Taylor's description of the beggars' life as one of 'right perpetuall motion').[21] Brome's 'crew' of beggars makes manifest the ways in which the mobile and the itinerant are constantly remaking the spaces they inhabit.[22] Several commentators have noted the implicit and explicit associations of the beggars with ideas of the performative and the creative, not least in the fifth-act household entertainment that takes place at Justice Clack's residence. There were ongoing links between travelling players and other categories of vagrant and vagabond throughout this period, but the play is equally alert to the unsettling aspects of both groupings' capacity for constant re-creation and the challenges to fixed or static ideas of community they therefore embodied.[23] The play makes great artistic capital from a contrast between Oldrents's eventually ill-fated attempts to create a fixed, static, and therefore predictable lifestyle versus the volatility of life on the open road (it is this effort which makes him, ironically, so vulnerable to the prophecies of the patrico that are already governing his restrictive and

---

[20] Sullivan, *The Drama of Landscape*, compares Springlove's assertions of being a surveyor and those of John Norden's *The Surveyors' Dialogue*, which claimed to mediate between the aristocratic lord and his lands, enabling him 'sitting in his chayre' to see 'what he hath, where and how it lyeth, and in whose use and occupation' (pp. 160–1). These discussions also bring into the frame the estate surveys being undertaken by Oldrents's real-life equivalents in the 1630s, such as William Senior's extensive work for the Cavendish estates.

[21] Taylor, *The Praise, Antiquity and Commodity of Beggery*, sig. C4r. Taylor's pamphlet may also have encouraged such elements of Brome's play as the emphasis on birdsong as a particular lure to the begging lifestyle (see the extended account of the engagement with the natural world afforded by the diet and mode of living of beggars on sig. C1r). Taylor's text also mentions the convention of sheltering in barns on country estates ('A begger will a Barne for harbour take, / When Trees and Steeples are o're-turn'd with winde', sig. B2r).

[22] Fumerton, *Unsettled*, p. 55.

[23] See, for example, the discussion in the joint introduction to *A Jovial Crew* in *Brome Online* by Richard Cave, Eleanor Lowe, Helen Ostovich, Elizabeth Schafer, and Brian Woolland, especially paragraph 9; see also related discussions of the analogy between actors and vagabonds in Keenan, *Travelling Players*. For an excellent consideration of these analogous mobilities from a historical geographers' perspective, see Brayshay, 'Waits, musicians, bearwards, and players'.

overprotective behaviour towards his two daughters in problematic ways at the start of the play). By extension, the rules and codes of the hedgerow community provide an alternative to the mainstream, connecting with what Catherine Richardson has described as the 'anti-house behaviour' associated with hedges, dikes, and ditches in this period.[24]

As well as deploying the site of encounter and social circulation that is the early modern inn, which we explore in the following section,[25] Jonson's *The New Inn* invokes ideas of vagrancy and mobility as a kind of anti-household gesture through a series of suggestive allusions. This allusivity is achieved partly through the back-story of Fly, the homeless 'inmate' of the Light Heart Inn. Goodstock the Host offers conflicting versions of this narrative: Fly was either someone he encountered in the process of his own extended travels around the country (5.5.92–100) or was literally signed over to him as part of the inn's inventory. Either way, Fly stands as an example of a placeless or homeless 'inmate' until the close of the play, when he is gifted the property in its entirety.[26] By the fifth act, Goodstock is revealed to be Lord Frampul, an aristocratic landowner who effectively went 'walkabout' following what he perceived as moral failures within his marriage. Failure to govern an estate properly becomes a stimulus to mobility in this particular version of moral and ethical geography. Frampul's wife, we learn, was also an aristocratic runaway; she, in turn, re-emerges in the play in the figure of the Irish Nurse, who attends to 'Frank', an adopted orphan who is cared for in the context of Goodstock/Lord Frampul's newly fashioned version of affective family and the benevolent household at the Barnet Inn.[27]

However, as the initial account of Goodstock's meeting with Fly 'on the road' suggests, the intricate relationship between homelessness and mobility explored by plays like *A Jovial Crew* is also raised by the Host's belated revelations of his rural travels prior to settling at the inn:

[24] Richardson, *Domestic Life and Domestic Tragedy*, p. 37.

[25] See McRae, *Literature and Domestic Travel*, p. 122 on the 'staging' of 'encounters within inns and alehouses' (p. 122) and for an extended discussion of the inn as staging post, see my introduction to *The New Inn* in *CWBJ*. Earlier versions of my research into the detailed representation of inn as social space in this play appear in '"The day's sports devisèd i'the inn": Jonson's *The New Inn* and theatrical politics', *Modern Language Review*, 91 (1996), 545–60 and in *Ben Jonson's Theatrical Republics* (Basingstoke: Macmillan, 1998), pp. 144–63.

[26] On 'inmate' as a term for paying lodgers in this period and as a particular example of informal parish poor relief which may also be reflected in the treatment of Fly in this play, see Hindle, *On the Parish?*, p. 311. See also McRae, *Literature and Domestic Travel*, p. 141. McRae notes that Fly 'stands as an index of the inn as a space of mobility and commerce' (p. 142).

[27] Cf. McRae, *Literature and Domestic Travel* in which he regards the play as in part a reinvestigation of ideas of family and the household, albeit one offering a 'distorted parody of home' (p. 124). It should be added that Frank will turn out to be biological family in that s/he is really the Frampuls' daughter Laetitia in disguise.

> I am Lord Frampul,
> The cause of all this trouble; I am he
> Have measured all the shires of England over,
> Wales and her mountains, seen those wilder nations
> Of people in the Peak and Lancashire;
> Their pipers, fiddlers, rushers, puppet-masters,
> Jugglers, and gypsies, all the sorts of canters
> And colonies of beggars, tumblers, ape-carriers,
>
> (5.5.91–8)[28]

Although Goodstock/Lord Frampul's description makes claim to his having sought the company of various marginalized and disenfranchised social groups, he actually describes his journey in the same terms of measurement and surveying that we have witnessed Springlove and others apply to the Oldrents estate in *A Jovial Crew*. For all of the implicit identification with mobile groupings such as gypsies and beggars, ultimately Lord Frampul's discourse is framed in the terminology of the landed estate. His careful recreation of the Barnet Inn as a micro-estate or household makes new sense in this light.

Andrew McRae has written with considerable resonance about early modern roads in terms of 'spatial knowledges'.[29] He stresses the ways in which local administration and government practised control over these potentially destabilizing networks of travel and connection, noting that every parish had to appoint a surveyor for roads and highways, and observing in the process that these 'prioritized systems of local knowledge'.[30] McRae acknowledges the way in which the threat of mobility, which we have been identifying in the heightened responses to the notion of a beggars' life on the open road in *A Jovial Crew*, was in some respects contained both by the literature of navigation (maps and itineraries, for example) as well as by official practice of these connecting highways.[31] The presence

---

[28] McRae remarks that 'In all the literature of the early modern period, this [speech] stands as a rare instance of acts of travel within the borders of England and Wales being articulated with the same discourse of wonder applied more commonly to foreign exploration' (*Literature and Domestic Travel*, p. 137), though it should be noted that Jonson described his own carefully stage-managed Scottish walk in 1618 as a 'discovery'. Equally striking is how readily Lord Frampul's list maps onto the itinerant entertainers who are the subject of Brayshay's research in the REED archive; see his ''Waits, musicians, bearwards and players', p. 431. This lends credence to readings that connect Jonson's play with an examination of theatre as it operates within a mobile or travelling situation, 'on the road' as it were.

[29] McRae, *Literature and Domestic Travel*, p. 75.

[30] McRae, *Literature and Domestic Travel*, p. 75.

[31] See also Catherine Delano-Smith, 'Milieus of Mobility: Itineraries, Route-maps and Road-maps', in James R. Akerman (ed.), *Cartographies of Travel and Navigation* (Chicago and London: Chicago University Press, 2006), pp. 34–45.

of homeless or of itinerant working communities (those living in what Fumerton refers to as a 'patchwork' economy[32]) on the stages of early modern drama was a reflection of the times and of its particular social anxieties, which manifested themselves in a concern with mobility, literal and conceptual. The 1620s and 1630s had witnessed a severe economic slump and, as a result, vast numbers of people were living in the kind of subsistence poverty depicted in Brome's play. *A Jovial Crew* is surely responding to the precise set of socioeconomic conditions that Fumerton suggests characterizes these decades: rising population and unemployment; the aforementioned economic depressions caused, in particular, by successive failed harvests; and an attendant decline in noble households and hospitality (to which Oldrents's benevolent estate is intended to stand in direct counterpoint); rising rents (and here again, Oldrents's nomenclature is suggestive of more benign traditional practice); the conversion of copyhold tenure to leaseholds; and an economic atmosphere of high prices and relatively low wages.[33] Brome's play responds in part, then, to what Fumerton articulates as 'a contemporary sensibility that vagrancy had reached new crisis levels'. There was, she says, a '*felt* increase in the number of dispossessed poor' and, therefore, this play's trajectory starts to make sense beyond a solely romantic, pastoral literary tradition, in which aristocrats 'play' at living a rural existence, although there are elements of that convention clearly embedded in the decision of Oldrents's daughters to escape from the patriarchal home into a life of 'performed' beggary.[34]

The crucial difference to Rachel and Meriel's pastoral 'motion' (2.1.32), in which they also enlist their respective suitors, Vincent and Hilliard, is that their escapist notions of the life of liberty 'on the road' are severely tested by the realities of endlessly sleeping on straw in barns and begging for a living on the open highway with all the personal dangers that that involves: Oliver nearly subjects them to a brutal sexual assault in 4.1; they are only rescued by Springlove's arrival and intervention. Martin Butler has written previously of the challenge to the 'escapist' reading of this play that discussions of flea bites, gnawing hunger, biting cold, and endless lack of sleep introduce.[35] It is exactly this testing of expectations that causes Springlove to respond with a degree of cynicism to the sisters' initial request to be accepted by him and his itinerant friends:

---

[32] Fumerton, *Unsettled*, p. xviii.   [33] Fumerton, *Unsettled*, p. 6.

[34] For a more extended discussion of the phenomenon, see my 'Beggars' commonwealths'; and also Gaby, 'Of vagabonds and commonwealths'.

[35] Butler, *Theatre and Crisis*, pp. 269–79 (272).

Oh I conceive your begging progress is to ramble out this summer among your
father's tenants; and 'tis in request among gentlemen's daughters to devour their
cheesecakes, apple pies, creams, and custards, flapjacks and jam-puddings. (1.1.197)

As well as suggesting that Rachel and Meriel's travel instinct will be strictly
limited to the safety of their father's landholdings, Springlove's terminology of 'progress' in this context is telling. The direct counterpoint to the
informed traversal of the national road network by beggars and itinerants,
one to which this play clearly alludes, was the royal summer progress. This
highly organized form of mobile ritual and ceremonial had taken place,
often on an annual basis, during the Elizabethan period and was sustained
as a practice by both Stuart monarchs in the early seventeenth century.
That these progresses regularly involved and inspired site-specific theatrical events, as well as theatricalized encounters in terms of commissioned
masques and entertainments, and stays at significant aristocratic households, has already been discussed. Sullivan has argued that the mobility
that Oldrents appears to embrace following Springlove's departure, and the
news that his daughters too have run away, while described by the home-
body Randall (who claims never to have journeyed more than twelve miles
from his birthplace, 4.1.906) in terms of wild transgression, 'tantivy all the
country over' (4.1.625), is in reality strictly limited to the controlled movements of a progress, as he moves between neighbouring estates. Even when
he travels for two days and a night to Clack's disappointingly inhospitable
household, it is still to a property belonging to someone of standing in the
community;[36] there is nothing radical about Oldrents's achieved mobility and this would seem to be in keeping with the conservative closure
to the play when all characters seem to return to their allocated place in
society.

*A Jovial Crew* would seem, then, to be effecting some clear demarcations
between types of travel and the different social groups which practised alternate forms of mobility, but there are interesting ways in which Springlove's
loaded vocabulary in the first act, as well as his actual behaviour in the play,
seeks to collapse some of these governing categories and distinctions. Mary
Hill Cole describes royal progresses as 'intentional wandering'; this statement effects an intriguing link with the activities of Brome's road-based
beggars and, like the previous analogies with surveying practices, begins

---

[36] Compare, for example, the presidential progress undertaken by the Earl of Bridgewater following
his installation as Lord President of the Council of the Marches which Chapter 2 argued is in part
the real life journey that lies behind Milton's Ludlow masque in 1634. That progress is discussed in
Brown, 'Presidential travels'.

to suggest something more radical in the decision of the beggars to live their lives within alternative social spaces and by alternative social codes. Cole's research into the forms of progress draws our attention to the careful civic choreography of entrances and departures, greetings and gift-giving ceremonies, embedded in these events; she refers to this in terms associated with theories of mobility: 'Moving, standing, approaching, and receiving, ascending and descending, all were physical actions that revealed political realities.'[37] A similar reading might be applied to the begging scenes in *A Jovial Crew* that the audience witness as carefully scripted and rehearsed encounters on roadways (see, for example, 3.1). While Brome's detailing of the 'performance' involved in begging corresponds with contemporary literature, which sought to represent beggars as cynical counterfeits, it is by means of these subtler analogies with other forms of performance, in the regions and on the national highways, that new readings are at least made available.[38]

The activity and performance of progress undoubtedly had a direct impact on the physical infrastructure of the nation, not least on its roads and highways. The most overt method by which the state deployed the road network in an official capacity was through the ceremonial of progress. This practice had its own ameliorative effects: the development and improvement of roads, particularly in more outlying regions from the governmental centres of Westminster and Whitehall, took place in preparation for royal visits. The Surveyor of the Ways would map the route, the Master of the Post would ensure information networks; gentlemen ushers prepared individual households to receive the King or Queen; and the yeoman of His/Her Majesty's Wardrobe would deal with transportation of clothing. While prior to such events, many common highways were little more than rutted mud-tracks, in advance of royal visits surfaces were smoothed and standardized and bridges constructed to enable the crossing of rivers and to ease royal movement through the landscape.[39]

One of the most significant acts of progress that Charles I made during his reign was his belated 1633–4 Scottish coronation trip, when he travelled

---

[37] Cole, *The Portable Queen*, p. 122.
[38] See William C. Carroll, *Fat King, Lean Beggar: Representations of Poverty in the Age of Shakespeare* (Ithaca: Cornell University Press, 1996).
[39] Daryl W. Palmer has demonstrated the ways in which significant public figures, including performers and writers, performed their own appropriative versions of these royal progresses, their journeys in part enabled by the improved conditions of the public infrastructure of roadways and bridges; see his *Hospitable Performances: Dramatic Genre and Cultural Practices in Early Modern England* (West Lafayette, Ind.: Purdue University Press, 1992). Jonson's 1618 walk to Scotland is one example of this, following, as it did, sometimes quite literally, in the footsteps of James VI and I's progress to Scotland the previous year.

with a considerable retinue to Scotland and back. Even this act was an act of performative imitation in some respects of his father's 'salmonlyke' return to Scotland in 1617.⁴⁰ Both the Stuart Scottish progresses occasioned considerable artistic and cultural response, not least in the form of specifically commissioned drama and poetry, often performed at significant households or 'staging-posts' on the journey. In the case of Charles's 1633 progress, we have already mentioned the Jonson-authored entertainment staged by Cavendish at his Welbeck Abbey estate in Nottinghamshire. The printed afterlife of many such artistic responses is proof that the social and cultural effects of progress can be registered in ways that extend far beyond the immediate moment of encounter. We might begin to think of these events as one way in which the idea of the nation and its specific geographies and regional identities were conveyed to a wider public; early modern drama, which engaged actively with ideas of mobility and travel, was clearly another.

*A Jovial Crew* is a particularly fascinating text in the ways in which it seeks to co-opt, to juxtapose, and at times to hybridize, a highly varied discourse and scale of mobility, from royal progress to begging through to land surveying practices, in order to encourage its audiences to imagine the wider nation.⁴¹ It is an intriguing side note to the play that we learn that Oldrents first encountered Springlove in his beggar's persona when he was on a trip in the northern provinces. We have a glimpse here of an Oldrents with a wider sense of the nation than his fixed notion of his place in the community at the start of the play would suggest. It is interesting to speculate whether Oldrents could have been one of the courtly retinue who would accompany a monarch north on an event such as the 1633 Scottish progress. If so, he becomes linked in the contemporary imagination with figures like the Earl of Arundel as well as Cavendish (one of

---

⁴⁰ The phrase was James's own in a letter to the Scottish Privy Council; see G. P. V. Akrigg, *The Jacobean Pageant: or The Court of King James I* (Cambridge, Mass.: Harvard University Press, 1962), p. 259.

⁴¹ A separate argument might seek to examine the ways in which Brome also encouraged audience awareness of the wider nation in complex and diverse ways through the medium of language. He was a playwright particularly invested in bringing accurate regional accents and dialects onto the stage; the Yorkshire dialect of Constance, the eponymous heroine of *The Northern Lass*, provides a particularly sustained example, but that play also features the Cornish language and *The Sparagus Garden* includes extended dialogue between characters conversing in Somerset dialect. *The Late Lancashire Witches* accords sustained Lancashire dialect conversations to two servant characters, Lawrence and Parnell. On Brome's engagement with northern idiom and dialect, in particular, see Katie Wales, *Northern English: A Cultural and Social History* (Cambridge University Press, 2006). For an extended discussion of Brome's interest in Yorkshire dialect and ideas of the north more generally, see my critical introduction to *The Northern Lass* in *Brome Online*.

Brome's key patrons at this time) and, in the process, actual Caroline practices of hospitality and mobility are measured directly against his.[42]

Springlove, in his teasing comment to Rachel and Meriel that they might eat their father's tenants out of house and home on their own projected 'beggars' progress', suggests, by implication, that these monarchical ventures drained local provisions and resources. There may be a vein of biting social commentary in this, but, as already noted, Springlove's statement collapses what might otherwise seem considerable perceptual and spatial differences between the community of the hedgerow beggars as depicted in *A Jovial Crew* and early modern understandings of the particular geographies of royal progress. The social impact of mobility in general and of the kinds of social encounter facilitated by the particular act of being in motion are considered from all angles in this play. This renders its specific invocations of pastoral convention highly political.[43] Different modes of mobility are brought into a complex dialogue with one another in ways that move beyond cliché. What it might mean to be 'on the road' in the 1630s and 1640s, either for aristocrat or for itinerant worker, is clearly under debate.

## INNS AND TAVERNS AS PROVINCIAL STAGING-POSTS: JONSON'S *THE NEW INN* AND MASSINGER'S *A NEW WAY TO PAY OLD DEBTS*

As social historians have amply demonstrated of late, the provinces and the 'metropolitan core' of London were more connected to one another in this period than discrete studies of each tend to imply. The traffic of material goods, ideas, and people (not just the itinerant workforce discussed in the previous section, but also the nobles and gentry who moved consistently between the capital and their rural estates for reasons of business and pleasure) has characterized discussions of flow elsewhere in this study.[44]

---

[42] One of the individuals who was also part of the retinue that travelled north with Charles I in 1633 was William Harvey. In his *Anatomical Exercitations*, published in 1653, he would recount how, while in the far north of Scotland, he stood upon 'a rugged and dangerous Clift', Bass Rock in the Firth of Forth: 'Overhead, clouds of flocking birds swirled so thick that', he wrote, 'they darken and obscure the day' and he became fascinated in the perilous nesting practices of the guillemot, with its single egg placed precariously on a rock ledge; see Woolley, *The Herbalist*, p. 103; and see Keynes, *The Life of William Harvey*, esp. pp. 196–201. These encounters with the 'north' by members of the Caroline elite were presented back to a less mobile community in interesting ways. If we think of Oldrents as part of this grouping, someone with a knowledge of the worlds elsewhere that Springlove is keen to explore, an added dimension enters the play.

[43] See also Brome's *The Queen and Concubine* (1635), which configures vagrancy and pastoral through its handling of Eulalia's exile.

[44] See, for example, Thirsk, 'England's provinces', pp. 97–108; and Margaret Pelling's 'Skirting the city? Disease, social change and divided households in the seventeenth century', in Paul Griffiths

When plays such as *A Jovial Crew* or, indeed, Massinger's earlier Caroline comedy *A New Way to Pay Old Debts* opted to 'ground the scene' in rural Nottinghamshire, London theatre audiences may not have found this as remote or estranged a setting as has sometimes been implied.[45] Networks of communications such as the emergent postal system as well as improved methods of transportation, not least the wider availability of affordable coach travel, all served to expand contemporary understandings of the map of the country. Even so, some areas and regions of the country would have been more readily accessible to the mainstream of the English populace and, in particular, the metropolitan audiences of London commercial drama. Nottinghamshire, firmly located in the centre of England, is persistently described in Caroline literature as constituting the 'north', which would suggest that plays set even further afield from the capital, such as Heywood and Brome's dialect-riven 'docu-drama' *The Late Lancashire Witches* (1634), could have been presenting less familiar and therefore potentially unsettling geographies to spectators.[46] This in turn suggests that access to or knowledge of Nottingham and the Midlands region by a large of proportion of theatre audiences was highly likely.[47]

*A New Way to Pay Old Debts* makes repeated efforts to remind those spectators of its Nottinghamshire 'scene'. When Sir Giles Overreach mistakenly believes that he has made a lucrative marriage for his daughter Margaret to Lord Lovell, he dispatches Alworth to the nearby city of Nottingham to obtain a marriage licence (4.1.42). Elsewhere, he informs us that among many properties in the area that he has acquired in his rapacious policy of land-grab, he has a manor-house located in Gotham, a village

and Mark S. R. Jenner (eds.), *Londinopolis: Essays in the Cultural and Social History of Early Modern London* (Manchester University Press, 2000), pp. 154–75. The phrase 'metropolitan core' derives from Mark Brayshay, Philip Harrison and Brian Chalkley, 'Knowledge, nationhood and governance: the speed of the Royal Post in early modern England', *Journal of Historical Geography*, 24: 3 (1998), 265–88 (267).

[45] The phrase occurs in the Prologue to *A New Way to Pay Old Debts* (5), which demonstrates striking awareness of the politics of location. Since there has been no striking news from continental Europe of late, the playwright, it is claimed, has turned to the local: 'Corantoes failing, and no footpost late / Possessing us with news of foreign state, / . . . we are forced from our own nation / To ground the scene' (1–5). The edition cited is that edited by T. W. Craik for New Mermaids (London: A & C Black, 1964).

[46] 'Docu-drama' is Heather Hirschfield's suggestive phrase for this play that dealt with topical events; see her 'Collaborating across generations: Thomas Heywood, Richard Brome, and *The Late Lancashire Witches*', *Journal of Medieval and Early Modern Studies*, 30 (2000), 339–74. In *A New Way to Pay Old Debts*, Lady Alworth refers to Overreach's daughter Margaret being 'the richest match / Our north part can make boast of' (4.1.201–2).

[47] Cf. Brayshay, 'Waits, musicians, bearwards, and players', on the 'lively touring network of artists in the Midland and the North' who facilitated the flow of cultural and political ideas between metropolis and province (p. 435).

some eight miles south-west of the city (4.3.114); it is here that Parson Will-do is beneficed and the implication of his name, and his willingness to preside over an illegal marriage, is that he is beholden to Sir Giles for that position. Early on in the play, Lady Alworth's cook Furnace takes great pleasure in informing guests of the fine venison he has acquired from nearby Sherwood Forest (1.3.20–2). It is worth speculating as to why Massinger, like several of his playwriting contemporaries in the 1620s and 1630s, finds Nottinghamshire as a county particularly attractive as a setting for drama. In earlier discussions of work by Jonson and Brome, including *A Jovial Crew*, patronage provided one important explanation. Cavendish is a figure whose influence looms large in the work of several playwrights at this time and plays set in his own domains would have had particular attractions. Commercial drama, unlike more site-specific household commissions, could not afford to appeal only to the predelictions of a single individual, however, so there must be wider motives in play alongside the specific context of patronage networks.

In a fine essay exploring the 'systematized counterpoint' of the various households of *A New Way to Pay Old Debts*, Albert Tricomi has suggested that it is the setting of Timothy Tapwell's alehouse, in front of which we begin the play as he and his wife Froth refuse entry to bankrupt local gentleman Welborne ('No booze? nor no tobacco' is the striking opening line), that gives the clearest clue to Massinger's choice of the Nottinghamshire locale for his topical drama on social mobility.[48] Audiences will learn later that Tapwell, formerly a butler in the Welborne household, refuses to serve Welborne on the strict instructions of Marrall, a lawyer who works for the household of Sir Giles Overreach. Tapwell's alehouse, we quickly discern, is a site for illegal activities of various kinds; Welborne refers to the alehouse being the resort of 'whores, and canters, / Clubbers by night' (1.1.62–3) and Tapwell will later confess in private that the 'passages of our house' involved the 'receiving of stolen goods' (4.2.11,12).[49] It seems that Marrall, and, by extension, Overreach and the local Justice of the Peace, Greedy, who also appears to be in Overreach's pay, will turn a blind eye to this illicit activity, provided that Tapwell does their bidding.

Tricomi finds real-life counterparts for all this. Sir Giles Mompesson, the 1620s monopolist, whose activities are regularly cited by critics as the

---

[48] Albert H. Tricomi, '*A New Way to Pay Old Debts* and the Country-House Poetic Tradition', *Medieval and Renaissance Drama in England*, 3 (1986), 177–88 (182–3).

[49] Peter Clark suggests that alehouses, in particular, became associated with harbouring stolen goods in this period, especially stolen grain and poached animals, such as hares (*The English Alehouse: A Social History, 1200–1830* (London: Longmans, 1983), pp. 145–6).

inspiration for Massinger's remarkable dramatic creation of Overreach, had particular responsibility for the regulation of inns, taverns, and alehouses and was in fact nicknamed 'Lord of the Hosts' for his 'entrepreneurial, extortionate methods of dealing with England's inns and tavern-keepers'.[50] The proliferation of alehouses and taverns in Nottinghamshire, as elsewhere in the country in the 1620s, was a cause for concern in Parliament but Nottinghamshire had been a particular focus for the exploitation of patents and monopolies created by the crown, which gave the control of alehouse licences to individuals such as Mompesson and aides such as Francis Michell, the JP who was formally censured by Parliament for accepting bribes from innkeepers and whom Tricomi posits as the model for Justice Greedy in the play.[51] Inns and alehouses, then, serve as particularly resonant sites for thinking about a range of social issues, but especially the impact of social mobility.

*A New Way to Pay Old Debts* is keen to inform audiences that Overreach, a rapacious landlord who will wreak physical damage on neighbours' estates in his attempts to obtain them (2.1.34–9), hails from London and therefore from its new proto-capitalist social mores. In many respects, he is the direct opposite of Oldrents in *A Jovial Crew*, a figure, as we have argued, of fixed geography and sure morals. Even within the play, Massinger offers several contrasting examples to Overreach in the form of Lord Lovell, an aristocrat of ancient blood lines, and Welborne's late lamented father, who was the model of civic duty and community responsibility:

> Old Sir John Welborne, justice of the peace, and *quorum*,
> And stood fair to be *custos rotulorum*;
> Bare the whole sway of the shire, kept a great house;
> Reliev'd the poor, and so forth.                    (1.1.34–7)

The 'great house' in the rural shire serves as one significant site of collective memory through which the impact of social change can be registered, and plays such as *A Jovial Crew* and *A New Way to Pay Old Debts* clearly pay testimony to that fact.[52] That Cavendish's personal politics would appear sympathetic to this stress on 'older' values lends weight to the sense that his patronage might also have played a shaping role in some of the Nottinghamshire geopolitics of these plays, though Massinger's own upbringing as the son of a servant for the Pembroke family and therefore,

---

[50] Tricomi, '*A New Way to Pay Old Debts*', p. 183. See also Conrad Russell, *Parliaments and English Politics, 1621–29* (Oxford: Clarendon Press, 1979), p. 102.
[51] Tricomi, '*A New Way to Pay Old Debts*', p. 183.
[52] Pierre Nora, *Les lieux de mémoire / sous la direction de Pierre Nora* (Paris: Gallimard, c. 1984–1992).

presumably, with access to their Wilton House estate in Wiltshire should also be borne in mind as a strong influencing factor.[53]

*A New Way to Pay Old Debts* is fascinated by the spatial relationship *between* places; we are regularly informed what the precise distance is between different properties and what the best mode of transportation would be to reach them (on foot or by horse; see, for example, 2.3.60–2, 3.1.100). In this way the play serves to make links between places and to suggest that a community is best served by the wholesome maintenance of those links, usually enacted through forms of hospitality and exchange. We do see the great household of Lady Alworth performing hospitality, not least through the efforts of her cook, Furnace, to serve extravagant meals to all comers, but also in the welcome that is provided to guests by the steward Order and the usher Amble. Elsewhere, Massinger seems to offer anti-types of this benevolent form of community, anti-households even: Overreach's self-aggrandizing household is one obvious example, but Tapwell's alehouse, which operates along corrupt and covert lines, is equally significant in this regard. Inns and alehouses presented in both negative and positive light on the early modern stage prove a fertile site for analysis of the ways in which early modern drama sought to engage with the anxieties and concerns that surrounded the new mobility and free circulation of early seventeenth century society as well as the opportunities for encounter and exchange that mobility provided.

*The New Inn* takes place in an inn-house called 'The Light Heart' in Barnet in the county of Middlesex and engages in a very direct way with many of these ideas. The Barnet setting alone would have alerted audiences in the late 1620s to the play's engagement with issues of mobility. Just a few years earlier, Heywood had shown great glee in setting a central scene of *The English Traveller* (*c.* 1626–7?) in a Barnet ordinary, a place serving food that was, like the alehouse or tavern, slightly lower down the social scale from an inn. In the process he offered the audience a character reference for the sorts of activity, social and sexual, enabled by this location:

> This Barnet is a place of great resort,
> And commonly upon the market days
> Here all the country gentlemen appoint
> A friendly meeting; some about affairs
> Of consequence and profit, bargain, sale,
> And to confer with chapmen; some for pleasure,

---

[53] Michael Neill discusses this aspect of Massinger's biography in his introduction to his Arden Early Modern Drama edition of *The Renegado* (London: Methuen, 2009).

> To match their horses, wager in their dogs,
> Or try their hawks; some to no other end
> But only meet good company, discourse,
> Dine, drink, and spend their money.
>
>                              (3.3.1–10)[54]

This is exactly the kind of 'communal nexus' that Peter Clark's seminal research has demonstrated that the English alehouse, and its more elite counterpart the inn, provided in this period, offering a range of facilities and services including food and entertainment, but also financial credit, support structures for the poor, and a focus for communication and exchange.[55]

Inventories and accounts for actual households at this time provide access to those journeys undertaken by the real-life equivalents of Oldrents or, indeed, Lady Frances Frampul and her chambermaid Prudence in *The New Inn*. Those account books for 1632 kept by the first Viscount Scudamore's steward (and it is intriguing how often the figure of the steward proves our mediator in the archive as much as in these plays engaging with the operations of the noble household) indicate, for example, a journey undertaken from the family estate in Herefordshire to London. It took four days and we can determine that the family stayed at inns in Gloucester, Farringdon, and Henley en route to the capital. Detailed expenses, including the amount and type of food consumed (pork, rabbit, partridge, fruit, and cheese) are provided, as well as – in ways redolent of *A Jovial Crew* – the performance of charity and alms-giving to beggars and inn-workers encountered on the way.[56]

There is undoubtedly a deeply practical and pragmatic function to Jonson's emplacement of *The New Inn* in a suburban inn.[57] Such sites had become by the 1620s popular resorts for Londoners seeking temporary refuge from the cramped and noisy conditions of the city, as well as all

---

[54] The edition of *The English Traveller* cited is that contained within Paul Merchant (ed.), *Thomas Heywood: Three Marriage Plays* (Manchester University Press, 1996).

[55] Clark, *The English Alehouse*, p. 139. Elsewhere, Clark comments on the 'matrix of economic, social and cultural activities' offered by the alehouse (p. 339).

[56] Hereford Cathedral Library, MS 6417, pp. 49–51. Payments are made to 'poore theves' in Gloucester but also to chamberlains and ostlers working in the inn, suggesting that a culture of gift-giving was one of the lubricants in these social situations where people of mixed backgrounds came into direct contact. These accounts have been partly transcribed by F. C. Morgan in the *Transactions of the Woolhope Naturalists' Field Club: Herefordshire*, vol. 33 (1949–51) (Hereford: Hereford Times Ltd, 1952). See also Scudamore Account Books LC 647.1, vols. 1–3 (1635–7; 1640–2; 1641–2) in Hereford Central Library for comparable entries.

[57] While it might be argued that 'suburban' is an anachronistic usage in this context, my intention is to stress that the proximity of Barnet to the metropolis is central to its operations and allure in *The New Inn*.

the opportunities for covert social and sexual activity, as well as personal role play, that a space outside of the everyday enabled. The play's central motif of the 'Parliament of Love', in which Prudence the chambermaid plays the role of Queen for the day and presides over a hearing in which Lord Lovel is forced to persuade Lady Frances of his affections, is one way in which the performative capacity of the inn is made viscerally present for audiences; elsewhere, the Host takes great delight in invoking the idea of the inn as theatre (1.3.132–3), playing, in turn, on the notion that prior to the establishment of purpose-built London playhouses, many inns and inn-yards had doubled as spaces for performance, as well as acknowledging that some of these, such as the Red Bull, were still in operation as late as the 1620s.[58]

Early scenes depict a series of potential 'actors' arriving at the inn and later in the play the ultimate form of sexual role play will be presented in the memorable shape of the tailor's wife, Pinnacia Stuff (the play alludes at several points to her height, giving us some clue to the physiognomy of the male actor who would have taken the role). Pinnacia has purloined a beautiful dress made by her husband for a direct commission from Lady Frances to be worn by Prudence as part of the 'day's sports devisèd i' the inn' (1.6.44) and, once attired in the clothes of her social superiors (a fact about which she demonstrates little concern, in stark contrast to Prudence, who is worried by the sartorial implications of dressing like her mistress), she pretends to be a Countess who is, in turn, seduced by her footman (her husband, the tailor Nick Stuff, also in erotic fancy dress):

> It is a foolish trick, madam, he has;
> For though he be your tailor, he is my beast.
> [ . . . ]
> When he makes any fine garment will fit me,
> Or any rich thing that he thinks of price,
> Then I must put it on and be his countess
> Before he carry it home unto the owners.
> A coach is hired and four horse; he runs
> In his velvet jacket thus to Romford, Croydon,
> Hounslow, or Barnet, the next bawdy road;
> And takes me out, carries me up, and throws me
> Upon a bed –                                    (4.3.63–74)

---

[58] The connection between inns and playhouses in this period is a subject of ongoing critical debate. The Red Bull appears, for example, to have ceased to function as an inn once it became a theatre. For the most recent research on the inn as playhouse conundrum, see David Kathman, 'Inn-yard playhouses', in Richard Dutton (ed.), *The Oxford Handbook of Early Modern Theatre* (Oxford University Press, 2009), pp. 153–67 (160). I am grateful to Lucy Munro for discussion of this issue.

The implications of Pinnacia's access to newly affordable coach travel will be explored later; suffice to say at this point that she stands in the play as a literal embodiment of anxieties about the new mobility of the lower classes, not least the craft communities of London's wards and neighbourhoods. Her punishment for transgressing older norms of staying in one's place is brutal; she is sentenced to be stripped naked and 'carted' around the streets, displayed as a common prostitute, and rendered subject to the random violences of the watching crowds. It is a grim inversion of the freedom to travel which she has elsewhere asserted.

As well as serving as a leisure resort, however fraught in terms of valence, for aristocrats and citizens alike, early modern inns served as staging points to and from the city in other important ways. It is the description of Jug the tapster in the 'Persons of the Play' when *The New Inn* was published in octavo form in 1631 that serves as an important indicator in this regard. Jug is called the 'thoroughfare of news' (Persons of the Play, 52), which could suggest a number of facts about him. Certainly, as *The English Traveller* suggested in its embedded description of the Barnet ordinary frequented by Young Geraldine and others as a space of 'discourse' (3.3.10), and in 3.3's portrayal of the chambermaid Bess relaying gossip about Wincott's wife to Geraldine as 'new[e]s' (56), inns and alehouses enabled the circulation of gossip and social chit-chat.[59] We can certainly position Jug in the context of this particular network of social circulation; but the exchange of 'news' in the early seventeenth century operated in more formal ways through the emergent infrastructure of the postal network. Historical geographer Mark Brayshay has brilliantly detailed the ways in which the postal network provided a form of 'spatial bonding', operating as an 'interface between the everyday insular world of provincial England and both the affairs of other far-off places and the loftier overarching concerns of the State itself'.[60] Inns were crucial sites within this matrix; as Brayshay goes on to note: 'England's provincial post rooms were frequently located in inns with attached livery stables and postmasters were usually innkeepers.'[61] This maps almost directly onto the spatial footprint of 'The Light Heart' as it is enacted as a space in *The New Inn*, so, while the delivery of post is not explicitly cited, we can use the operations of the postal network as a point

---

[59] Cf. Brayshay *et al.*, 'Knowledge, nationhood and governance', p. 264.

[60] Mark Brayshay, 'Royal post-horse routes in England and Wales: the evolution of the network in the later sixteenth and early seventeenth centuries', *Journal of Historical Geography*, 17: 4 (1991), 373–89 (374).

[61] Brayshay, 'Royal post-horse routes', p. 380. See also Brayshay *et al.*, 'Knowledge, nationhood and governance'.

of access to the kinds of mobility, social and cultural, that the play seeks to analyse.

The published writings of Jonson's contemporary, John Taylor, bring to life for us the world of the early modern roads and highways that forms a kind of spectral geography to *The New Inn*, shaping, shadowing, and standing behind its onstage events and actions. In 1637, Taylor published *The Carriers Cosmography*, a fascinating compendium of which inns in London held and dispatched post to which areas of the country. The Black Bull in Smithfield, for example, was the recipient of post coming to and from Bingham in Nottinghamshire, with carriers available for collections on Fridays.[62] In this text, Taylor provides us with yet another intriguing form of social cartography, mapping the postal routes and networks of early modern England in the moment just prior to the formation of a national system, and linking us back, in turn, to the world of *The New Inn*, where 'The Light Heart' is clearly located on one of the main postal networks in and out of London (Barnet stood on the Great North Road). Jug stands in metonymic relation to the inn-house as a recipient of gossip, news, and information, as a site of circulation.

Another inn-worker to whom Jonson dedicates a notable amount of stage time and attention is Peck the ostler. While no scene takes place directly in the space of the stables where he works, Jonson provides us with a lengthy scene in which Peck's colleagues discuss the various scams that the ostler has performed on guests in the past: the 'pranks of ale and hostelry', as they are resonantly referred to (3.1.125).[63] In the process, audiences are invited to register the importance of ostlers and of stabling facilities and provision in an inn, as well as realizing that this was an area open to abuse.[64] As Joan Thirsk has indicated, horses had always been a significant part of medieval and early modern culture. Horses were required not only for the purposes of road transportation, but also when the river was used, since they were the easiest means of embarking and disembarking goods and commodities. In the era of widespread coach travel, horses retained and even increased their significance to early modern mobility.[65] The costs of

---

[62] John Taylor, *The Carriers Cosmographie* (London, 1637), sig. A4v.

[63] I discuss the politics of Jonson's making visible the labour in this play through the characterizations of the inn-workers and coach-drivers in 'Jonson and space', in Eugene Giddens (ed.), *The Oxford Handbook to Jonson* (Oxford University Press, forthcoming).

[64] Cf. Ostovich *et al.*'s analysis of the importance of the provision both in inn-house theatres and great households of stabling facilities in the introduction to Helen Ostovich, Holger Schott-Syme, and Andrew Griffin (eds.), *Locating the Queen's Men, 1583–1603* (Burlington, Vt. and Aldershot: Ashgate, 2009), p. 14.

[65] Joan Thirsk, *Horses in Early Modern England: For Service, for Pleasure, for Power* (University of Reading, 1978), p. 5.

stabling these horses, in addition to paying for the staff to maintain them and their uniforms or livery, was considerable and these costs necessarily increased when owners were on the move, staying at inns and taverns like The Light Heart on the common highways. A horse required 141 lbs of hay per day along with 7 lbs of straw, a peck of oats (a peck was a specific measurement, equivalent to a quarter of a bushel), and half a peck of peas.[66] The aforementioned accounts of Viscount Scudamore's steward indicate the outlay at a Farringdon inn in 1632 on hay, oats, beans, and mash for the horses that drew the family coach, as well as individual payments to ostlers, which may indicate that the family hoped through this act of 'gift giving' – 'Gifts' is the category assigned to these entries by Scudamore's scrupulous steward – to stay in good favour with the men responsible for stabling their horses.[67]

In a brilliant, if sometimes overlooked, scene, Jonson brings all of these realities on to the stage of *The New Inn* when he depicts the appropriately named Peck, whose role it is to take care of guests' horses, reflecting on his ingenious scams, designed to deprive those same guests of their money. Pierce the drawer offers the audience considerable detail:

PIERCE:                              When,
         You know the guest put in his hand to feel
         And smell to the oats, that grated all his fingers
         Upo' the wood –
         [ . . . ]
         You were then there,
         Upo' your knees, I do remember it,
         To ha' the fact concealed. I could tell more:
         Soaping of saddles, cutting of horse tails,
         And cropping – pranks of ale and hostelry –        (3.1.117–25)

A 1636 pamphlet in the form of a dramatic dialogue by Henry Peacham, *Coach and Sedan*, made reference to similar hustles and scams in the observations of his knowing character of the 'Brewer's Cart'. He stresses that 'Coach' should take care of the horses he relies upon to pull him:

See your man give to his horses their due allowance in Hay and Oates, and that he beguiles them not [ . . . ] Your man also shall leave that old knavish tricke of tying a horse haire very straight about the [ . . . ] feete (which present will

---

[66] Thirsk, *Horses in Early Modern England*, p. 7. In 1574, she notes that Sir Henry Sidney spent 1s 5d for stabling in Reading for one night and 2s 7d for another night in Warwick.

[67] See Hereford Cathedral Library MS 6417, p. 50. Payments are made to two chamberlains, two 'oslers', plus a drawer and a tapster, the very same combination of workers that make up Jonson's dramatis personae in the Barnet inn of his play.

make him halt) then to tell your Master hee is lame, and will not serve his turne. (sig. F3r)

At the Light Heart, Peck has clearly been covering over sawdust with good oats and charging for a full bucket of provender. We may never see the stables of the inn directly onstage, then, but in all kinds of ways the discussions between the inn-workers in 3.1 enable us to imagine what this space is like and how it connects to the wider issues of social mobility with which the play seeks to engage.[68]

### RUNNING ON WHEELS

The 1620s and 1630s constituted a moment when the arrival of widespread coach travel began to impact not only on the habits but also on the social relations and even the built environment of the world in which Jonson and his contemporaries moved. Jonson lived through the period in which coach travel was not only introduced to England, but became mainstream, so much so that by the 1630s so omnipresent were coaches and carriages in the streets of London that there were protests against them and a, perhaps, inevitable stream of parodic and polemic literature in response.

According to Taylor in his 1623 prose pamphlet *The World Runs on Wheels: Or, Odds betwixt Carts and Coaches*, the first coach had been brought to London in 1564. In the early days, usage of these expensive items was limited to the most wealthy of noble families and, even then, coaches were regularly shared between estates. Yet, by the 1620s, they had become so commonplace that hiring of them was open to those of all social ranks and levels, much to Taylor's expressed disgust and concern:

when euery *Gill Turntripe*, Mrs *Fumkins*, Madam *Polecat*, and my Lady *Trash*, *Froth* the Tapster, *Bill* the Taylor, *Lauender* the Broker, *Whiff* the Tobacco seller, with their companion Trugs, must be Coach'd to *S. Albanes, Burntwood, Hockley- in-the Hole, Croydon, Windsor, Uxbridge*, and many other places, like wilde Hag- gards prancing vp and downe (sig. B3v)

In 1636, the Privy Council attempted, with limited success, to restrict use of coaches, establishing a minimum journey length of three miles for hired coaches, and to limit usage to customers of higher social rank. As coaches proved key to new modes of 'urban sociability' such as household visiting

---

[68] Brayshay *et al.*, 'Knowledge, nationhood, and governance', where they talk of the 'appreciation of a wider geography' the emergent postal network encouraged (p. 264).

and performative coach rides in places like Hyde Park, such regulations proved impossible to administer.[69]

The fact that Taylor's text is dedicated to his fellow watermen, whose trade was threatened by the rise of coach travel, offers some explanation for its hyperbolic claims; it blames coaches for all manner of ills in contemporary society, from a dearth of natural resources (on account of all the timber felled to create the coaches and maintain their wheels) to widespread obesity and ill-health due to the reliance on coaches to carry people from place to place. Nevertheless, this is a text that gives us a direct glimpse into what were massive social transformations taking place in the early seventeenth century and of which coach travel might at least be regarded as a symptom, if not the sole cause. The places catalogued in Taylor's complaint are all located to the north of London and register a shift of perspective away from the Thameside locations explored in Chapter 1 and towards the ever-expanding suburban areas to the north. A similar map is provided by Peacham's *Coach and Sedan* (see Figure 9), in which he has a coach and a sedan chair debate who is superior, only to be bested by the passing Brewer's Cart. In the guise of describing all that he does not do, the sedan chair makes a list of the lower rank members of society and the dubious social locations served by the coach which is remarkably similar to that described in Taylor's earlier pamphlet as is the negative foregrounding of gender:

> we carrey no Lackquies or Footboyes, when we are emptie, nor have we to do with *Dol Turn-up*, and *Peg Bum-it*, your silken wenches of *Hackney*, to carry them to the *Red | Bull*, and other Play-houses, to get trading, or Citizens wives to *St Albanes, South-mimmes, Barnet, Hatfield, Waltham, Ilford, Croidon, Brainford*, and other places.[70]

As we have seen, through the plot lines surrounding Pinnacia Stuff, *The New Inn* makes huge comic capital from this social phenomenon. A central strand, and, indeed, property, of that play is the dress, commissioned from

---

[69] J. F. Larkin (ed.), *Stuart Royal Proclamations* II (Oxford: Clarendon, 1983), pp. 494–6; also cited in Mark Jenner, 'Circulation and disorder: London streets and hackney coaches, *c.* 1640–1740', in Tim Hitchcock and Heather Shore (eds.), *The Streets of London: From the Great Fire to the Great Stink*, (London and Sydney: Rivers Oram Press, 2003), pp. 40–53 (41). Jenner notes that the 'regulatory energy' around coaches is an indication of the 'ways in which the conflicting uses of London public spaces were being renegotiated' (p. 42). See also Merritt, *The Social World of Early Modern Westminster*, p. 170. Merritt notes that Daniel Featly denounced 'idle visits' in coaches from the pulpit of Westminster Abbey in the 1630s (*Clavis Mystica*, London, 1636, p. 277).

[70] [Henry Peacham], *Coach and Sedan Pleasantly Disputing for Place and Precedence* (London, 1636), sigs. C1r–v.

Figure 9: Woodcut frontispiece to Henry Peacham, *Coach and Sedan Pleasantly Disputing for Place and Preceden[ce]. The Brewers Cart Being Moderator* (London, 1636).

Nick Stuff for the purposes of the planned playacting at the Barnet inn, which has failed to materialize at the start but which will eventually appear on stage as part of Pinnacia's performance as a countess. A coach also proves central to this storyline. An earlier scene in the fourth act has prepared audiences for Pinnacia's rather wholehearted approach to her aspirational acting. Barnaby the coachman has arrived bedraggled and browbeaten at the inn, in need of a stiff drink (or two). He explains to the Light Heart employees how his hat had blown off en route at Highgate and how his mistress: 'Would not endure me 'light to take it up, / But made me drive bare-headed i' the rain' (4.1.16–17). The reason for this prohibition is understood by the inn-workers, who rapidly comprehend the social semiotics that declared that only those coachmen who worked for noble families went bare-headed. Pinnacia's access to coach travel is encouraging exactly the kinds of social blurrings about which Taylor's and Peacham's pamphlets seem so anxious.

Historians of new technologies such as coaches have argued that their impact can be registered not only on the street maps of early modern cities, as new provision for access and parking had to be made, but even within interior domestic space as coachmen became regular members of elite households, both rural and urban.[71] *The New Inn* suggests as much through the presence not only of the hired coach driver Barnaby among the cast of characters, but also Trundle, who is directly employed by – and therefore is presumably a live-in resident of – the Light Heart. Trundle proves a crucial actor in the plot line involving 'Frank' and 'his' organized disguise as Prudence's waiting-woman for the day's sports. At Pru's instruction, Trundle transports an empty carriage from the inn, only to return under the pretence of carrying a passenger:

> Good Trundle, you must straight make ready the coach,
> And lead the horses out but half a mile
> Into the fields, whither you will, and then
> Drive in again with the coach-leaves put down
> At the back gate, and so to the back stairs,
> As if you brought in somebody to my lady,
> A kinswoman that she sent for.       (2.3.1–7)

---

[71] See Jenner, 'Circulation and disorder', esp. pp. 42–4. Julia Merritt observes that 'the provision made for stables and coaches was one of the selling points of houses built in Covent Garden in the 1630s' (*The Social World of Early Modern Westminster*, p. 172). On the ways in which coaches and the need for coachmen contributed to changes in the household economy and the reconfiguring of houses and buildings, I am grateful to Alison Smith's research presented in her paper 'Women and their coaches in seventeenth-century Verona', presented at the Renaissance Society of America conference, Venice, April 2010.

The potential for illicit activities in the concealed space of a coach, as alluded to here in the reference to putting the coach-leaves down, was a subject for many contemporary bawdy allusions, often focusing on the female sex; once again the erotic element of Pinnacia's storyline can be seen to be reconfiguring contemporary anxieties and social stereotypes for theatrical consumption.

The opportunity for illicit sexual encounter was just one aspect of the ways in which coaches had become associated with increased female agency and mobility in the Caroline period. Julia Merritt notes that 'Access to sedan chairs and the family coach potentially gave elite women greater levels of freedom'; contemporary diaries indicate the rounds of social visiting, often entailing women visiting women, or indeed visiting, in the company of other women, sites of public display such as Spring Gardens or Hyde Park, that coaches facilitated.[72] It is exactly this kind of mobility that Carol jealously guards in Shirley's *Hyde Park*: 'Ile not be / Bound from Spring garden; and the Sparagus', she notes (sig. E1r), in turn invoking parallel sites of mobility such as the Sparagus Garden. It is no coincidence that *The Sparagus Garden* is also a play interested in mobility, symbolized most obviously on stage by a sedan chair which appears as a portable property in the fourth act.

Once again, early modern drama proves a superb barometer of emergent social practices; the rhythms and social circulations of Shirley's 1635 Town comedy *The Lady of Pleasure* are dependent on the world of easy access to coach travel on the part of its female characters. In the first act, Madame Decoy, for example, cannot resist dropping in on Aretina, even though she is clearly on her way to another location: 'Alas, the coach, madam, stays for me at the door' (1.1.170). With this particular form of social circulation come other kinds of exchange, not least of gossip. In this way coaches act as a mobile facilitator of the news and exchange we have elsewhere seen moving through the fixed but porous sites of inns and alehouses. Aretina, a character acutely conscious of the need for social display as part of her efforts to rise up through the ranks of London society, is described by her husband as making a nuisance of herself in her personal coach in the city's cramped medieval streets:

---

[72] Merritt, *The Social World of Early Modern Westminster*, p. 171. She proffers the specific example of Lady Anne Halkett, who, in the 1630s, made trips with female friends to Spring Gardens. A contemporary ballad 'News from Hide-Parke' tells the story of an encounter between a 'North-Country Gentleman' and a 'Lady of Pleasure'. He, having met her in the Park, conducts her '(in her own Coach) home to her Lodgings' (London, 1631). Cf. Gowing, 'The freedom of the streets'; and on gender and spatial practice more generally, see Doreen Massey, *Space, Place, Gender* (Cambridge: Polity Press, 1994).

> whose rude postilion
> Must pester every narrow lane, till passengers
> And tradesmen curse your choking up their stalls,
>                                                   (1.1.183–5)

There is a witty inversion here of more common complaints by the London elite about the aggressive spatial behaviour of tradesmen and hackney (or hired) coach-drivers.[73] The type of noblewoman whose public acts of display in a fine coach Aretina seeks to emulate is brought directly onto the stage in the very next scene, when the audience witnesses Lady Celestina disputing with her steward over what she regards as his false economizing on her behalf in the matter of the furnishing and decoration of her private carriage. When she learns that he has not lined it with the (expensive) 'crimson plush' she specified but with a far cheaper and cruder cloth, she lets rip:

> Ten thousand moths consume't! Shall I ride through
> The streets in penance, wrapped up round in hair-cloth?
> Sell't to an alderman; 'twill serve his wife
> To go a-feasting to their country house,
> Or fetch a merchant's nurse-child, and come home
> Laden with fruit and cheesecake. I despise it.   (1.2.29–34)

The precise social geographies of Celestina's contempt make clear that it mattered as much where coaches travelled as the manner in which they were adorned.[74] Having fallen short of her high standards in its decoration, her coach is now fit only to serve as a common hackney carriage to ferry the likes of Pinnacia Stuff out to a Barnet inn or at least its equivalent on the eastern edges of the city:

> To market with't;
> 'Twill hackney out to Mile-end, or convey
> Your city tumblers [prostitutes] to be drunk with cream
> And prunes at Islington                      (1.2.41–4)

With a similarly assertive social politics, Celestina expresses in no uncertain terms the route-ways she desires that coaches belonging to other inhabitants of the city might take past her carefully located window on the street side of the Strand; all other coaches will be made to do obeisance at her window:

---

[73] Compare Jenner, 'Circulation and disorder', p. 44, with its subtle analysis, deploying the theories of Pierre Bourdieu, of the 'coachmen's heixis, the bodily regime by and in which they pursued their livelihoods', p. 44. See also Stuart Piggott, *Wagon, Chariot and Carriage: Symbol and Status in the History of Transport* (London: Thames & Hudson, 1992).
[74] Cf. Whyman, *Sociability and Power*.

'my balcony / Shall be the courtier's idol' (1.2.94–5). That she also insists on owning a sedan chair and liveried 'men-mules' (1.2.52) to carry her in it further embeds her in this world of radical new forms of urban transportation and its social consequences.

Increased access to coach travel, and the concomitant increase in the sheer number of coaches travelling the city's streets and the country roads, had a palpable impact on local and national geographies, leading to a general upgrading of the national road network to cope with the traffic, but also the establishment of new kinds of spatial knowledge and 'competencies' as locations, including the capital's first coach-hire rank near Temple Bar, were established and popular 'rides' to sites such as Hyde Park altered the physical experience of the city's streets and connecting neighbourhoods.[75] It is to this alternative transitional site of mobility and encounter, the park or green space, that the discussion now turns.

## 'NEERE LONDON': THE TRANSITIONAL SPACE OF PARK AND SUBURB

Urban historian Margaret Pelling has delineated the concept of 'skirting', by which she refers to the way in which early modern residents of London regularly moved between the city and its more rural hinterlands, as a means of better understanding the relationship between urban space and its rural counterpart in this period.[76] Many people, she stresses, were not convinced urbanites; they were town-dwellers, perhaps, but ones with considerable mobility and a 'skirting mentality'.[77] Craftspeople, herbalists and botanists, household servants, and, not least, women, were more accustomed to semi-detached modes of living than we sometimes give credit.[78] Attention to 'skirting' practices necessarily requires that we develop a subtler understanding of the kinds of mobility enabled at the edges of urban space: for example, thinking about the access to 'green lungs' through trips to parks

---

[75] 'Competencies' is the phrase used by Lefebvre, by way of Noam Chomsky, to describe the kinds of knowledge that arise from repeated spatial practices; see *The Production of Space*, p. 33. On the 'Maypole' hackney carriage site, run by Captain Bailey in 1634, see Merritt, *The Social World of Early Modern Westminster*, p. 169; and Woolley, *The Herbalist*, p. 117. Tim Hitchcock and Heather Shore make the point that the knowledge of hackney coach drivers enabled Londoners to move around the city without the aid of maps; in this way they were themselves guides to material space ('Introduction' in Tim Hitchcock and Heather Shore (eds.), *The Streets of London: From the Great Fire to the Great Stink* (London and Sydney: Rivers Oram Press, 2003), pp. 1–9 (5).

[76] Pelling, 'Skirting the city', p. 154.   [77] Pelling, 'Skirting the city', pp. 154, 156.

[78] Laura Gowing makes parallel arguments about female mobility in her essay in the same volume as Pelling's: '"The freedom of the streets": women and social space, 1560–1640', in Paul Griffiths and Mark S. R. Jenner (eds.), *Londinopolis: Essays in the Cultural and Social History of Early Modern London* (Manchester University Press, 2000), pp. 130–51.

and walks located on the outskirts; the 'simpling' trips of apothecaries and herbalists, many of which were recorded in contemporary publications; and the concomitant development of pasturage, market gardens, and orchards not only to feed central London but also to satisfy the demands of visitors to these edge locales.[79] Mapping this increasingly constructed environment and its presence in early modern drama enables us to chart new kinds of mobility and spatial practice at the very moment of their emergence.

Tottenham Court, the eponymous subject of the 1633 play by Thomas Nabbes, furnishes us with a particular example of the kind of site that contributed to a 'skirting mentality'. 'Tottenham Court', as evidenced by its appearance as a referenced site (home of Squire Tub and his widowed mother) in Jonson's *A Tale of a Tub*, was ostensibly a manor house and estate, but the name came to refer to the wider region, a semi-rural location within easy access of the city and yet associated with 'extra-daily' behaviour of various kinds, as the Prologue to Nabbes's play makes clear: 'Y'are welcome, Gentlemen, to Tottenham Court, / Where You (perhaps) expect some lusty sport' (1638 edn, sig. A4r). The Prologue goes on to link the area with cream cakes, ale, and Mayday-like festivities. Tottenham Court was one of those resorts which were the destination of London-dwellers who either walked there or hired coaches for the purpose. The play *Tottenham Court* is partly set in the transitional space of Marylebone (or 'Marrowbone') Park: the 'scene', as the printed edition of 1638 instructs us, is 'Tottenham Court and the fields about it'. This was ostensibly a large green space with areas set aside for commoners to put their livestock to pasture, and was, as a result, both the practical resort of small-scale agriculturalists like Cicely the milkmaid, who is the daughter of the Park's Keeper, and of city types seeking recreation of various kinds (often illicit, if the insinuations of characters like the Keeper are to be believed: 'Mere recreation / To walke for health seldome invites young Gallants, / To leave their beds so early' [1.6. sig. C1v]). To serve these visitors, domestic households adapted to become temporary alehouses and sellers of provisions. When the play begins, the Park is also a locus of escape for country dwellers, Worthgood and Bellamie, young romantics who are escaping Bellamie's overweening uncle. In the opening moments, they reflect that they 'are arriv'd neere London' (1.1. sig. A4v) and it is this 'neere London' setting that is crucial to my analyses when exploring the ways in which plays reflect, and, in some

---

[79] Pelling, 'Skirting the city', p. 158.

respects, set the pattern for various kinds of mobility in contemporary culture.

Worthgood and Bellamie are travelling under cover of darkness, for fear they will be pursued by her uncle; in the following scene we will see that uncle employing various tenant farmers and neighbours from his lands to hunt down the eloped couple. The pair's first sense of reaching close to the city is, strikingly, an aural one: 'Sure I heare / The Bridges Cattaracts', says Worthgood (though possibly what he thinks is the running water of the Thames is only the wind in the trees; the somatic experience can be a misleading one). In the confusing darkness the lovers lose each other and, as a result, Bellamie is forced to introduce herself to a passing milkmaid – Cicely – as a 'distrest maid' (1.4. sig. B3v). Cicely, up early, as is the nature of her trade, is surprised by this encounter: 'A maid of your years, and so neere London.' She reflects that this must mean that Bellamie is 'distressed', in the sense of being a broken or bankrupt woman, come to this recognized site of illicit liaison near the city in order to prostitute herself for the purposes of financial gain: 'Never an early walking gallant to take you up this morning. The Parke here hath fine conveniences: or Totenham Court's close by [ . . . ] I will to my Cowes, and leave you to the fate of the morning' (1.4. sig. B3v). The implication is that both the Park and nearby Tottenham Court are recognized sites for such activities and this is confirmed by Slip's comment later that 'A wench is growne a necessary appendix to two pots at Totenham Court'.[80]

Another 1630s drama that re-performs the space of a park on the early modern commercial stage is Shirley's *Hyde Park*. In its print version the play was dedicated, as Adam Zucker has noted, to Henry Rich, Earl of Holland, the titular if not the labouring keeper of Hyde Park, which was itself a former royal deer park.[81] This play invokes the space of the park as a site for sexual encounter in a manner akin to Nabbes. Hyde Park also

---

[80] What Cicely thinks she recognizes or identifies in Bellamie is a type familiar from other early modern plays; the rural woman forced by desperate circumstances into prostitution in the city. Brome had presented just this 'type' in the figure of Camitha Holdup in *The Northern Lass*. Brome elicits considerable sympathy for Holdup's situation, forced as she is, as a single mother, not only to suffer the humiliation of arrest and the threat of whipping or the workhouse that was a common punishment for prostitutes, but also the sexual attentions of the Middlesex JP Sir Paul Squelch (his bad breath and all) who tries her. Brome invokes a stereotype, but then puts flesh on its bones, revealing some serious social double standards in the process.

[81] Zucker's fine chapter on *Hyde Park* is forthcoming in *The Places of Wit* (Cambridge University Press, forthcoming 2011). I am grateful to Adam for permission to read and refer to his work prior to publication. My thanks also to Eugene Giddens who is editing the play for the Revels Plays series for conversations on related themes.

functions here, during the third and fourth acts which take place entirely within the parameters of the park, as a site of memory. Lord Bonvile, in a knowing invocation of Petrarchan metaphors of the hunt, informs Julietta:

> This place, the place were good enough
> If you were bad enough, and as prepared
> As I. There have beene stories that some have
> Strucke many deere within the Parke.
>
> (4.1. sig. F4r)

The park's ample size is indicated not least by the swirling flow of multiple characters across the stage; this is a location that can hold many people. Shirley also makes imaginative use of proxemics – as indicated in Bonvile's lines above: '*This* place, *the* place' – to place his many characters (and therefore the audience) in different parts of the park at different times. At the start of 3.1, Lord Bonvile welcomes Julietta and gives an indication of the season as well as the aural soundscape that may well have been recreated in the Cockpit Theatre when the play was first performed: 'Lady, y'are welcome to the Spring, the Parke / Lookes fresher to salute you, how the birds / On every tree sing . . .' (sig. E2r). Elsewhere, the kinetic geography of these acts is performed through reference to acts of walking, or, more precisely, *promenading*, undertaken by Julietta and Bonvile, among others: 'Let's walke . . . Let's walke a little further' (4.1. sig. F4v); 'Whither will you walk my lord? you may engage / Your selfe too farre and lose your sport!' (sig. F4r). The sense implicit in Julietta's words in that last quotation – that one can get lost in the park – is itself an indicator of literal size and acreage, as well as of the tests of moral and sexual fortitude that she and several other characters are forced to undergo in the course of the play's multiple plot lines.

A further way in which the size and scale of the Park is conveyed to the audience, and made a crucial element of the play's dramaturgy of encounter and confusion, can be registered in the staging of the horse-race. Hyde Park, as well as being a space in which people arranged to meet and to see and be seen in their coaches or in a pedestrian context, was a site for gambling on foot-races and horse-races, both of which take place during the course of Shirley's drama. Whereas in Act 3 the physical dynamics of this are fashioned from the sending of runners across the stage ('*The Runners, after them the Gentlemen*', s.d. sig. F1r), in the fourth act the larger scale event of the horse-race is created in an imaginary offstage space, the audience being invited to commit their imaginations to its production through the dialogue of those watching from onstage and the intermittent traversal of the stage by muddied riders and disappointed punters. It is a skilful piece of choreography that serves to conjure up a wider sense of space for the watching spectators both onstage and in the auditorium.[82]

An additional part of the onstage dance of characters involves those who do not simply use the space of the Park for social and leisure purposes but depend upon it for their livelihood, workers such as the keepers and those who sell victuals to visitors. In 4.1, the stage direction declares: '*Enter Milkemaide*'. She is ostensibly selling syllabub, one of the numerous dairy products that, as we have already seen in scornful comments made by Lady Celestina in *The Lady of Pleasure*, were commonly associated with edge-city green spaces such as Hyde Park or Islington and Tottenham Court; the specific reference, however, to its derivation from a 'red Cow' (sig. G3r) suggests that it is, in fact, wine that the dairymaid is selling on the sly to the park's wealthier guests. Wine, too, was part of the overall scene of social aspiration in this period; its consumption in sites such as Hyde Park, or the Sparagus Garden on Bankside that so fascinated Brome, serves to emphasize the delicate fusion of site, object, and desire that so often took place in the context of cultural performance.

For Zucker, one of this play's more acute commentators, the dairymaid is further evidence of Shirley's tendency to present a 'labourless London'.[83] Although Shirley takes the trouble to put her on the stage, for Zucker she remains marginal and marginalized. While she is a 'participant' in the economy of the Park, she is merely 'peripheral', even to the extent of existing only in a marginal stage direction in the printed edition. Nevertheless, I would want to turn that argument on its head and note that Shirley takes the trouble to make these 'peripheral workers' visible onstage, reminding us in the process of the wider economy and, indeed, the 'broader urban world' that Zucker feels is 'so often written out of Caroline London comedy'. As with Jonson's inn-workers, there is a politics of representation and mobility at stake in the presence of the working world in the spaces and sites depicted in these place-conscious dramas. What Pelling's delineation of 'skirting' mentalities with which I began this section or the writings of cultural geographer and environmental historian William Cronon remind us is that, in looking at any particular site, be it inn-house or public park, the story that needs to be told refers not only to the site as a hermetically

---

[82] I have written elsewhere of a particular interest in the offstage space in Jonson's Caroline dramaturgy: '*The New Inn* and *The Magnetic Lady*: Jonson's dramaturgy in the Caroline context', in Brian Woolland (ed.), *Jonsonians: Living Traditions* (Aldershot: Ashgate, 2003), pp. 51–66.

[83] Once again I am grateful to Adam for allowing me to work with his chapter on *Hyde Park*, forthcoming in *The Places of Wit*.

sealed space but also to those roads which lead in and out of that space. Edges and peripheries matter as much as centres in a narrative that is about flow and encounter, in a narrative about mobility rather than stasis.[84] The dramaturgy of Shirley and Nabbes actively understood those facts and in the process paid attention to the architectonics required to put these theatrical choreographies into place in ways that would bring those ideas alive in the context of performance.

INNS, TAVERNS, AND ORDINARIES IN THE CITY

One of the ways in which mobility is suggested and implied in *Tottenham Court*, alongside the night-time woodland wanderings of Worthgood and Bellamie, and the early rising of the park employees such as the Keeper and his milkmaid daughter, is through the movements of those tenant-neighbours employed by Bellamie's uncle to track down the eloping couple. When we first witness these tenants in 1.2, two are already bored with the chase, as well as disgruntled with their parsimonious employer:

1 TEN[ANT]: Stay, neighbour, let him goe. Shall wee rob our carcasses of sleepe all night that have been sufficiently tyr'd with the dayes toyles, for his reward? What will that be thinke you? a Christmas dinner; with a Chine of his great Oxe? (1.2. sig. B2r)

The second neighbour contributes to this comic speculation, suggesting that they might be served up a 'stale hare' or a sad goose 'that broke her necke, creeping through the hedge into the Parson's stubble' (1.2. sig. B2v). The two men decide to hang back and sleep the night out in a thicket, rejoining the search party in the morning.

   With deft economy the tenants' exchanges provide the audience with a working idea of the place from which these characters derive: the tenanted fields of a rural estate, with its hedges and hard work. Furthermore, where the tenant-farmers end up in their efforts to absent themselves from the chase gives us insight into a lower-status variation of the kind of drinking establishment sketched in Jonson's *The New Inn*. In the fifth act, we learn that, rather than sleep in the hedges like beggars or vagrants for the night, these rural farmers have knocked on the door of a cottage, prevailing on

---

[84] My thinking here is particularly shaped by William Cronon's essay 'Kennecott Journey: The Paths Out of Town' in William Cronon, George Miles, and Jay Gitlin (eds.), *Under an Open Sky: Rethinking America's Western Past* (New York and London: Norton, 1992), pp. 28–51 (esp. p. 33, where he stresses the need to walk the paths out of town to understand a place like Kennecott, a largely abandoned Alaskan mining town).

the residents to offer them shelter. One of them then reflects on the deep sleep they fell into once there: 'And dreamt we were in Cranborne Church at a drowsie Sermon' (5.1. sig. I1v), only to be woken later by sudden loud noise: 'The house was presently full of Gallants with Musicke, and to dancing they went' (5.1. sig. I1v). There is the usual suggestive contrast here between the peace and quiet of a country life as compared to life lived nearer to the capital. The tenants have, it seems, stumbled on an alehouse, premises usually held in domestic homes and known about partly by word of mouth. This particular Tottenham Court establishment is clearly very popular and highly successful in economic terms; there is much discussion of the inflated prices the widow-hostess and her tapster charge, akin to the quarrels over the 'reckonings' in Brome's urban drinking establishment in *The Sparagus Garden* (3.50–6). On further investigation, it is striking how many scenes, or, indeed, entire plays, in early modern drama focus on sites of consumption of various kinds, on the 'socioeconomic and organizational phenomenon' of food and the 'spatial and symbolic contexts in which consuming was located', to invoke Sara Pennell's suggestive phrases.[85] From the scenes already analysed in *The New Inn*, where the varying social designations of guests consume drink served by Pierce and Jug, to the alfresco consumption of asparagus and wine in the carefully sketched Asparagus Garden of Brome's play, the scene of victualling is consistently performed on commercial and amateur stages between the 1620s and 1650s.[86]

The consumption of food but also inns, taverns, and alehouses as sites proved a convenient way of bringing together a mixed ensemble of characters and individuals on the stage. Jonson's Barnet inn was populated with a variety of workers, both resident like the inn-workers, including Peck the ostler and itinerants like Barnaby the coach-driver, and visitors, from the tailor and his wife to aristocrats including Lords Lovel, Latimer, and Beaufort, and attendant servants such as Prudence. The Host's concealed identity merely adds to this sense of a mixed community. Beyond the dramatic possibilities enabled by the deployment of such a setting, these

---

[85] Sara Pennell, '"Great quantities of gooseberry pye and baked clod of beef": victualling and eating out in early modern London', in Paul Griffith and Mark S. R. Jenner (eds.), *Londinopolis: Essays in the Cultural and Social History of Early Modern London* (Manchester University Press, 2000), pp. 228–49 (p. 229). Brayshay *et al.*, 'Knowledge, nationhood, and governance', discuss the 'social and economic importance of victualling houses in early modern England' (pp. 283–4).

[86] Although Joan Thirsk makes a dismissive reference to the 'opportunism' of plays of this kind as merely capitalizing on contemporary fashions in their 'modish' titles, I would argue that they are sustained analyses of new practices of consumption as well as the spatial sites in which this consumption took place; see her *Food in Early Modern England: Phases, Fads, Fashions 1500–1760* (London: Hambledon Continuum, 2007), p. 95.

victualling establishments fostered the analysis of tendencies and trends in contemporary society, not least ideas of sociability, and, I would argue, mobility:

> Locales of leisured eating were clearly escapist venues, where the anonymising bonds of labouring life in the capital might be temporarily laid aside, and in which an otherwise fragmentary social cohesion might be sought through sociability; they capitalized on conceptions of food forged for the consumer in the midst of necessity.[87]

The alehouse in which Nabbes's tenant farmers unexpectedly find themselves is the same Tottenham Court property that Frank Changelove and Stitchwell reach after their running race in 2.5. Changelove observes that it is a 'handsome room', asking the audience to imagine the blurring of domestic space implicit in semi-commercial properties of this kind (2.5. sig. D4r).[88] Worthgood and Bellamie have also reached this place, though Bellamie is noticeably appalled by its lowly status, describing it condescendingly as 'A common alehouse' (2.6. sig. E1v). It is equally telling that her uncle has lodged himself in a rather finer class establishment, a London inn; this is revealed in 5.1. (sig. I1v), when the tenant farmers describe how they sent news of the discovery of his niece to the uncle at his expensive city lodgings. Bellamie is by now disguised in Cicely's clothes, so George mistakes her for the milkmaid with whom Frank is in love. The alehouse is also occupied by some Inns of Court gentlemen, as well as other tailors and London citizens. Sam, Bellamie's brother and a diligent student, is anxious to get back to his studies, but his companion James has other ideas. James is clearly a representative in the play of a loose liver (possibly in both senses of the term!) and there is some fun in-joking in his professed love of theatre:

> Hang cases and bookes that are spoyled with them. Give me Johnson and Shakespeare, there's learning for a gentlemen. I tell thee, Sam, were it not for the dancing-schoole and playhouses, I would not stay at the Innes of Court, for the hopes of a chiefe Justice-ship. (3.1. sig. E3r)

None of the sites mentioned, the playhouses or the Inns of Court, is an actual setting in this play but they are conjured as part of the daily and cultural cartographies of characters. Characters are partly defined through

---

[87] Pennell, 'Victualling and eating out', p. 243.

[88] Cf. Louise Hill Curth and Tanya M. Cassidy, '"Health, strength, and happiness": medical constructions of wine and beer in early modern England', in Adam Smyth (ed.), *A Pleasing Sinne: Drink and Conviviality in Seventeenth-Century England* (Cambridge: Brewer, 2004), pp. 143–59, where they note that 'Alehouses were closer to being domestic settings than taverns or inns' (p. 145).

the spaces they occupy and practise; Stitchwell, for example, is anxious to stress that he is a tailor of standing, since his shop is located in the Strand, revealing in the process the petty rivalries of city life:

A Taylor in the Strand; and I am as good a man there as Deputy Tagg in the City, though he thinke himselfe an Alderman's fellow, and no Cuckold. (3.1. sig. F1r)

The Tottenham Court alehouse is no exception to this rule. Even within its confined space, there is a distinction between guests in terms of the room in which they are located. Sam as an Inns-of-Court gentleman has enough status to request a private room in which to talk with his sister following their mutual recognition (sig. F2r), whereas the tailor's wife finds herself subject to George's attempted seduction in the washhouse: 'Pray, sir, forbeare. Is this a place to make one's husband a Cuckold in?', she laments (3.[4] sig. F2v).

The location of the washhouse is economically confirmed for the audience by the entrance and exit of a 'Wench' with a bucket of water, which she pours into the tub where George is unfortunately hiding after his fumbling encounter with Mistress Stitchwell has been interrupted by the arrival of her husband, who is much the worse for wear from the drink he has consumed. Stitchwell's wife instructs him to go and throw up in the fields so that she does not lose face with the servants (though she is actually preventing the hastily concealed George from being covered in the process): 'Emptie it in the fields, then; let not the servants take notice you are such a sloven' (3.[5] sig. F2v). As with the work of the ostler in *The New Inn* or Cicely the early rising milkmaid in *Tottenham Court*, or, indeed, the littermen of *The Sparagus Garden*, who are employed to transport a cross-dressed Timothy Hoyden around the London wards and streets in a sedan chair, this is another striking example of labour being made visible through the making of space on the early modern stage. The wench's response to a half-drowned George emerging from the tub is to remark on her wasted effort: 'Mischief on you, sir; you have spoiled mee a pile of conduit water, cost mee many a weary step the fetching [ . . . ]' (3.[6] sig. F2v). This is, of course, a blatant scene of farce, but in terms of its spatial dynamics it is resonant, conjuring for the audience a very real sense of the surrounding landscape of the tapster's house, as well as the various rooms and occupants – both paying guests and employees of the property itself.

Literal settings or locations are one overt way in which early modern drama engaged with and enacted ideas of cultural geography, but, as the example of coach travel indicates, there were also specific acts of mobility that performed or produced space on the stage in provocative and potentially transformative ways. In the final section of this chapter, we step down quite literally onto the streets and thoroughfares of early modern London to consider the act and art of walking as it was represented by the playwrights of the day.

## WALKING IN THE CITY

The forms of mobility, and, even more precisely, of walking practised by the crew of beggars that Springlove joins on their seasonal migrations in Brome's *A Jovial Crew*, would seem to bear out de Certeau's influential formulation of the spatial politics of perambulation that 'To walk is to lack a place', but that analysis of walking and its attendant geographies, cultural and material, is only partially accurate as an account of early modern cultural geography.[89] As Karen Newman's comparative research on early modern London and Paris has indicated, hedgerow beggars constitute a very different epistemological category to the urbane sociable walkers for whom the practice of promenade was very much an assertion of power and place, a performance of spatial control.[90] Plays such as *The Sparagus Garden* and *Tottenham Court* prove once again to be at the vanguard of representing the sociocultural development of urbane walking as a leisure practice and may even have promoted the activity through their conscious staging and restaging of this form of modish mobility.

It is at the start of the second act of *Tottenham Court* that the audience first encounters Frank and George. These two gallants are, early in the morning, 'walking to Totenham Court' philosophizing on the way about the 'Chymistry of Love' (sig. C3v). Frank is in love with Cicely, even though his male companion considers them socially ill-matched. Cicely is living proof of the opportunity for encounter with people from all social levels that comes from operating at the 'street level' required by pedestrianism as compared to the physical separation provided by modes of mobility such as coaches. En route to Tottenham Court, Frank and George meet other early day walkers, including Stitchwell, the Strand tailor, and his wife. Stitchwell is trying to encourage others to race him

[89] de Certeau, *The Practice of Everyday Life*, p. 103.
[90] Karen Newman, *Cultural Capitals: Early Modern London and Paris* (Princeton University Press, 2007), p. 17. See also Michelle O'Callaghan, *The English Wits: Wit and Sociability in Early Modern England* (Cambridge University Press, 2007), p. 28; and Karen Newman, 'Walking capitals: Donne's First Satyre', in *The Culture of Capital: Properties, Cities, Knowledge in Early Modern England* (London: Routledge, 2002), pp. 203–21.

to Tottenham Court for a wager; he will exit the stage running. This matrix of characters and the dynamics of their meeting both on the way to and within the space of Tottenham Court are, then, like the various characters who move around the locale of Hyde Park in the third and fourth acts of Shirley's play, embodied proof of Newman's claim that 'Traversing urban space . . . was the chief pastime of the early modern city dweller'.[91] These plays, and comparable contemporary dramas such as Brome's *The New Academy* (1636) are frequently discussed in terms of capturing the emergence of the Town district of London as a distinct cultural neighbourhood in the early seventeenth century.[92] What they help to indicate is how 'The city's expansion from east to west produced new social topographies . . .'[93] The 'new technologies of movement' as well as the revised social perspectives provided by hackney carriages has already been explored, but the redefinition of walking or promenading as a leisurely and elite bodily practice can equally be seen as a marker of social change. What the movements of Frank and George in Nabbes's play indicate, for example, and perhaps why the action of walking in this way proved so perpetually attractive to Caroline dramatists seeking to map their contemporary city, is the novel space of encounter that this form of perambulation opens up.

These encounters are not without their dangers in early modern drama, of course, not least for immigrants, incomers to a place who are less familiar with its quotidian practices and therefore far less able to navigate its thoroughfares with protective knowledge. In 2.1 of *The Sparagus Garden*, we learn that Timothy Hoyden, newly arrived into Hammersmith by way of his home in Taunton Deane in Somerset, has been set upon by a confederate in crime of Sir Hugh Moneylacks: 'my Spring has seized him upon the way' (234). Tim is a fairly stereotypical example of the gullible incomer at whom Henry Peacham aimed his prophylactic pamphlet *The Art of Living in London* in 1642, or, as its subtitle put it, 'A Caution how Gentlemen, Countrymen and Strangers, drawn by occasion of businesse, should dispose of themselves in the thriftiest way, not onely in the Citie, but in all other populous places'.[94] Walking encounters in these plays are

---

[91] Newman, *Cultural Capitals*, p. 59.

[92] R. Malcolm Smuts, 'The court and its neighbourhood: royal policy and urban growth in the early Stuart west end', *Journal of British Studies*, 30 (1991), 117–49; see also Zucker, 'London and urban space'. On Brome in particular, see Steggle, *Richard Brome*.

[93] Newman, *Cultural Capitals*, p. 63.

[94] For a fuller discussion of possible relationships between Brome's play and the content of Peacham's 1642 pamphlet, see my critical introduction to the play in *Brome Online*, especially paragraphs 1 and 2.

not always as wholly manipulative as Hoyden's waylaying in Hammersmith or Peacham's negative appraisals of city space might suggest. One familiar plot device is, for example, for a character simply to happen upon a place, a person, or an event; the act of walking is often an obvious promulgator of plot momentum. In *The New Academy*, for example, Valentine will claim that he spies Camelion's shop (and his wife within it) when 'Walking by chance' in the environs of the New Exchange (2.1.250). Valentine's walking may be more than just a plot enabler; his participation in urbane walking – walking in the city for the pure sake of walking in the city – immediately locates him for the audience as a member of a certain social grouping, one with the leisure time and inclination to traverse the town streets near the Strand in this way.

Elsewhere, the more regular perambulations of city inhabitants provide a reliable map or rhythm of expectation on which other characters depend. As already noted, in *The Sparagus Garden* the rival JPs Touchwood and Striker meet regularly in the streets for what turns out to be a therapeutic quarrel. Striker will claim that his health depends on these encounters: 'I met with my physician, dog-leech Touchwood / And cleared my stomach, and now I am light at heart' (2.2.374). It is the regularity of this pair's movements around the neighbourhood that ensures that they can meet for their 'daily constitutional'; as Touchwood notes of Striker at 2.2.347: 'This is his usual walk'; this category of practice and allusion evokes personal maps but also shared kinetic maps of the city.

As well as suggesting the daily circulations and notional cartographies of the city performed by the act of walking, the example of Striker and Touchwood draws our attention to the association of walking and health in the bodily and regulatory regimes encouraged and promoted in this period. John Taylor expressed his very pragmatic concern that increased coach travel would lead to people becoming obese when *The World Runs on Wheels* was published in the 1620s, but in 1631 Thomas Taylor extended that analysis of mobility into more metaphorical and spiritual terrains when he expounded on his idea of 'Circumspect Walking' in a pamphlet of the same name.[95] For him, all good Christians had to 'take heed' of their 'owne walking', and 'provident walking' would enable them to foresee and protect against all kinds of danger and evil.[96] What is intriguing, however, are the obvious ways in which his discursive strategies in this pamphlet

[95] Thomas Taylor, *Circumspect Walking: Describing the Severall Rules, as so many seuerall steps in the way of wisedome* (London, 1631).
[96] Taylor, *Circumspect Walking*, p. 3.

map onto more literal accounts of walking (and mobility more generally) as material and social practice at this time. Peacham's *The Art of Living* is similarly an invitation to 'take heed' and be provident about dangers on the London streets; and we register in contemporary anxieties about the issue of increased female mobility and agency, notable in several of the plays under discussion here, comparable concerns to those expressed by Thomas Taylor that women should 'be not gadders, but housekeepers'.[97]

It is certainly striking, the number of conversations about issues of personal health and fitness that occur in relation to all the walking being undertaken in *Tottenham Court*. Stitchwell recommends exercise regimes to the young apprentices and journeymen who lodge in his house-cum-workshop:

> I tell you Master Changelove though I am a Taylor I keepe servants that are stout knaves. I love them well, and they looke well to my businesse. On holydayes I give them leave to use exercise. (2.1. sig. D1r)

This exchange allows Stitchwell's wife to lament her lack of a similarly rigorous workout in the marital bed, but also to reflect, with suitable innuendo, on the various physical attractions of the young men employed by her husband ('your finisher is as pretty a fellow as ever did tradesmen or his wife service [ . . . ] He pitcheth the barr, and throws the stone; it does me good to think of it', 2.1. sig. D1r). The audience receives in the process a veritable geography of apprenticeship as Stitchwell sketches the character of his youthful employees; he notes:

> I have a Cornish-lad that wrestles well, and hath brought home Rabbets every Bartholomew-tide these five yeares. At stoole-ball, I have a North-west strippling shall deale with ever a boy in the Strand. (2.1 sig. D1r)

As well as thinking about the particular act of mobility represented by walking and exercise, we are cast here into the world of mobile labour and temporary lodgings that in part characterized urban space at this time. Equally, although we never hear these apprentices and journeymen speak in the same dialectical variation that characterizes the stages of Brome's plays, that linguistic complexity is nevertheless suggested by Nabbes via his offstage conjurations of the contemporary city. Through these various representations of perambulation, all kinds of other geographies, places, and spaces, as well as the bodily practices they produce or stimulate, are made visible.

---

[97] Taylor, *Circumspect Walking*, p. 68.

Contemporary theoretical engagement with the act and art of walking and the kinds of spatial knowledge it promotes, not least of urban geography, locate a very modern sensibility in the subversion and appropriation of city space.[98] Nevertheless, the writings of de Certeau and Lefebvre, among others, have their roots (and routes) in more classical sources. Aristotle was associated with a philosophical grouping known as the Peripatetics, so called because of their practice of offering instruction while walking round an educational site – a precedent cited directly by the character of Crasy in Brome's 1629 play *The City Wit* (2.1.141).[99] What the sustained attention of playwrights such as Brome and Nabbes to walking suggests is that its capacity as a practice to produce, as Zucker has so suggestively termed it, new 'cultural competencies', new kinds of spatial knowledge and behaviour, was something of which early modern dramatists were only too aware and keen to capture and examine in, and through, their dramaturgy.[100]

A consideration of the engagement with and representation of various forms of mobility in this diverse sample from early modern drama reveals a number of important things about the ways in which ideas of movement and motion figured on the early modern stage and in the imaginations of spectators. Mobility and travel are, on occasion, substituted for by dramatic representation of travel; on occasion, prior or shared spatial and geographic knowledges on the parts of audience members are supplemented and even challenged by these plays. Brome's work offers us direct examples of how contemporary anxieties about itinerancy were challenged by their juxtaposition with that most elite performance of mobility, the royal progress. Jonson's, and, indeed, Massinger's, provincial and suburban-based Caroline dramas manifest a repeated investment in making visible the new intraregional connections in the nation, not least those enabled by new modes of transportation and communication. Even in those plays which have at their core a wish to represent the actual geographical sites and spaces in which audiences would have operated, London-located plays by Brome and Nabbes not least, we have seen how the action frequently tests and explores the ways in which mapping and cognition shaped everyday

---

[98] One excellent set of critical interventions in this discussion is the collection of essays in D. J. Hopkins, Shelley Orr, and Kim Solga (eds.), *Performance and the City* (Basingstoke and New York: Palgrave, 2009).

[99] I am grateful to Elizabeth Schafer for drawing my attention to this reference; see her edition in *Brome Online*.

[100] Cf. Zucker, *The Places of Wit* and cf. Jean Howard, *Theater of a City: The Places of London Comedy, 1598–1642* (Philadelphia: University of Pennsylvania Press, 2007). See also Lefebvre, *The Production of Space*, p. 33, where he determines that successful and coherent production of spatial practice requires a degree of 'competence'.

behaviour; not only how people understood their locality but also the relationship of that locality to the wider social and political geography of the city and, by extension, the nation.

If mobility is essentially a way of thinking about encounter, with places and with people, then it seems obvious that drama, which holds at its generic core the sheer potential of encounter, not least with a live audience, would be drawn to this particular form of geographical imagining. Melanie Ord has observed that when, in 1620, Sir Francis Bacon published his scientific treatise *The New Organon*, he offered a version of the intellectual encounter with the natural world that was a form of active personal engagement, recall, and imagination: 'In Bacon's writing, nature is repeatedly seen as an area to be cognitively mapped: traced with metaphorical goalposts, signposts, and resting-places and scored over with journeys made and yet to be made'.[101] It strikes me that this description serves equally well as an account of early modern drama's vibrant engagement with the spaces and places of the English landscape through its plot lines of literal and social mobility. In the inns, ordinaries, and staging-posts of plays by Jonson, Massinger, Nabbes, Heywood, and Brome, in the roadside encounters of dramas such as *A Jovial Crew*, in the imagining of journeys to the further reaches of the nation in London-staged plays such as *The Late Lancashire Witches*, or in the highly localized social and urban cartographies of London-based plays such as *The Sparagus Garden* or *Tottenham Court*, we witness a version of these tracings and scorings of the complex connectivities and networks of early modern cultural geography. Early modern drama is an actor-agent in these networks, shaping as much as reflecting the practice of these spaces, suggesting modes of cognitive mapping and journeys to be made to a responsive audience alert to the personal and political geographies in which their own lives operated.

[101] Melanie Ord, *Travel and Experience in Early Modern English Literature* (Basingstoke: Palgrave Macmillan, 2008), p. 89.

CHAPTER 5

# Neighbourhoods and networks

In any study of the cultural geography of early modern drama, the city of London necessarily looms large as the performance location, and frequently the prime subject matter, of commercial drama. However, as Chapter 3 indicated, the purpose-built playhouses were far from being the only sites for theatre in this period. Equally, the sites and spaces engaged with and 'mapped' by the dramatists of the age were not confined to urban locales, even in the canon of a playwright such as Jonson, who is frequently presented as the urban dramatist par excellence.[1] There has been important work done of late to redress a perceived metropolitan bias in the study of early modern drama; this has contributed to a much needed complicating of the map of early modern playing as art and aesthetic, and the places and spaces which that art sought to capture and represent.[2] However, there remain important ways in which literary scholarship can be inflected by the advances made within other disciplines in terms of thinking about how we understand and experience cities (cultural geography and performance studies are both essential touchstones in this respect) and the ways in which those spaces were historically conceived of, constructed, and practised (here, urban and social history have, perhaps, most to offer).

[1] In thinking about the sociospatial context for communities and also the drama that sought to imagine and represent those communities for a viewing public, there has been considerable interest in the early modern city as a site. Important recent work by Jean Howard has constructed a number of city dramas in relation to the 'spatial stories' that they both mobilized and legitimized (see *Theater of a City*) and Janette Dillon has limned the specific spatial categories of theatre, court, and city, while arguing for the significant interaction and overlap between them (*Theatre, Court and City*). The essays edited by Lena Cowen Orlin under the suggestive title *Material London, ca. 1600* have, in turn, done much to nuance and complicate our notion of the metropolis as site and space, not least in its interactions with its rural hinterlands and provinces. Some of the discussion of the multiple meanings of 'household' in Chapter 3 invited us to think about metropolitan places and spaces in dialogue with rural and provincial communities and in many respects this chapter is an extension of that argument. On Jonson's urban psychology, see, for example, Martin Butler, 'Jonson's London and its theatres', in Richard Harp and Stanley Stewart (eds.), *The Cambridge Companion to Ben Jonson* (Cambridge University Press, 2000), pp. 15–29.
[2] Keenan, *Travelling Players*; Findlay's *Playing Spaces*.

By thinking of London as a city in terms of particular zones or districts, such as Covent Garden, or in terms of specific streets as providing and defining communities and subcommunities – The Strand proves a particularly rich example, housing as it did many of the significant courtiers of the day, but also offering major opportunities for shopping, consumption, and trade in the form of the New Exchange – we begin to break down any monolithic sense of the city as a singular or static site. Donald Lupton, writing in 1632, recognized as much in his attempts to understand the 'global city':[3] 'She [London] is grown so great. I am almost afraid to meddle with her [ . . . ] she is certainly a great world, there are so many worlds in her.'[4] The two specific locations of Covent Garden and The Strand will form the focus of the following and concluding chapter, but one of the ways in which a monolithic reading has been resisted in recent urban historical research has been through an attention to the different spatial or organizational categories by which London was divided into smaller units. These units often constituted administrative categories, alternatively defined by ecclesiastical or civic authorities. A ward was a governmental division (what we would now think of as part of a political constituency). The parish was an area defined by its having its own distinct church and clergy and the accoutrements of those institutions such as a parish council and officials. A hundred was a comparable subdivision that tended to exist within the county or shire and which might also have its own court or means of legal jurisdiction. Within the hybrid, overlapping, or contiguous spaces of the near suburbs of the city of London in the early modern period, people might well perceive of themselves as belonging to either category, or to both. There is, as this reveals, an acute difference between inner and outer suburbs in classifying these spatial groupings. The relationship between the 'village' of Westminster and the City of London, to which it was directly proximate, has been the focus of extensive research by Julia Merritt and the records of activities within the area during the 1620s and 1630s reveal a number of the contradictions and potential conflicts of interest that these different social categories fostered. Westminster regarded itself as autonomous from the city, but inevitably its activities were impacted by decisions made within the capital. There were also shifting parish boundaries within Westminster at this time and therefore the sense of identity its residents held was

---

[3] The phrase is Crystal Bartolovich's; see her essay '"Baseless Fabric": London as "World City"' in Peter Hulme and William Sherman (eds.), *The Tempest and its Travels* (London: Reaktion, 2000), pp. 13–26.

[4] Donald Lupton, *London and the Country* (London, 1632); cited in Harkness, *The Jewel House*, p. 1.

constantly evolving.[5] Covent Garden, for example, was on Westminster's boundaries and did not become a parish in its own right until the early 1640s.[6]

Even within the city proper, as well as on its outer edges or in its developing hinterlands, there were areas that were beyond its formal jurisdiction. The 'Liberties' have been the focus of considerable attention from early modern scholars in the wake of Steven Mullaney's ground-breaking study, *The Place of the Stage*, which raised all kinds of important questions about the relationship between centre and margin in city government and legislation as well as theatre's status within and reaction to the same.[7] That a number of these zones were located within the city walls or on its edges, in particular the religious and theatrical precinct of the Blackfriars, and also the legal district that constituted the Inns of Court, further complicates the picture. All of these sites and spaces were, as we will see, the raw material for drama at this time. There is a danger that our understanding of the relationship between these different urban and social categories, often overlapping categories as I am suggesting, has become too ossified, ignoring in the process a complex interplay between different senses of belonging and identity that pertained in early modern communities. While the literal map of the city at this time, an artefact or entity that was often prescribed by administrative or official requirements, is one useful tool in thinking about the ways in which people understood and, in turn, represented the city in which they existed, it is just one of several ways by which people 'mapped' their sense of belonging. To that end, what I want to offer in this chapter is the labile category of the 'neighbourhood' as a particularly enabling means through which to think about early modern urban practice. In my definition, 'neighbourhood' combines spatial elements – people did identify neighbours and neighbourhoods according to the places in which they lived and worked – with the social and cultural aspects of the term.[8] People regarded their 'neighbourhood' as orientated as much by the affective bonds

[5] Merritt, *The Social World of Early Modern Westminster*, offers the particular example of the contested parish boundaries (which in the 1630s included Covent Garden) of the St Martin's in the Field district (pp. 208–9).

[6] Merritt, *The Social World of Early Modern Westminster*, p. 3. See also Steggle, *Richard Brome*, p. 48.

[7] Steven Mullaney, *The Place of the Stage: Licence, Play and Power in Renaissance England* (Ann Arbor: University of Michigan, 1995 [first published by University of Chicago Press, 1988]).

[8] This thinking is strongly influenced by Jeremy Boulton's *Neighbourhood and Society: A London Suburb in the Seventeenth Century* (Cambridge University Press, 1989). Joseph P. Ward in his introduction on 'Situating identity' to *Metropolitan Communities: Trade Guilds, Identity, and Change in Early Modern England* (Stanford University Press, 1997), pp. 1–2, talks of how 'recently scholars have decreased the significance of locality in their models by viewing communities as flexible groups marked by ties of allegiance and affection rather than physical proximity'. My method, as will be clear, arises from a preference for a combination of both these models rather than a choice between them.

between those individuals and groupings whom they lived alongside, or by the space in which they carried out professional or institutional activities (it should not be presumed that residency and trade activity necessarily overlapped). If we start to apply this social anthropological model of the 'neighbourhood' to the different parts, zones, and versions of London that are regularly reconstituted and reconfigured on the early modern stage, we can bring the subcommunities and localities of the city into clearer view and with that offer fresh attention to the particular practices and insights to which they give rise.[9]

We began in the chapter on households, using terms prevalent both from historical geography and from new biographical studies, to think in terms of neighbourhoods and networks as more useful social and geographical formations for understanding how ideas of community operated both in drama and in everyday life. In this chapter, I seek to extend that thinking by taking us into early modern London and demonstrating the ways in which playwrights such as Brome, his mentor Jonson, and Shirley not only became expert recorders of these spaces, sites, and streets, but were agents in the ways in which people conceptualized and engaged with them.[10] I am offering a version, then, of the 'thick description' or 'fieldwork' that ethnographers such as Clifford Geertz and James Clifford introduced in the 1980s and which bore such sway over the practices of New Historicism.[11] Instead of deploying that kind of descriptive process to reinscribe the 'city' as a monolithic and stable site inculcated in the power structures of the early modern state (the kind of 'centres' versus 'margins' mapping that Mullaney's work pioneered),[12] I want to deploy the fieldwork that takes us into the heart of particular communities, households, streets, neighbourhoods, and parishes of the time as a means to unpack the complex and often contradictory operations of both the drama and the dramatists that sought to engage with and to understand the contemporary city.[13]

---

[9] My model is akin to Harkness's 'multisited ethnography' in *The Jewel House*, p. 255. I am also indebted to more contemporary works of social anthropology in the metropolitan context, in particular Daniel Miller's *The Comfort of Things* (Cambridge: Polity Press, 2008).

[10] Cf. Harkness, *The Jewel House*, p. 2: 'To understand how London helped to bring about such a change, it is helpful to return to her streets.' The phrase also brings to mind Roy Porter's pioneering idea of 'doing medicine from below' and getting the patient's eye view in 'The patient's view', *passim*. It could be argued that in the play Hoyden's plot line enables just such a vantage point for the 1630s audience.

[11] James Clifford *et al.* (eds.), *Writing Culture: The Poetics and Politics of Ethnography* (Berkeley: University of California Press, 1992).

[12] Mullaney, *The Place of the Stage, passim*.

[13] Particular acknowledgements need to be made here of the work of Harkness, who in *The Jewel House* writes of her own method as 'thick description and the mapping of social and intellectual networks among individuals and between communities of practitioners' (p. 8); and see Margaret

PARISH POLITICS AND JONSON'S *A TALE OF A TUB*

Very few early modern Londoners, those who wrote in journals and notebooks such as artisan woodturner Nehemiah Wallington, or those whose lives briefly and partially appear in the court depositions of the day, described themselves as belonging solely or wholly to the city. More frequently, people would identify themselves as belonging to a particular parish. As Keith Wrightson has indicated, people tended to know the topography of their parish 'intimately' and this contributed not only to their 'sense of place' and identity, but was a central part of their modus operandi.[14] As well as being a religious unit of administration and belonging, as we have already noted, the parish was a social system, albeit one in the constant process of construction by means of ongoing structures of negotiation and 'accommodation'.[15]

One way of rethinking the map of early modern London in terms of smaller zones, subunits, and communities, is, then, to think of the 'parish' as the key facet of understanding that often shaded into or operated as a 'neighbourhood'.[16] Deborah Harkness has written about the ways in which the idea of the parish contributed to and, in part, defined an 'urban culture of criticism and accountability'.[17] Identities were often fashioned through a sense of belonging and accountability to the parish as a unit of religious and spiritual administration, but also in more practical and cartographic terms as a marker of the geographical parameters of a neighbourhood. One of the plays that makes manifest this idea of the parish, and, indeed, the looser social arc of the parish neighbourhood, is Jonson's 1633 play *A Tale of a Tub*, set as it is on a frosty St Valentine's day morning in the parish of St Pancras, or, as the dramatis personae has it, in the scene of the 'Finsbury hundred'. Jonson immediately draws attention in this naming and citing (and, indeed, siting) of different 'areas' to those variant forms and administrative terms that were available for understanding local geography.

Pelling in *Medical Conflicts in Early Modern London: Patronage, Physicians, and Irregular Practitioners 1550–1640* (Oxford: Clarendon Press, 2003), where she strives for 'intimacy' and describes her project as trying to 'recapture the social, economic, and cultural experience of ordinary people' (p. 8). She is as a result interested in 'small-scale structures' (p. 8).

[14] Keith Wrightson, *English Society, 1580–1680*, 2nd edition (London: Routledge, 2002), p. 48.
[15] Wrightson, *English Society*, p. 73.
[16] See Steve Hindle, 'Parishes, provinces and neighbourhoods', in Julie Sanders (ed.), *Ben Jonson in Context* (Cambridge University Press, 2010), pp. 134–43.
[17] Harkness, *The Jewel House*, p. 224.

People in this play live in hundreds, in parishes, in villages, and even regard themselves as communities belonging to particular streets or clusters of housing. The central landholding family of the play, the Tubs, are based in Totten[ham] Court (the area where Tottenham Court Road is today); the local constable Tobias Turf belongs to Kentish Town; Justice Preamble (also known as Bramble in the play) represents Marylebone; John Clay the tile-maker belongs to Kilburn, which was well known in this period for its tile-works (often serving as the subject of local petitions claiming noise and olfactory pollution of the surrounding environment).[18] Other characters, like Clay, belong to areas that, like their names, are indicative of their professions and trades. Rasi Clench the farrier (a clench is a kind of nail used in the process of shoeing horses) is from Hampstead; In-and-In Medlay the cooper is from Islington; To-Pan the tinker is from Belsize. Given a map of London and its outlying districts in the 1630s, an ordinary person might well have identified certain areas or streets by the crafts or trades with which they were linked and Jonson plays with this form of associational geography in his cast list. As well as being 'a carefully constructed cross-section of Stuart local government', as Martin Butler has noted (many of these men are holders of local office: Turf is the constable, Medlay the headborough, and To-Pan the thirdborough), the various characters are a locational guide to the workings of the city and its outlying districts.[19]

There is inevitably some slippage between what is understood as a 'parish' in strictly jurisdictional terms and the ways in which individuals or groups of individuals might perceive of themselves as belonging to a parish 'community' or 'neighbourhood'; in Harkness's terms, for example, neighbourhoods were often centred on 'one or more parishes, and were anchored by a parish church'.[20] This form of social mapping is borne out in *A Tale of a Tub*. The play opens with Chanon Hugh, who is Vicar of St Pancras church, at the heart of the diocese, and the events which unfold in this play surround the (mostly failed) attempts of Turf to see his daughter

[18] Ward, *Metropolitan Communities*, discusses attempts by the city authorities to move the offending works out into the suburbs as part of the New Corporation of the Suburbs in 1636 (see, e.g., pp. 36–8). Merritt notes that the use of Westminster fields for brickmaking and the sourcing of clay for the industry was a cause of concern in the 1630s (*The Social World of Early Modern Westminster*, pp. 185–6). As the city hinterlands grew and, with them new housing developments, residential areas were brought into ever closer contact with industry. In a subtle way, *A Tale of a Tub* explores some of these tensions.

[19] The comment is made in a commentary note to Martin Butler's edition of the play for *Selected Plays of Ben Jonson*, vol. 2 (Cambridge University Press, 1989), p. 423, n. 15.

[20] Harkness, *The Jewel House*, p. 140. For an excellent examination of this syndrome, see Merritt, *The Social World of Early Modern Westminster*, esp. pp. 212–22.

Audrey married. Hugh's church, although never actually represented on stage, is the constant focus of attention and direction in the play as various characters are instructed to head there, sometimes with the aim of marrying Audrey, more often than not with the intention of thwarting her nuptials. In terms of associational geography, however, audience imaginations will have been actively imagining, 'reading', and interpreting this site from the moment Hugh steps onstage. St Pancras Church was renowned at this time for bearing witness to a high number of irregular or illicit marriages.[21]

This geographical context is conceivably the background to the name of the curate in Brome's *The Sparagus Garden*: Pancridge. This links him by association to illicit weddings, as well as explicating, in part, his anxiety to appear as an upstanding member of his community. It may also provide a context for his seeming cynicism in Act 5 about the institution of marriage. He both refers to Rebecca Brittleware's 'light' heels, implying her tendency towards adultery, and in the next breath describes the impending wedding ceremony (forced marriage?) of Annabel and Cautious over which he is due to preside in the following terms: 'I am now going to yoke a heifer to a husband' (5.2. 1089, 1091).[22] There are similar veins of reference in Nabbes's *Tottenham Court*, which takes place in locales adjacent to those in which Jonson's *Tub* unfolds. Discovering his eloped niece Bellamie in hiding at an alehouse, the uncle is at the same time introduced to his new daughter-in-law, Cicely the milkmaid, who has, during the interim, married his son, Sam: 'Yet more plots!' he remarks with horror, 'Sure the Parson of Pancrace hath been here' (5.6. sig. K2r). Ironically, by the close of *Tottenham Court*, further business will have been secured for St Pancras Church, which is where the Keeper of Marylebone Park intends to marry the widowed hostess of the alehouse which becomes the locus of reunion in the play (5.7. sig. K4r).[23]

The implication in *A Tale of a Tub*, then, is that Hugh makes a tidy sum from ministering over dubious marriages and couplings. The audience is encouraged simply by knowing the church he represents to suspect Hugh of self-serving intentions from the beginning and this expectation is not disappointed. Hugh has come from St Pancras on an errand from Squire Tripoly Tub, who is one of several suitors to Audrey Turf in the play, and who is keen to delay her impending wedding to John Clay, decided on by a Valentine's day lottery by her parents. Hugh has happily accepted

---

[21] See Butler, *Selected Plays of Ben Jonson*, p. 423, n. 1.

[22] See related discussions in the notes to my edition of *The Sparagus Garden* in *Brome Online*.

[23] On the centrality of the parish church to ideas of community or neighbourhood, spatial and social, see Merritt, *The Social World of Early Modern Westminster*, pp. 212–22.

payment for this work, but is also keen to increase his earnings potential by encouraging Justice Preamble to get involved in the action as well:

> Oh for a choir of these voices, now,
> To chime in a man's pocket, and cry chink!
> One doth not chirp: it makes no harmony.
> Grave Justice Bramble next must contribute.
>
> (1.1.90–3)

Hugh is presumably handling a coin in his pocket at this point (an 'angel' in early modern parlance was a coin depicting the image of St Michael). We soon witness Hugh's desires being satisfied when, in 1.5, we observe him trying to persuade the Justice to halt the wedding. Preamble – his proper title; the 'Bramble' used by many characters is a disparaging nickname – has his sights set on Audrey himself, although he begins by suggesting that Hugh go against the wishes of the neighbourhood in seeking to prevent Audrey's marriage to Clay: 'Subtle Sir Hugh, you are now in the wrong, / And err with the whole neighbourhood, I must tell you [ . . . ]' (1.5.9–10). He proceeds to offer a 'brace of angels' to ensure that Hugh works for him and not for the Squire in this matter. Hugh is quickly swayed to new loyalties:

> And I of this effect of two to one;
> It worketh in my pocket 'gainst the Squire
> And his half bottom here, of half a piece,
> Which was not worth stepping o'er the stile for.
>
> (1.5.63–6)

Hugh expresses loyalty in physical terms in this speech. Loyalty to an individual such as the Squire involves Hugh travelling outside of his parish and therefore he seems to expect some form of pecuniary reward (a limited sense of loyalty, at best).

*A Tale of a Tub* persistently invokes the offstage action of characters crossing stiles in order to convey to audiences the idea of how parish edges and property boundaries were perceived and practised. This is indicative of the ways in which the play engages, in its convoluted plot lines and its stage action – in which the stage community moves around various geographical spaces in the enacting of daily business – with what in earlier contexts I termed the 'kinetic geography' of neighbourhood. We get a very immediate sense of the frosty fields and town streets through which Lady Tub dispatches Pol-Martin to pursue her wayward son, for example (1.6.49–51), and of Turf's home, where the food for the wedding dinner is being prepared. We are asked to imagine the street that has been strewn with sweet-smelling bay leaves and rosemary fitting to the time of year for the nuptials, and the barn on Turf's property where Clay will later hide from the hue and cry that wrongly pursue him as a robber. From the central gathering point of St Pancras Church to the grand estate of the Tubs, where the final 'motion' restages the events of the play as a wedding masque for Audrey and her eventual groom, Pol-Martin, Jonson's text asks us to imagine a whole district and community, its built environment, and its social and jurisdictional structures.

Hugh's opening speech has similarly drawn our attentions to the community of parishioners, when he mentions the freezing cold keeping people in their beds that morning:

> Now o'my faith, old Bishop Valentine,
> You ha' brought us nipping weather: *Februere*
> *Doth cut and shear*; your day and diocese
> Are very cold. All your parishioners
> As well as your laics, as your quiristers,
> Had need to keep to their warm feather beds,
> If they be sped of loves. This is no season
> To seek new makes in.　　　　　　　　(1.1.1–8)

This is a play rife with the language and operations of 'neighbourhood', but also with all of its potential breakdowns. Audrey's marriage becomes a particular focus of these tensions. It becomes clear that Turf has resisted the attentions of the local squire (Tripoly Tub) towards his daughter because he considers his family to be from a different social level and therefore unsuitable for intermarriage. Turf practises a somewhat random form of 'endogamy' by insisting instead that his daughter marry a local tradesman whose name was selected in the aforementioned lottery (there is a sense of historical precedent, since it is how Turf and his own wife Sybil were matched thirty years previously). Audrey rather charmingly echoes her father's views at 3.8 when she declares to the possessive Lady Tub on the subject of her son:

> I know myself too mean for his high thoughts
> To stoop at, more than asking a light question
> To make him merry, or to pass his time.
>　　　　　　　　(3.8.12–14)

The acute awareness of the social categorization provided by rank in Audrey's and her father's reactions to a potential coupling with Squire

Tub suggests that 'neighbourhood' in this community is severely curbed by the familiar obstacles of wealth and power.

There is, however, a strong sense of the neighbourhood as a geographical and social entity in this play and of people's proximity to each other, as they move between houses and residences; Turf enters on stage having heard the merry exchanges between his neighbours from the privacy of his garden (1.3.1–2), a very tangible realization of living conditions in this parish. With this literal and physical proximity of the neighbours comes a sense of shared histories and knowledges: witness To-Pan on Rasi Clench as an unofficial local historian:

> You are a shrewd antiquity neighbour Clench!
> And a great guide to all the parishes!
> The very bell-wether of the hundred here
> As I may zay.                    (1.2.29–32)

The linguistic manifestation of locality in the form of To-Pan's dialect is yet further evidence of the careful way in which Jonson limns a very specific community within the larger cartographic category of London's suburbs.[24] The saltpetre works on which the Tub family wealth is founded is part of the geological, economic, and personal history of this place. The former owner, Sir Peter, is now dead, but the traces of his works live on in various ways within the Tub household – both in the metaphors used to describe his widow (Hugh's less than kindly remarks are that she is 'all dried earth / *Terra damnata*, not a drop of salt / Or petre in her!' (1.6.68–70), but these lines also capture something of the physical desecration of the local landscape enacted by digging for saltpetre) and in the shape of Pol-Martin, Lady Tub's handsome young usher, who previously went by the name of Martin Pole-cat when he was a basket carrier in the works (1.6.26–34). Basket Hilts, the governor and companion to Squire Tripoly, may also bear in his name traces of the family trade.

The resonance of *A Tale of a Tub*'s engagement with questions of local administration and governance during the period of the so-called 'Personal Rule' has been discussed in detail elsewhere, but it is important to register in this context the ways in which local office-holding is seen to place pressures on the villagers and townsfolk who assume those roles.[25] The

---

[24] To-Pan's dialect approximates to dialect patterns more usually associated with the West Country at this time. Jonson was a playwright who demonstrated considerable interest in accent and dialect, but was not averse to relocating certain geographical models to highlight a sense of 'difference' between characters living in close proximity.

[25] See Martin Butler, 'Late Jonson', in Gordon McMullan and Jonathan Hope (eds.), *The Politics of Tragicomedy* (London: Routledge, 1992), pp. 166–88; and Julie Sanders, '"The collective contract

188 Neighbourhoods and networks

tension is a direct product of geography, of the proximity to neighbours that the play has elsewhere made so visible;[26] Toby Turf is frequently having to take decisions relating to people he knows directly (such as when 'Captain Thumbs', really Chanon Hugh in disguise, insists that the hue and cry be set on Audrey's prospective bridegroom as a thief; this in turn provokes Preamble effectively to place Turf on trial and to cite the respect of neighbourhood in the process: 'And I am sorry too for your neglect / Being my neighbour' (4.1.16–17)) and he is constantly seeking the support and endorsement of his neighbours as a result, though noticeably not his wife, whom he tells to 'mind your pigs o' the spit at home' (2.2.111). At one point, Turf laments the responsibility he has to bear in the local community, wishing instead to be the 'scavenger', that is to say the lowliest official appointed in the parish system:

> Passion of me, was ever man thus crossed?
> All things run arsy-varsy; upside down.
> High Constable! Now by Our Lady of Walsingham
> I had rather be marked out Tom Scavenger,
> And with a shovel make clean the highways
> Than have the office of a constable.         (3.1.1–6)

The appeal to 'Our Lady of Walsingham' suggests yet another form of community, which is that conjoined by ideas of faith. Notionally set in an earlier historical period, the early years of the Elizabethan reign, *Tub* is able to explore the pull of older ties of neighbourhood and pre-Reformation identity and practice on the interpretation of place and space.[27] Of course, it would be wrong to suggest that the kinds of intimacy and proximity which drive the plot line of *A Tale of a Tub* were limited to rural parishes.[28] Jonson, quite deliberately, as with the Barnet setting of *The New Inn*, locates his play within striking distance of the city in order to remind spectators that, for all the drama's superficial hiding behind the various masks of local

---

is a fragile structure": local government and personal rule in *A Tale of a Tub*', *English Literary Renaissance*, 27 (1997), 443–67.

[26] There are important links to the ideas of social proximity as explored, with specific relation to gender, in the work of Laura Gowing, *Common Bodies: Women, Touch and Power in Seventeenth-Century England* (New Haven and London: Yale University Press, 2003).

[27] This idea of vestigial or residual traces of older religious and social practice in the early modern landscape has been thoughtfully explored in recent research. See, for example, Jennifer Summit, 'Leland's *Itinerary* and the remains of the medieval past', in Gordon McMullan and David Matthews (eds.), *Reading the Medieval in Early Modern England* (Cambridge University Press, 2007), pp. 159–78; and Phebe Jensen, *Religion and Revelry in Shakespeare's Festive World* (Cambridge University Press, 2008).

[28] Wrightson, *English Society*, p. 64. He gives the specific example of Stepney, where, between 1606 and 1610, 63 per cent of all marriages were between partners from the parish.

dialect and the past, the operations of neighbourhood and parish that it depicts are, in reality, remarkably close to home.

If, as Keith Wrightson suggests, and plays such as *A Tale of a Tub* appear to endorse, 'Localism was an important element in both the social experience and the mentality of sixteenth- and seventeenth-century people', then the ways in which the locality was both understood and practised will surely provide a point of entry to the cultural geography of those localities as mobilized by contemporary drama.[29] The main concept when thinking about this is the 'neighbourhood'. Unlike the more institutionally inscribed unit of the parish or the county, the 'neighbourhood' was wholly more nebulous and indistinct and yet, as we shall see, it was a very active means by which people understood and attempted to negotiate their direct social and material environment. To quote Wrightson: '"Neighbourliness" . . . is a somewhat vague concept . . . Yet it was a notion much employed by sixteenth- and seventeenth-century people.'[30] Catherine Richardson talks about the rhetorical force of the concept of neighbourliness: 'Spatial proximity produced intimate knowledge, and the rhetoric of "neighbourhood", meaning everyone's charge to ensure the moral uprightness of their local community, turned that knowledge into a currency with which to purchase local honesty'.[31] Ideas of 'good neighbourliness' were powerful social forces and, according to Wrightson, not just a matter of 'residential propinquity' but a 'mutual recognition of reciprocal obligations of a practical kind'.[32] It is exactly this kind of 'neighbourhood' that *The Sparagus Garden* so brilliantly mobilizes and depicts, although the lack of honesty active among its members is partly what drives the various plot lines of this lively play as well as its rhetoric of neighbourliness.

While not geographically exact in terms of identifying, in the way that Jonson's *Tub* does, the specific parish or parishes in which the events of the play unfold, there are, nevertheless, sufficient geographical markers and hints to locate a reasonably knowledgeable person in particular zones of London, and, by extension, to think about the version of 'neighbourhood'

---

[29] Wrightson, *English Society*, p. 59.     [30] Wrightson, *English Society*, p. 59.
[31] Richardson, *Domestic Life and Domestic Tragedy*, p. 34. A key book in this field is Boulton, *Neighbourhood and Society*; ostensibly a case study of a Southwark community, its findings have implications for and applications to a range of sites and situations.
[32] Wrightson, *English Society*, p. 59.

and 'neighbourliness' that *The Sparagus Garden* represents. As Chapter I evidenced, the Lambeth marshes on the south side of the Thames are, for example, the most likely location both for the asparagus plots that provided the new edible commodity that forms the central symbol of the play as well as the riverside pleasure palace itself. Visitors to the Lambeth site include the Brittlewares, who run a china shop close to the new shopping heartland of The Strand. Somerset innocent Timothy Hoyden has passed through Hammersmith, a village to the north-west of London and on the main connecting road with his county of origin, on his way to the Brittlewares' household, where Sir Hugh Moneylacks is a long-term lodger; and, as already mentioned, the curate conjures up morally complex associations with the suburban parish of St Pancras. My intention, though, is less to pinpoint specific areas of the built environment in the play with reference to available maps of seventeenth-century London than to think about the ideas of neighbourliness that it seeks to interrogate and even promote.

*The Sparagus Garden* is expert at creating a material and physical sense of the neighbourhoods in which it takes place. This is often achieved through specific props, objects, or commodities, including the aforementioned asparagus. Sara Pennell has demonstrated the centrality of foodstuffs and victualling practices to the ways in which space was developed and used in the city and its environs:

Suburban development of the City, Westminster, and the liberties south of the Thames brought with it demographic pressures upon the spatial and temporal organization of non-elite labour and thus of domestic life. High concentrations of individuals living in lodgings, singly, or in fluid, often non-familial groups, and the presence of that prototypical "consuming" population, domestic servants, often in search of food on their free days or to spend their board wages, made extra-domestic victualling inevitable.[33]

The Asparagus Garden as a site contains and promotes all of these social and demographic shifts. As Chapter 4 indicated, this play is rich in its engagement with new ideas of personal transportation in an urban context, full, as it is, of references to the novel phenomenon of the sedan chair. Moneylacks is investing in sedans, Rebecca Brittleware will escape down the Strand in one in Act 4, and Tim Hoyden will even be carried (crossdressed) onstage in one. As well as creating a sense of space through what some cultural commentators refer to as the 'social life of things', the play creates a vivid sense of the ways in which particular networks of streets

---

[33] Pennell, 'Great quantities of gooseberry pye', p. 230.

connect with one another and in the process connect individuals and neighbourhoods.[34] It is not until the fifth act that we realize that Striker's housekeeper, Friswood, is also Rebecca's aunt and that their proximity to each other is as much a matter of kinship relations as the dense dwelling conditions of early modern London.

The key 'relationship' in the play, however (and I place that term in quotation marks partly because it is a relationship that appears utterly dysfunctional from the opening moments of the play, defined as much by its breakdown in communication as by any sense of reciprocity or mutual obligation) is that between the two elderly JPs, Striker and Touchwood. The cultural stereotype of the JP was a convenient means in early modern drama of inviting audiences to think about community structures and operations (and, in the case of corrupt justices such as Thrifty in the Osborne manuscript play or Clack in *A Jovial Crew*, about their concomitant failures, fissures, and breakdowns). As *A Tale of a Tub* revealed, the structures of local officialdom enable deep insight into social relationships and the specific cultural geography of certain areas, districts, and parishes. The example of Sir Paul Squelch from Brome's earlier play, *The Northern Lass*, is yet further illustration of the fact that these depictions of the (often dubious) power of local officialdom were far from limited to rural or outlying parishes and often extended into the space of the city of London itself.

Striker and Touchwood are in some respects figures of deep stability in their respective neighbourhood. They have been resident for at least thirty years, as several references make apparent; but their deep-set feud with one another has endured almost as long: Gilbert notes to Touchwood in the opening scene: 'Troth, sir, the point is this: you know (and the town has ta'en sufficient notice of it) that there has been a long contention betwixt you and old Master Striker your neighbour –' (1.1. 20). Their quarrel has become as much a part of their self-definition as their roles in the local judiciary. Touchwood introduces us to the quarrel (if not the reason for it) in his opening exchange with Walter and Gilbert; and it becomes the compelling reason for both men striving to separate the play's young lovers, Sam (Touchwood's son) and Annabel (Striker's biological granddaughter but now his ward and quasi-daughter, owing to the early death of her mother and her father's financial and emotional profligacy).

---

[34] The phrase derives from Arjun Appadurai's work, *The Social Life of Things: Commodities in Cultural Perspective* (Cambridge University Press, 1988). For a specifically early modern discussion of this concept, see Patricia Fumerton and Simon Hunt (eds.), *Renaissance Culture and the Everyday* (Philadelphia: University of Pennsylvania Press, 1998).

What this account of the 'relationship' fails to convey, however, is the way in which the play is equally explicit in making clear to the audience the deep need both men have of each other – as the examination of urban perambulation in the previous chapter began to suggest, their quarrel has become their reason for existence and they structure their days, and even their geographical movements around the neighbourhood, accordingly.

In 2.2, Striker longs for another vituperative encounter with his rival and actively seeks him out, believing that his general health depends on this regular stimulation. The idea of relationships, be they positive or negative, as central to the functioning health of a community is prevalent in this play. Striker knows where to find Touchwood, since both men take regular daily perambulations of the same sections of the parish; we are witnessing an everyday version of the customary practice of Rogationtide or 'beating the bounds'.[35] Touchwood says of Striker: 'This is his usual walk' (2.2.347), and we understand from this the habituation of these two men to specific routes and rituals. Similarly, in 3.1.438 of this play, Gilbert and his young male friends know exactly where to find Sir Arnold Cautious when they need him. Prying on women at the Asparagus Garden is his 'daily haunt'; De Certeau's concept of everyday practice comes into clear view here.[36]

The scene between Striker and Touchwood at 2.2 is a brilliantly written duologue in which the surface invective is belied by the shared rhythms of the exchange; the old men echo each other's terminology and trade insult for insult like a bickering married couple:

STRIKER: Sirrah, sirrah, how dar'st thou keep a son that dares but look upon my niece? There I am wi'ye, sir.
TOUCHWOOD: Sirrah, and sirrah to thy withered jaws and down that wrinkled throat of thine: how dar'st thou think a son of mine dares for displeasing me look but with foul contempt upon thy loathed issue?
STRIKER: Impudent villain, I have heard he has seen her.
TOUCHWOOD: Has he but seen her? [*Aside*] ha, ha, ha, I fear I shall out with it: I would not be forsworn. I'll keep it in if I can.
STRIKER: Yes, malapert Jack, I have heard that he has seen her, but better hadst thou pissed him 'gainst the wall than he presume to love her: and there I am wi'ye, sir. (2.2.356–60)

---

[35] Merritt has demonstrated the importance of the Rogationtide ceremony to the parish identities and communities of Westminster in the 1620s and 1630s. St Martin's in the Field went so far as to commission a parish map in 1624 in order to reduce internal conflicts over boundaries (there were tax collection implications); *The Social Life of Early Modern Westminster*, pp. 208–12. On this tradition, more generally, which survives into present times in some areas, see Sullivan Jr, *The Drama of Landscape*.

[36] Cf. de Certeau, *The Practice of Everyday Life*.

Striker has hinted at this dependency on the quarrel with Touchwood in an earlier exchange with his housekeeper (and secret lover) Friswood on the possible affair between Sam and Annabel; he also describes that relationship in terms of neighbourhood: 'that miscreant whose hatred I would not lose for all the good neighbourhood in the parish' (1.2.135). That Striker would sacrifice his standing in the local community to maintain the relationship with Touchwood, even when it is founded on enmity and insult, is telling.

The reliance of the men on one another is further borne out by their later 're-match', when Touchwood visits the residence of a supposedly ailing, possibly dying, Striker. The visit would seem to perform the customary practice of good neighbourliness, of visiting the sick and comforting the dying. Friswood wonders at this sudden change of behaviour on Touchwood's part:

Nay, good sir, say not so after so many messages and entreaties, by all the best of the parish, and an exhortation made to you by the minister himself: did you vouchsafe to come, and will you now come short to see my master, now the doctors give him over and he is dying? (4.1.731)

Her words indicate that Touchwood (and presumably Striker) have been subject to the criticism and counsel of their parish neighbours who have urged them to end their longstanding fight. We are further informed that the parish priest has become involved in this arbitration process and this starts to explain why Brome suddenly introduces the Curate as a new character in this same scene. Master Pancridge – his name, as already noted, suggesting a link to the questionable mores of St Pancras Church – is pleased that his ministrations appear to have worked, assuming that Touchwood's visitation is a sign of good neighbourliness pending reconciliation between the querulous pair: 'See, sir, your neighbour Touchwood comes to be reconciled to you' (4.1.739). Touchwood asserts that he has no such amicable intentions, although there is considerable irony in the fact that his visit 'cures' Striker, who is noticeably revived by their exchange of invective. Initially, at least, Touchwood has come to gloat over the situation. In order to sway him from that cruel task, the curate invokes the topographical concept of the neighbourhood: 'For neighbourhood and charity, speak lower' (4.1.791). The minister invokes a sense of communal judgement – not just the parish or neighbourhood, but the world; he deploys an idea of the 'theatre of the world' that was current in theological texts, so we can see how directly Brome is imitating contemporary religious and communal discourse here: 'Best look into yourself, sir. The world's a stage on

which you are both actors and neither to be his own judge' (4.1.743).[37]
Brome enjoys playing with the clichés of religious language elsewhere, for
example in *The Demoiselle*, but in *The Sparagus Garden* the decision to
introduce the figure of the curate at this point does appear to have been
a direct outcome of the explorations of neighbourhood in which the play
is so deeply invested. On the surface the curate is a standard spokesperson
for the parish as a religious institutional unit, yet, in terms of the imaginative geography of the play, he expands to embody wider, more secular
operations of neighbourhood as well.

The fifth act will unravel the history behind the Striker–Touchwood
enmity – in particular, the tragic outcomes of a sexual relationship between
Touchwood and Striker's sister that resulted in an unwanted pregnancy and
deep cruelty on the part of Striker towards his pregnant sister, whom he
evicted from the family home. Noticeably, Friswood acts as moral con-
science in the relating of this back-story to the audience. It is worth noting
the special forms of agency that Brome ascribes to women in the various
neighbourhoods of his plays: Rebecca and Friswood in *The Sparagus Garden* and Trainwell, a housekeeper figure akin to Friswood in *The Northern
Lass*, are obvious instances of women who shape as well as are shaped by the
communities in which they reside and work. They are embodied examples
of the ways in which London functioned, as Margaret Pelling has argued, as
a 'network of neighbourhoods' in which those neighbourhoods 'structured
social practice'.[38] Pelling's specific focus was the medical and medicalized
neighbourhoods of London, which will be the subject of the next section.
*The Sparagus Garden*, as will be seen, structures its particular onstage communities through these alternative modes of spatial identity and belonging
as well as through the mechanisms of neighbourhood already invoked.
Through plotlines of bloodletting and purgation as well as by means of the
central symbolic item of asparagus, Brome's play engages with the ways in
which the monitoring and treatment of health became a chief contributor
to the ways in which people 'belonged to' or identified themselves with
specific places and spaces.

From these opening ideas about neighbourhood as a physical and mental
space, I want to move on to look not just at the 'cartographies of disease'
that Pelling and others have identified as operating in times of plague
(there were key outbreaks in 1627, 1628, 1632, and 1634 during my focus

[37] For example, Pierre Boaistuau's *The Theatre of the World in the which is Discoursed at Large the
Many Miseries and Frailties Incident to Mankinde in this Mortall Life*, dating from the sixteenth
century and originally published in French, was translated into Spanish and then English during
the seventeenth century.
[38] Pelling, *Medical Conflicts*, pp. 9, 337.

time period), but the ways in which particular medical collectives and communities were identified with, and to an extent shaped by, the areas of London in which they operated. In the process, I want to consider the ways in which Brome and Jonson, among others, in plays such as *The Sparagus Garden* and *The Magnetic Lady*, sought to capture and even influence these spatial and affective communities.

## MEDICALIZED NEIGHBOURHOODS AND COMMUNITY HEALTH

In an article published in 2000, Pelling suggested that there had been a tendency in urban history up to that point to concentrate on the physical fabric of the city, rather than its residents. There had, as a result, she determined, been a dehumanizing effect on the scholarship.[39] By contrast, drama often achieves a 'street-level' intimacy with the topics and debates of its day and this is why in this section I am interested in the intersection of maps and medicine in three focus plays, Jonson's *The Magnetic Lady* (1632), Brome's *The Sparagus Garden*, and Nabbes's *The Bride* (1638). I am interested in identifying these intersections not just because it is useful, or even enlightening, to register the ways in which plays engaged with the medical debates of their time, or how, in doing so, they engaged in particular ways with the topography, material and social, of the city of London, but because I believe that these plays are significant agents within those debates, part of the cultural forces shaping early modern thinking about both medical practice and the practice of the city.

The idea of neighbourhood that is to the fore in this section is that created by medical practices, then, both in terms of the providers of medical care – interpreting that category in its widest sense to include official and unofficial practitioners as well as those who provided the plants necessary for remedies and botanical simples – and the recipients or users of medicine and healthcare provision. As I hope will become clear, the provision, but also the receipt, of medical advice was one way in which communities were spatially and socially organized in the early modern city. The anxieties of particular communities around illness could serve as cohering beliefs at times of particular crisis, such as plague, and therefore contribute to particular senses of 'neighbourhood', but, in addition, a map of the various wards and parishes of London in our focus decades reveals the concentration of medical and related botanical practice in certain areas and suggests that there were also particular places conceived as medicalized neighbourhoods.

---

[39] Pelling, 'Skirting the City' ('it is easy to make the physical fabric of the town . . . serve as a proxy for human activity', p. 155).

It is, perhaps, advisable to pause at the outset to establish the different kinds and social tiers of medical practitioners that existed in the 1620s and 1630s and therefore the different and often rival neighbourhoods of medicine at this time – in particular, the triad of groups that went by the collective titles of the College of Physicians, the Society of Apothecaries, and the Company of Barber Surgeons. This idea of individuals working and thinking as collectives also contributed directly to contemporary ideas of networks and neighbourhoods. We might think about this triad on a sliding scale of legitimacy. All were, it is true, recognized as licensed companies of some sort, but it was the College of Physicians which had, if you like, the royal stamp of approval; indeed, one of the leading lights of the College in these years was William Harvey, who published the first major tract in England on the circulation of the blood in 1633, ideas deriving from lectures he first gave in 1618 but which received very little attention from the scientific or medical community at that time.[40] In our focus decade, Harvey was the chief physician to Charles I, accompanying him on the 1633 coronation progress to Scotland, among other things. He was also one of the chief 'censors' of the college, which meant that he had direct responsibility for policing the practice of medical support services such as apothecaries' shops – which were subject to frequent unannounced 'raids' at this time – to ensure that 'impure' recipes were not being sold to the public, that is to say, that they were abiding by the standard and approved medical recipes that were outlined and endorsed in the London Antidotary published in Latin under the title *Pharmacopoeia Londinensis*, in 1618.[41]

Apothecaries were one particular form of rival medical practice whose efforts and achievements within the community the College sought to curb and control; the herbalists, with whom they often worked in tandem in the production of herbal remedies, were another.[42] Despite Pelling's

---

[40] Benjamin Woolley notes that in the College *Annals* for that period there is no mention of this important set of findings; only concerns about the chaotic publication of the *Pharmacopoeia* and the discovery of 'impure' medicines on various raids and searches of apothecaries' shops; see *The Herbalist*, pp. 67–8. See also Keynes, *The Life of William Harvey*.

[41] These were only translated into the vernacular some years later by radical herbalist Nicholas Culpeper, who in 1632 was at Cambridge aged 16. He would therefore have been an apprentice in an apothecary shop in London in the late 1630s, so was absolutely shaped by the world I am describing here.

[42] Botanical simples, the experimental gardens, and also the 'simpling' expeditions that defined these communities have drawn the attentions of several historians of late. See, for example, Anna Pavord, *The Naming of Names: The Search for Order in the World of Plants* (London: Bloomsbury, 2005); Woolley, *The Herbalist*; and Leah Knight, *Of Books and Botany in Early Modern England: Sixteenth-century Plants and Print Culture* (Aldershot and Burlington, Vt.: Ashgate, 2009).

understandable hesitation about allowing buildings to serve as a proxy for the populace, the 'physical fabric' in which these rival medical groups operated can provide a means for understanding this triad of competitive practitioners and their different social status. By looking at the varying kinds of locale and residence they inhabited, and therefore the different kinds of mobility within the city that they enacted, we begin to register both their distinct nature and the distinct public perception of them. The apothecaries, for example, were most readily associated with their shops (Nicholas Culpeper worked as an apprentice in several of these in the 1630s; one being Simon White's property at Temple Bar, where he worked in 1637, a significant geographic locale in its own right, serving as a kind of conduit between lower and higher status medical establishments and areas). The locations of these shops on certain streets would be a key to the standing of the individual – Thomas Johnson, for example, whose expanded edition of John Gerard's *Herbal* became the must-buy book of the field in 1633, had well-to-do premises on the Strand; others, such as Simon White, were more humbly located. The shops were micro-theatres, their window displays hung with exotic items to draw customers. Johnson is famous, for example, for displaying the first bunch of bananas in 1633, an item he was given by the Chief of the College of Physicians, John Argent, who had himself received it from a merchant just returned from the Bermudas.

As already noted, the apothecaries were in turn linked with the herbalists, who supplied the stock for their premises. The herbalists were renowned for their experimental gardens, which provided the raw materials of their trade. Many of these, as Harkness has shown, were located in the Lime Street area of the city, which ran from Fenchurch Street in the south to the parish church of St Andrew Undershaft in the north (near Cornhill Street).[43] These were, then, lives lived more on the outskirts of the city, rather than in its power centres like the Court, the connecting thorough-fare of the Strand, or, as the 1630s developed, the areas around emergent sites such as Covent Garden. These groups of herbalists provide working examples of the 'skirting' mentality, as Pelling has defined it, and that was evoked in Chapter 4's discussion of urban mobility.[44] These individuals and groups gained frequent access to the countryside from their city residences, not least for research and fieldwork, and were also mobile in terms of their internal movements around the capital for the purposes of work

---

[43] Harkness, *The Jewel House*, p. 20.
[44] Cf. the idea of 'skirting' advanced by Pelling in 'Skirting the City'.

and practical exchange.[45] This sense of living on the edge of mainstream space was possibly exacerbated by the fact that these herbalists' groups or neighbourhoods tended to be immigrant and diasporic communities with their own internalized and externalized networks of correspondence.[46]

Barber surgeons were also linked to shops and therefore to the selling of wares; in *The Sparagus Garden*, John Brittleware, the barber surgeon become china-shop owner, though clearly struggling in various ways in his professional and domestic life, becomes an important bridging figure, representing the multi-tasking world of Londoners as well as the dubious social standing of barber surgeons. The reaction of the lawyer Trampler on hearing of Brittleware's mixed professional identity is telling: 'A surgeon? I took you for a china shopkeeper, Master Brittleware; these by-trades are for some by-purposes and I smell knavery' (5.2.1103).[47] Harkness notes that there was a thin line between barber surgeons and mountebanks in the public perception; all tended to sell their wares on raised platforms, temporary structures within the city, and there was an air of fakery and provisionality that automatically attached to such procedures and actions.[48] What these kinds of geographical as well as individual slippages do is to accustom us to associating medicine with commodification, identifying its practice as an item for sale as much as any other in the vibrant trade of the London markets.

By contrast with the more peripatetic existence of a barber surgeon, dependent on renting shop space or erecting temporary scaffolds from which to ply his trade, the Royal College of Physicians and later the formalized Society of Apothecaries tended to operate out of purpose-built buildings. The College, for example, was located on Knightrider Street near to the social and culture epicentre of St Paul's; Inigo Jones would design a hall for the barber surgeons by the end of the 1630s, a marker of their increasing acceptance into the mainstream, although this in some sense curbed their considerable freedoms. Harkness has noted that their

---

[45] Joseph P. Ward also writes about the mobility of particular crafts and tradespeople in *Metropolitan Communities*, p. 2.

[46] Cf. Harkness, *The Jewel House*.

[47] Harkness gives the example of Gresham's Royal Exchange, a place where the elite barber surgeons plyed their trade (*The Jewel House*, p. 3). George Baker was a barber surgeon who extracted teeth, set bones, and performed surgical procedures at the Royal Exchange (p. 9); this presents medicine as a commodity for sale as much as the china that Brittleware sells in his shop in Brome's play.

[48] Harkness, *The Jewel House*, p. 57. Theatre had a strong history of encouraging these links too – witness Volpone's performance as Scoto of Mantua in Jonson's eponymous 1606 play. The phrase 'mountebank' is used to describe a barber surgeon in Nabbes's *The Bride*, 1638 (5.[4]. Sig. H4v), suggesting that the associations were still current in the 1630s.

company was responsible for overseeing the quality of medical goods and services and policing those who transgressed their rights, but by the 1630s they were in competition with and being out-policed themselves by the College of Physicians.[49] The Society of Apothecaries had been in temporary premises at the Painters-Stationers Hall until 1632, when it moved into its own premises on the Blackfriars site of the former priory and liberty (it had been under City of London jurisdiction since 1608 but retained elements of independence), a geolocation that still fed, therefore, on that idea of a collective operating on the edges of the norm. That this location placed the Society's premises literally next door to one of the major theatres of the day is surely not a geographical coincidence that can be ignored when exploring the engagement of Caroline drama with medical subject matter. Playwrights such as Jonson and Brome can have expected apothecaries to be a familiar sight and contact for many audience members, and even to form part of that audience. The opportunities for in-jokes and references were abundant. Also specific to that moment in 1632, however, was the coming together of doctor and apothecary as a mandatory professional team.[50] From that point onwards, the College of Physicians insisted that all apothecaries work in tandem with doctors – perhaps this ruling was a product of jealousy of the Society of Apothecaries' new standing with their purpose-built offices and all. It certainly confirms the controlling and censorial impulses of the College, which increased the frequency of its checks and raids, its inspections of paperwork and searching of storerooms, post-1632. All of these facts, geographical and procedural, surely influenced the decision of Jonson to include in his Blackfriars performed and located play of 1632, *The Magnetic Lady*, the characters of Dr Rut and his apothecary and sidekick, Tim Item.

It should be stressed that both Rut and Item are fairly reprehensible figures, partly designed to evoke audience laughter, although they also evince the painful acts of recognition that are often so essential to successful social satire. Compass sketches Rut's character for us in the first act before we have even seen him in action on the stage: he is the 'young physician to the [Loadstone] family', who seems to have taken up almost permanent residence in the household and who is, we are informed, 'licentious in discourse' (1.2.39–40). He is also, as his name implies, a 'professed voluptuary' who indulges in obscene language and thinks himself a great wit (1.2.41). There is little to endear him to the audience in this, but things get steadily worse when we actually meet with Rut in the flesh. In 2.3 he comes to

[49] Harkness, *The Jewel House*.   [50] Woolley, *The Herbalist*, p. 123.

attend Lady Loadstone's 'niece' Placentia (the events of the play will indicate why those quotation marks around Placentia's identity are required) since she is apparently suffering from an extreme form of indigestion and bloating. Dame Polish her governess informs Rut that she is 'Puffed, blown [ . . . ]' (2.3.9). He diagnoses wind and suggests that she be 'released' with a peg or a faucet and that the getting of a husband will be the best solution of all:

> A wind bomb's in her belly, must be unbraced.
> And with a faucet, or a peg let out,
> And she'll do well: get her a husband.
>
> (2.3.20–2)

Audiences may well laugh, but in some sections of early modern society young women's ailments were ascribed to the untested state of virginity and the attentions of a husband presumed to be a general cure-all (attempts are made to solve Constance's suicidal love-melancholy by comparable means in Brome's *The Northern Lass*, for example). As later plot developments make clear, Rut actually suspects the truth – that Placentia is pregnant – but he will only make this point known to her uncle and ward Sir Moth Interest in the hope of gaining financial reward. There seems little care of the patient in this self-serving diagnosis.

The arrival of Rut's 'learned apothecary' and now mandatory professional sidekick Tim Item in Act 3 – tellingly, while Rut himself is feeding his face in an offstage dining room – does little to alleviate the situation. The two work in harness to their own benefit rather than that of the patient. At this stage Tim is asked to attend to Placentia, who is about to give birth prematurely following the shock of the violent contretemps between Sir Diaphanous Silkworm and Captain Ironside that has occurred offstage at the dinner table. Sir Moth Interest has fallen into a swoon in the face of all these unexpected events and Dr Rut's solution is both heavy handed and verbose. He first tries to punch Interest out of his fainting fit (as Polish wryly observes: 'What a brave man's a doctor / To beat one into health' (3.5.14–15)) and then recommends purging:

> Gi' me your hand, Sir Moth. Let's feel your pulse.
> It is a pursiness, a kind of stoppage,
> Or tumour o'the purse, for want of exercise,
> That you are troubled with; some ligatures
> I'th'neck of your *vesica* or *marsupium*
> Are so close-knit that you cannot evaporate
> And therefore you must use relaxatives.

> Beside, they say you are so restive grown,
> You cannot but with trouble put your hand
> Into your pocket, to discharge a reckoning,
> And this we sons of physic do call *chiragra*
> A kind of cramp or hand-gout. You shall purge for't.
>
> (3.5.30–41)

This will confirm to knowledgeable members of the audience that Rut and Item adhere to the rather old-fashioned and morally suspect Galenic practices of the College of Physicians (Item has previously advised the 'three high ways; / That is by sweat, purge, and phlebotomy', 3.5.43–4). The Galenic model of the four humours encouraged the 'letting' or purging of any humour deemed by medical science to be in superfluous abundance in the body; an excess of blood, for example, was believed to be a cause of choler or volatile temperament.[51] Debates around this topic were not uncommon on the Caroline stage, as we will explore further in a moment through an examination of the characters and plot lines of *The Sparagus Garden*, performed just three years after Jonson's play.

There is, of course, scabrous wit in the diagnosis of Sir Moth's 'tight wallet' syndrome – the events of the play depict him constantly attempting to seize Placentia's trust fund for himself – but it also exposes the medical profession, which seeks by diagnoses to open purses and wallets for pecuniary ends. In practice, the 'purge' that Rut recommends is of Interest's money through gambling with cards rather than a genuine phlebotomy or bloodletting, but the play has effectively established the dubious nature of medical professionals. This ensures that by the time we are exposed to the 'amateur' and unlicensed midwives who attend the illicit birth of Placentia's baby boy – Mother Chair, in particular – their personalized and vernacular mode of medicine scarcely seems more dubious than that which is represented by the professionals. Although these women may seem bawdy and outspoken – Polish quickly falls to railing on Chair as a 'witch / Bawd, beggar, gipsy' (4.4.1–2) – and full of remedies and superstitions with their talk of caudles and cures (4.7.7–9) and their covering up of evidence ('smock-secrets') via careful blanching of the bedlinen (4.7.41), they at least work on behalf of the patient, unlike the 'errant learned men' (3.4.64) (as Polish sharply refers to them) who represent official medicine.[52]

---

[51] There are related themes in the 1608 play *The Family of Love*, attributed by some to Thomas Middleton; see Gail Kern Paster, 'Purgation as the allure of mastery: early modern medicine and the technology of the self', in Lena Cowen Orlin (ed.), *Material London c. 1600* (Philadelphia: University of Pennsylvania Press, 2000), pp. 193–205.

[52] See Julie Sanders, 'Midwifery and the new science in the seventeenth century: language, print and the theatre', in Erica Fudge, Ruth Gilbert, and Susan Wiseman (eds.), *At the Borders of the Human:*

For a comparable theatrical scene in a household entertainment context, we can look to Sampson's *The Vow-Breaker*, discussed in Chapter 3 as
an example of Nottinghamshire geo-specific drama, but one which shares
intriguing kinships with Jonson's 1632 commercial drama in its interest in
the space of the birthing room. In 4.1, Anne Boot, the female protagonist,
is depicted, having recently given birth, surrounded by midwives and gossips, presumably drawn from the local community as was the tradition.
Like Jonson's Mother Chair, these women bear suitably suggestive nomenclature: Magpie, Prattle, and Long-tongue all imply the propensity for idle
chatter with which the midwife was stereotypically associated. Prattle's discourse on the foodstuffs that might be provoking Anne's nightmares links
her by extension to the world of natural medicine:

as Beanes, long Peason Lentills, Coleworts, Garlicke, Onions, and the like; Leekes,
Chos-nuts, and other opening Rootes, as Rad-dish, Carrets, Skirrets, Parsenips;
now there is some flesh is provocative too; as the Hart, the Bore, the ould Hare,
and Beefe; and then of the fowles as the Crane, Ducke, Drake, Goose, and Bustard.
(4.1. sig. H1r)

Prattle's extensive catalogue is comic but in practice not so dissimilar to the
accretive gatherings of household 'receipts' that were a common item in
early modern households, compilations, and anthologies that were often
produced by the women of the house.[53] The household medicine that plays
such as these depict cannot be so easily dismissed in the face of authorized
medicines: just as Mother Chair is correct in her handling of the Placentia
pregnancy in many respects, so it is the local knowledge of Prattle and her
fellow gossips that enables them to track poor Anne when she walks out in
the snow (though sadly not in time to save her from hypothermia). For all
the engagement of stereotype in scenes of this kind, there is a more nuanced
assessment of medical practice taking place than we might initially assume
and one which in turn invokes ideas of neighbourhood, community, and
belonging that cut across official categories.

    While the charges of misdiagnosis that Needle lays at Item's and Rut's
door in *The Magnetic Lady* are themselves a gross instance of self-protection
(he will turn out to be the biological father of the child), these assertions
allow Jonson to indulge in the kind of baiting of professionals that must

*Beasts, Bodies and Natural Philosophy in the Early Modern Period*, (Basingstoke: Macmillan, 1999),
pp. 74–90; see also Helen Ostovich's introduction to her forthcoming edition of the play for *CWBJ*.
I am grateful to Helen for permission to use this work in advance of publication and for discussion
and correspondence on this theme.
[53] Lynette Hunter, 'Women and domestic medicine: lady experimenters, 1570–1620', in Lynette Hunter
and Sarah Hutton (eds.), *Women, Science and Medicine, 1500–1700* (Stroud: Sutton Publishing, 1997),
pp. 89–107.

have been common on the streets of the Blackfriars parish. Tim suspects the doctor of poor judgement: 'Our doctor's urinal-judgement is half-cracked then' (5.1.16). This phrase is in itself a reference to actual practice whereby illness was diagnosed from examination of a patient's urine and faeces. In turn this was often tied to readings of almanacs and the position of the stars.[54] Notably, towards the end of the play, Rut still clings to astrology as a method of diagnosis (5.10.13–14).[55] What allows or enables Rut's professional judgement to be challenged so successfully is his own disassociation from 'women's matters' and his refusal to collaborate with midwives and 'amateurs' like Mother Chair. He has concealed the real truth to serve business ends and this makes it easier to charge him with failed judgement later. He does not seem to learn from this; as late as 5.7 he is diagnosing Needle's 'sleepwalking' tendencies in the following terms:

> It is the nature
> Of the disease, and all these cold dry fumes
> That are melancholic, to work at first
> Slow and insensibly in their ascent
> Till being got up and then distilling down
> Upo' the brain they have a pricking quality
> That breeds this restless rest, which we the sons
> Of physic call a waking in the sleep.      (5.7.5–12)

Admittedly, Rut and the tailor are in league by now, but this is still a fairly roundabout way to diagnose sleepwalking and is further evidence, were it needed, of Jonson's acerbic attitude towards the medical profession. It is clearly an attitude inherited by his one-time amanuensis, Brome, in that, just a few years later, his mind too is on medical issues and debates; *The Sparagus Garden* is brimful of plotlines engaging with contemporary medical controversies, not least those questioning the adherence to Galenic theories of the humours versus the newer, experimental, and experientially based, natural medicines of the herbalists such as Gerard in the late sixteenth century and Johnson and others in the moment of the play's composition and first performances. There might be a case for identifying targeted satire of significant individuals in these debates, figures like Harvey and his College of 'horseback physicians' or prominent herbalists like Johnson in the 1630s, but I am most interested in the atmosphere of febrile debate on which Brome is picking up, and in some sense promoting.

---

[54] On the significance of almanacs to early modern society, see Smyth, *Autobiography in Early Modern England*, pp. 15–56.

[55] A comparable character, Stargaze, can be found in the dysfunctional Frugal household in Massinger's *The City Madam* (1632), attendant upon Lady Frugal and her socially ambitious daughters.

The purging plot lines of *The Sparagus Garden* are one of the most obvious ways in which Brome engages with contemporary medical issues. They contribute, I would argue, to the way in which the play conveys the different networks and neighbourhoods of the London it is staging. In 2.1 we have the entrance of Tim Hoyden. He has come in search of his true identity; he believes that he is the son of a city gentleman, but is anxious to rid himself of his country upbringing in the process. This fact – and the £400 he rather too readily offers as recompense to anyone who can do him this service – is encouragement to Moneylacks and his crew to suggest purging him of his rural blood. Brittleware as a former barber surgeon can speak the required discourse of 'purging and bleeding' (2.1.281) and is employed to this end. Hoyden rather warily concedes: 'I like all excellently well, but this bleeding [ . . . ]' (2.1.298).

Hoyden's character is that of the archetypal ambitious and yet innocent incomer to London, but he is also a type specific to the 1630s. The purging plot line of *The Sparagus Garden* is equally up to the minute in terms of reflecting contemporary medical anxiety, even though, as Jonson's canon alone proves, humour plays had a considerably longer precedent. Hoyden is exactly the type of gullible and vulnerable incomer towards which Peacham aimed his *The Art of Living in London*.[56] That document describes London as 'a vast sea (full of gusts) fearefull dangerous shelves and rocks' (sig. A1v), but what Brome's play evidences is that the spatial and social construct of the 'neighbourhood' operates as much to exclude and to victimize as to offer a sense of belonging and identity. Interestingly, it is not only Hoyden in Brome's play who raises links to the humours theory: phlegm was a condition associated with old age and is embodied in the play by Striker, who is regularly seen hacking out his heart in altercations with his arch-rival Touchwood – original stage directions invite the actor to 'cough' throughout the querulous exchange in 2.2, for example:

STRIKER: Dar'st thou speak so, thou old reprobate?
TOUCHWOOD [*Aside*]: Thou dost not hear me say it is so, though I could wish
   it were with all my heart because I think it would break thine.
STRIKER: Hugh, hugh, hugh. *Cough[s]*
TOUCHWOOD [*Aside*]: I hope I shall keep it within the compass of mine oath;
   yet there was a touch for him
STRIKER: Oh, thou hell-bred rascal thou; hugh, hugh. *Cough[s] and spit[s]*. (2.2.
   362–6)

---

[56] I have argued that Brome's play and the fate of Hoyden may even have been a direct influence on the theatre-going Peacham when devising his pamphlet; see the 'Critical introduction' to my edition of the play in *Brome Online*.

Touchwood's name is also an indication of his quick temper and therefore links him in turn to the choleric humour. Brome is not merely adhering to old-fashioned medical precepts here; as already noted, Galenic practices were strongly upheld and enforced by the members of the College of Physicians. They held in suspicion the botanically and herbally led 'natural' medicine of their amateur rivals.[57] We might imagine that Brome's adherence to the rules of the four humours in the fashioning of Touchwood and Striker's characters indicates that he was a believer in Galenic systems, but other events and comments in the playtext, not least relating to ideas of community, must give us pause.

The purging and bloodletting rituals to which Hoyden is subjected are scarcely presented as rigorous medicine, diagnosis, and treatment; instead, these are the wayward schemes of the conman, Moneylacks, who is eager to restore the fortune he has frittered away before the start of the play. An earlier exchange between Moneylacks and the Brittlewares on the subject of doctors, and, in particular, remedies for infertility, prompts a fairly cynical discussion of the medical professionals plying their trade in 1635 London. Discussing ways to remedy Rebecca's profound pre-natal (in fact, pre-pregnancy) cravings, he suggests that she might find satisfaction in eating the new fashionable delicacy of asparagus. Once again Moneylacks has an ulterior financial motive – he is paid to 'gather' guests for the new property selling asparagus to paying customers – but he tricks it up in the form of a quasi-medical diagnosis:

MONEYLACKS: Have you this spring eaten any asparagus yet?
REBECCA: Why, is that good for a woman that longs to be with child?
MONEYLACKS: Of all the plants, herbs, roots, or fruits that grow it is the most
    provocative, operative, and effective. (2.1.205–7)

The authorities that Moneylacks cites on this matter are revealing. He invokes modern herbalists (as noted, Johnson's expanded edition of Gerard's *Herbal* had been published with great success in 1633 and Moneylacks certainly seems to have imbibed his copy in considerable detail):

All your best (especially your modern) herbalists conclude, that your asparagus is the only sweet stirrer that the earth sends forth, beyond your wild carrots, cornflag or gladioli. Your roots of standergrass, or of satyrion boiled in goat's milk are held good; your clary or horminium in diverse ways good, and dill (especially boiled in oil) is also good: but none of these, nor saffron boiled in wine, your nuts of

---

[57] Related works were also published in this period by John Parkinson, *Paradisi in Sole Paradisus Terrestrius* (1629) and *Theatrum Botanicum* (1640). On the interrelation of book culture and everyday culture and practice, see Knight, *Of Botany and Books*.

artichokes, rocket, or seeds of ash-tree (which we may call the kite-keys), nor thousand such, though all are good, may stand up for perfection with asparagus. (2.1.209)

Moneylacks claims to have had all this information from a professional, licensed, medic: 'I have it from the opinion of most learned doctors, rare physicians, and one that dares call himself so' (2.1.211). The use of the term 'physicians' seems very deliberate, evoking as it does the operations of the College.

John Brittleware's response is equally telling: 'What doctor is he, a fool on horseback?' (2.1.212). Horseback was the main mode of travel for these doctors and a public marker of their wealth. What we witness through the Brittlewares' responses is a view from 'street level' of poorer people's distrust of this expensive (and status-driven) form of medical dispensation. The doctor from whom Moneylacks claims to have his diagnoses on authority is one 'Doctor Thou-Lord' and Rebecca provides a neat characterization of him:

yes, we know Doctor Thou-Lord, though he knows none but lords and ladies, or their companions. And a fine, conceited doctor he is, and as humorous I warrant you. And will 'thou' and 'thee' the best lords that dare be acquainted with him: calls knights 'Jack', 'Will', and 'Tom' familiarly; and great ladies 'Gills' and 'sluts' too and they cross him. And for his opinion sake and your good report, Sir Hugh, I will have sparagus every meal all the year long, or I'll make fly for't. (2.1.214)

This is more likely to denote a type rather than be a criticism of a particular, identifiable individual, but what is conveyed in this short sequence is the social power and position of the medical fraternity in London neighbourhoods. To be treated by a doctor on horseback (or to have a family physician as in Lady Loadstone's household in *The Magnetic Lady*) is all part of the complex aspirational structures of both the Hoyden scenes of this play and Rebecca's 'cravings'. The latter manifest themselves in the shape of yearnings for the latest fashion or conspicuous display of wealth – and often the two are indistinguishable – such as travel in sedan chairs or the consumption of a seasonal delicacy such as asparagus. Medicine becomes part of this framework of desire, as much aspiration as necessity.

Moneylacks's involvement in the bloodletting and fasting treatment of Tim Hoyden – 'when this is done, and your new blood infused into you, you shall most easily learn the manners and behaviour' (2.1.309) – embeds him in contemporary medical debates. Phlebotomy had become a major bone of contention in the competitive rivalry between barber surgeons and physicians in London and was the subject of numerous petitions and complaints.⁵⁸ Physicians and surgeons were worried over boundary disputes in the practice of physic, but whereas the College of Physicians clung to bloodletting techniques, many barber surgeons were adopting and promoting Paracelsian diagnoses and therapies.⁵⁹ After the bleeding has taken place (the metaphorical idea of being 'bled dry' is surely also operative?), Moneylacks asks Tim:

And how do you feel yourself, Master Hoyden, after your bleeding, purging, and bathing, the killing of your gross humours, by your spare diet and your new infusion of pure blood by your quaint feeding on delicate meats and drinks? How do you feel yourself? (3.1.576)

Tim is scarcely in a fit state to judge, but the later recounting by Coulter of his master's ritual humiliation to Tim's half-brother Tom (an exchange conducted in their shared Somerset regional idiom, another marker of 'outsiders') tells the audience all they need to know:

And you had zeen't, you would ha'be pissed yourzelf vor woe, how they
    blooded him.
[ . . . ]
And then how they spurged his guts out.                    (4.1.683, 685).

If Jonson's medical concerns in *The Magnetic Lady* in part find their explanation in specific geographic and legal occurrences in 1632 (the new rulings on apothecaries and the movement of the Society of Apothecaries into the Blackfriars precinct), why does Brome choose in 1635 to explore medical issues on the stage? Admittedly he shows a pronounced interest in the subject in a number of plays, not least issues of depression and pathology which find their way into texts as early as *The Northern Lass* in 1629 and as late as *The Antipodes* in 1639, but there may still be something specific to the moment. There was the general atmosphere of increasing attempts at control in medical as in many other areas of Caroline policy in the 1630s, but, more precisely, 1634 had been a major plague outbreak year and this kind of event always threw into relief the practice, behaviour, and more mercenary or moneymaking tendencies of doctors, of the genuine and the quack varieties.

Good examples of this phenomenon can be found if we flip back briefly in time to the even more serious plague outbreak of 1625. Two texts, in

---

⁵⁸ Harkness, *The Jewel House*, p. 60. In personal correspondence, Lucy Munro also draws my attention to the contemporaneous poem by John Collop entitled 'Against phlebotomy to a leech'.
⁵⁹ Harkness, *The Jewel House*, p. 61.

particular, occasion remarkable insight into the impact, emotional, geographical, and spatial, of plague on the city of London and its inhabitants:
Thomas Dekker's *A Rod for Runaways*, published in London that same
year, which includes a striking frontispiece, and John Taylor's previously
cited *The Fearful Summer*. Dekker's pamphlet is dedicated to a surgeon,
presumably not one of the reprehensible types that he, along with Taylor,
exposes for taking financial advantage of the plight of poorer city residents
(the texts are similarly scathing in their criticism of wealthy individuals
who escape to their country residences with little thought for their poorer
neighbours to whom they could at least have left money and access to food
stores). Taylor notes how:

> On many post I see a Quacke salver's Bills
> Like Fencers challenges to shew their skils:
> As if they were such Masters of defence
> That they dare combat with the Pestilence.
>                                         (sig. A7v)

'Their Art' he says 'is a meere Artlesse kind of lying / To pick their living out
of others' dying' (sig. A7v), though he is quick to disassociate these 'Rat-
catchers' from the better kinds of 'Paracelsians', 'Galenists', or 'Herbalists' –
intriguing, too, that he links together these groups who were so keen to
distinguish themselves from each other in their own accounts (sig. A7v).
These pamphlets offer us an eye-witness account of the new geographies
of the city created by each plague epidemic, the cultural cartographies
of disease. From the mass graves (Dekker strikingly compares them to
warehouses of cloth, so full of winding sheets is the earth, sig. A2v) or the
novel signage of the bills of mortality that announced each week's losses
to the empty and boarded-up shops and houses, we are invited to walk
around these reconfigured spaces. The pamphlets present only a few moral
individuals taking care of their neighbours, while others mostly flee to
protect themselves and their belongings or refuse charity to others if they
find city refugees arriving at their door (Harvey was, incidentally, one of
only three College physicians who stayed in London in 1625 to treat the
sick).

   While there is no comparable set of documents for 1634, which was
admittedly a slightly less brutal epidemic, Brome was still writing *The
Sparagus Garden* in the immediate aftermath of a major plague outbreak.
The play's depiction of the neighbourhood's more exploitative capacities,
manifested both in its medicalized and sexualized plotlines, could be a
cynical response to real-life circumstances where the positive and supportive

side of neighbourliness seemed to break down at the first opportunity. Presumably, the same appalled sense of social justice that we receive from Dekker's and Taylor's pamphlets, their recording of people's selfishness in the wake of plague outbreaks, haunted theatre audiences' recent memories. Brome seems to play on this by coupling medical concerns with an ethically driven set of anxieties about neighbourly relationships. There is the danger of packaging up a city comedy such as *The Sparagus Garden* as some searing social indictment and that would be a falsehood in itself, but the resonance of its medical references and plot lines should not be underestimated.[60]

What we receive through both the plays discussed so far in this section is a carefully mapped sense of 'neighbourhood', albeit one under pressure – the deep-seated quarrel between Touchwood and Striker or the cruel scams of Moneylacks in *The Sparagus Garden* are simply different aspects of a parish community under pressure. Similarly, in *The Magnetic Lady*, Jonson creates yet another of his contained yet explosive households in which to unpack the workings of a community in micro-political terms: the church (in the form of the aptly named Parson Palate), the law (in the shape of Bias and Practice), as well as the medical profession and the concept of the family, all come under scrutiny. However, the limning or mapping of neighbourhoods in these plays may be more precise than even that account suggests. Their medical themes alone imply just how deeply embedded in particular areas of London these plays are and how they reflect the concerns of those neighbourhoods at a particular moment in time.

The asparagus garden that lies at the heart of Brome's eponymous play is clearly a space that can be linked to the physic and herb gardens of those involved in botany and medicine in the 1630s, those apothecaries and herbalists who in turn served the Royal College of Physicians. The play is not explicit in this regard; as we have seen, it links tangentially the garden and its chief produce of asparagus to contemporary medical debates and practices through the seductive discourse of Moneylacks in his efforts to gather guests for the proprietors. That the professional venture that is the 'garden' is run by the Dutch immigrant Martha offers a further conceptual link to the edge-city gardens of those herbalists who were from immigrant communities, many deriving from the Low Countries, and with

---

[60] There may be a link to the play's aristocratic dedicatee, William Cavendish, whose personal correspondence demonstrates a deep interest in medical issues and remedies. These ideas were first explored in the context of a paper given at the Oxford University conference on Cavendish, organized by Lynn Hulse and James Knowles: 'A sense of place in the writings of the Cavendish women', May 2002. The correspondence referred to is contained in the Portland Papers, University of Nottingham Department of Manuscripts; see for example, PW1.56; PW1.63; PW1.64.

continental European networks of exchange involving both correspondence and the literal exchanges of seed-swapping and a trade in bulbs and tubers.[61]

Comparable early seventeenth-century gardens to that depicted in Brome's play might include the Hackney garden of Edward la Zouche at the turn of the century or James Garrett's in the Lime Street area. Garrett was a Flemish apothecary and a renowned gardener, especially known for his tulips.[62] However, the best-known garden in the Lambeth region, whose fertile growing spaces of the marshes are, as we saw in Chapter 1, the likely locational association with the Asparagus Garden, was that belonging to royal gardener, John Tradescant and his wife, Hester. Their personal garden had been established at their house in South Lambeth in 1630 following the assassination of Tradescant's chief patron, the Duke of Buckingham, two years earlier. The house and garden became a magnet for public visitors, in part because of Tradescant's fine collection of botanical rarities, many of which he had collected as a botanizing sideline to diplomatic trips on behalf of the court, in the Low Countries, Muscovy, and on the Barbary Coast, but also because of his *wunderkammer* or 'cabinet of curiosities', a collection that was also referred to by contemporaries as 'Tradescant's Ark'. By 1634, just a year prior to Brome's play, the site had become well known enough for one visitor to record that he spent 'a whole day in peruseing, and that superficially, such as hee [Tradescant] had gathered together'.[63]

In Nabbes's *The Bride*, a play that was performed at Drury Lane in 1638, the year of Tradescant's death, there is a reference to just such a museum of 'rarities'.[64] It is here that Justice Ferret intends to pass some time while in London: 'Come Mistresse Bride, wee will walke and see some rarities and antiquities till they return. There is one in the neighbourhood is stored with them [ . . . ]' (3.2 sig. F2r). His wife offers an even more detailed account of the experience that the bride will have there:

The motion's good: it should have been mine. You shall see the feathers of a Phenix; beake of a Pelican, and the skins of birds, beasts, and fishes, stufft with hay, enough to bring down the market. For coynes and medalls he hath those that speake their date 500 yeeres before the use of letters. He hath the fingers and toes

[61] The 'economy of obligation', as Harkness terms it (*The Jewel House*, p. 44).
[62] Harkness, *The Jewel House*, p. 39.
[63] Arthur McGregor, 'Tradescant, John, the elder (d. 1638)', *DNB* (p. 4). The visitor was Peter Munday; see also R. C. Temple (ed.), *The Travels of Peter Mundy in Europe and Asia, '608–'667* (Hakluyt Series 2, vols. 45–6, 1919), 1–3. My thanks to Richard Cave for initial discussion of this link and for many rich suggestions that have fed into this chapter.
[64] Thomas Nabbes, *The Bride* (London, 1638). All references henceforth in parentheses within the text.

of a Colossus, and three hayres of a giants upper lip, each of them as big as a bull rush. Then he hath the members of a pigmie, that cannot be discerned but through a multiplying glass. Yet it is thought he would gladly part with all he hath for the Phylosphers stone; ay, or the unicorn's horne at Windsor. (3.2. sig. F2r)

This is a hyperbolic version of Tradescant's 'Ark', but, as with the asparagus garden in Brome's play, audiences would surely have enjoyed the frisson of contemporary associations. In the fourth act of *The Bride*, we meet the keeper of this collection, the suitably named Horten (his name connecting to 'hortus' meaning 'garden' in Latin), who reveals that he, too, keeps a physic garden at his property:

> From my garden, sir,
> I can produce those simples, shall outworke
> All the compounds of drugs, and shew like miracles
> Compared with them.            (4.1 sig. F4v)

Horten becomes a persuasive spokesperson for the seductive qualities of medicine, describing the particular store elite households place in recipes produced in the domestic space, though also implying in the process that medicine is a game of smoke and mirrors:

> Yet my Ladyes gentlewoman
> Bit by her monkey, swears by her lost maidenhead
> The world hath not a Balsame like to that
> Her closet yeelds, when 'tis perhaps but oyle
> A little aromatized for lamps.          (4.1. sig. F4v)

In the fifth act, Horten will claim to have the skills of a barber surgeon as well, when he seeks to attend to the wounded Raven. Mistress Ferret offers a character reference: 'Truly, sir, my neighbour is very skillful; he cured my little shock of the mange so perfectly that it hath famed him through the neighbourhood for an excellent dog-leech' (5.1 sig. H1v). In her usual style, Mistress Ferret deftly misses the criticism implicit in the label of 'dog-leech' that is accorded Horten by his neighbours, but in this way his characterization brings together all the complex associations of the medicalized spaces and places that this section has been exploring.

In the fifth act, Horten's more unofficial medical operations within the neighbourhood are brought into direct competition with a representative of the Royal College of Physicians, Plaster; as a servant notes: 'Here's Master Plaster, the learned Surgeon, that speakes nothing but Latine, because either he would not be understood, or not contradicted' (5.4. sig. H4r).

The scene evidences several examples of Plaster's obfuscatory use of Latin as he tussles with Horten over the treatment of Raven:

> where there is *continuitatis divertium*, you must consider whether it came *per contusionem, puritionem*, or how; and whether, a nerve, tendon, ligament, or artery be in danger. (5.4. sig. H4r)

The servant's loaded use of 'learned' when describing Plaster echoes attitudes adopted in Jonson's and Brome's plays. Once again, the 'street level' view of official medicine seems less than positive and also appears to work against traditional concepts of 'good neighbourliness'. As discussed in Chapter 4, Nabbes is an author whose plays were deeply embedded in the spaces and places that characterized contemporary London. In *The Bride*, he brings together the experimental gardens of herbalists on the city's outskirts and the medical neighbourhoods at its centre, not least through the invoked space of the Royal College of Physicians, in the process bringing the social mores and divisions they represented into potent dramatic collision. It is a dynamic and productive way of writing the cultural geography of the contemporary city.

Michel Foucault famously stated in a much-quoted passage of *The Order of Things* that the documents of the 'new history' would be 'not other words, text, or records, but unencumbered spaces in which things are juxtaposed: herbariums, collections, gardens [ . . . ]'.[65] The cultural geography of the plays analysed here bear that out in striking fashion, but they also invite us to think about the concept of 'neighbourhood' itself as one such unencumbered space, a site of juxtaposition, encounter, possibility, and production. The concluding chapter will therefore analyse some of the more familiar locations, spaces, and places of the early modern city, in particular the Strand and Covent Garden, through this particular enabling lens.

---

[65] Michel Foucault, *The Order of Things: An Archaeology of the Human Sciences* (London: Routledge, 2002), p. 143.

CHAPTER 6

# Writing the city
## Emergent spaces

This final chapter seeks to engage with the various cultural geographies, material and imagined, of the city of London in our focus decades. The aim is not to suggest a monolithic or unchanging map of the city, even within the relatively restricted time parameters under consideration. London had undergone recent massive transformations in terms of population increase and expansion of its physical fabric as well as the institutional structures required for that to function efficiently. This did not grind to a halt in the late Jacobean and Caroline periods: in many ways it continued to develop, not least in terms of the 'built environment' that will be the ostensible focus of the final sections of this chapter. The 1630s witnessed the conception and construction of Covent Garden and that area's significant contribution to the expansion of the West End district of the capital, a region referred to by many contemporaries as the 'Town'. Jonson had noted the embryonic development of that region in *Epicene* (1609), which takes place predominantly on the Strand and in neighbouring streets, a site which might be regarded, along with Covent Garden, as the heart of this social district. I will explore the ways in which the plays of the 1630s responded to the social phenomenon of the Town as well as contributing directly to the understanding and the practice of the social spaces and opportunities it afforded. This will be achieved via a detailed examination of the plays of Brome, Shirley, and Nabbes, in particular; plays which are self-consciously staged in the districts of the Strand and Covent Garden, and which themselves became prime agents in the ways in which the emotional and physical geography of the Town figured for inhabitants and visitors.

### THE STREET THEATRE OF THE STRAND

The significance of The Strand as a thoroughfare in any cultural mapping of early to mid-seventeenth-century London is now well established. If

*Epicene* had marked its emergence as a key physical and social bridge between the aspirations of the city and the preferment of the court – one such aspirant in that play Sir Amorous La Foole rents 'lodging in the Strand' (1.3.26) with the sole purpose of advertising his social ambition and intents, and even goes so far as to remark on another character's rooms that they would be perfect if only 'it were in the Strand' (1.4.8)[1] – then by the time of 1630s drama the street and its fashionable residences and shopping experiences were well established in the public imagination.[2] It might seem perverse to seek to categorize a 'thoroughfare' as a 'neighbourhood', but there were all kinds of resonant ways in which The Strand, which was in formal terms part of suburban Westminster and its parochial systems of administration, identified itself as a community and performed that role of a community back to itself and to the wider city.

Shirley bases his 1635 play *The Lady of Pleasure* in the fashionable enclaves of The Strand and devotes his two opening scenes to a staging of a virtual competition between two Strand women as to who can become most renowned for conspicuous displays of wealth and consumption. Aretina, in whose company we begin the play, has recently moved to London, escaping (as she sees it) from the confinements and vulgarities of a provincial existence:

> I would not
> Endure again the country conversation
> To be the lady of six shires!
>     [ . . . ] To observe with what solemnity
> They keep their wakes, and throw for pewter candlesticks,
> How they become the morris, with whose bells
> They ring all into Whitsun ales, and sweat
> Through twenty scarfs and napkins, till the hobbyhorse
> Tire, and Maid Marion, dissolved to a jelly,
> Be kept for spoon meat!          (1.1.2–3, 10–16)

The scornful catalogue of customs she provides in this tirade is meant to contrast heavily with the refined world of the city, or, more specifically, the Town, to which she has relocated and it soon becomes clear from the sheer weight of material objects and purchases mentioned in this opening scene the gusto with which Aretina has thrown herself, and the family finances, into this new urban existence. Her long-suffering husband Bornwell lists

---

[1] For a parallel discussion of these instances in the play, see Richard Dutton's introduction to his edition of *Epicene* (Manchester University Press, 2003), p. 11.

[2] Further details of this are explored through the archival records in Merritt, *The Social World of Early Modern Westminster*, pp. 140–5.

furniture, paintings, mirrors, perfumes, extravagantly embroidered clothes, jewels, and that key accessory of Caroline urban life, the coach, among other purchases. Despite this identifiable excess (perhaps enhanced by the presence onstage of significant props such as looking-glasses to emphasize the implicit vanity of Aretina?), in the following scene we see Aretina outdone by a woman of higher social station and therefore purchasing power, the Lady Celestina. When we first meet her, she is railing on her steward's attempts at fiscal efficiency in the furnishing of her coach's interior with inferior 'crimson camel plush' (1.2.28):

> Ten thousand moths consume't! Shall I ride through
> The streets in penance, wrapped up round in hair-cloth?
> Sell't to an alderman.                    (1.2.29–31)

What looks like a familiar form of crass stereotyping in these scenes, however – the depiction of spendthrift women frittering money away on superficialities – is challenged by what follows. Celestina, in particular, proves in many ways a very attractive character, one with a degree of moral integrity and heart to whom Bornwell is drawn. Aretina will admittedly find herself heavily compromised by the end, following a covert sexual liaison with town gallant Alexander Kickshaw, but the play is not without sympathy towards her even then. Shirley's central female characters prove to be multifaceted personalities and their opening scenes of fiscal extravagance are determined to be the product of the place and space in which they live. Celestina asserts:

> Here, and abroad, my entertainments shall
> Be oftener and more rich. Who shall control me?
> I live i'th'Strand, whither few ladies come
> To live and purchase more than fame. I will
> Be hospitable, then, and spare no cost
> That may engage all generous report
> To trumpet forth my bounty and my bravery
> Till the court envy and remove.        (1.2.77–84)

The deictic emphasis of 'Here' asks the audience to place Celestina and her actions securely within the context of the Strand neighbourhood and its competing world of pleasures and entertainments.

If Shirley's play takes us into the heavily brocaded and strongly per-fumed domestic interiors of Strand houses, then it gives us equal insight into the operations of The Strand as a distinct neighbourhood in the early metropolitan context. The houses themselves operated as sites of memory,

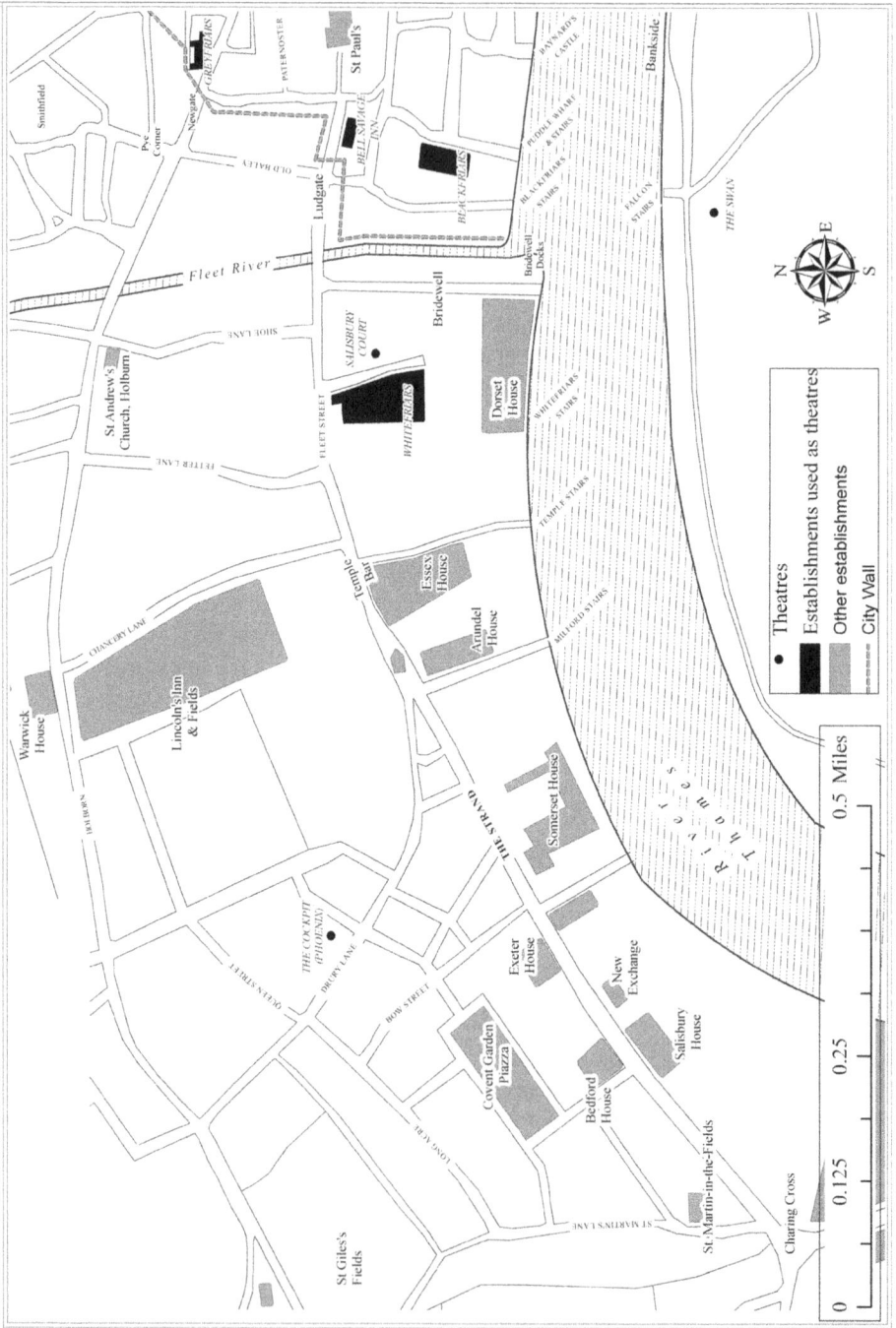

Figure 10: Map of The Strand and its environs c. 1640s.

*lieux de mémoire* in Pierre Nora's resonant phrase.[3] As former religious houses in the pre-Reformation period, their re-purposing into the symbolic residences of many of the most significant courtiers of the day rendered them repositories of previous usage and signification. The world of the pious could implicitly be read against the new world of commercial enterprise that the Strand embodied. A map of the neighbourhood indicates the proximity and therefore combined effect of these residences (see Figure 10). A walk along the Strand from the city in the direction of Westminster and the court starting at Temple Bar in the 1630s would have brought you swiftly past the Hay family base at Essex House, the Talbots' at Arundel House, Henrietta Maria's own court 'removed' from the Whitehall centre at Somerset House (this may indeed be the buried allusion in Celestina's hope that her 'bounty and [ . . . ] bravery' (1.2.83) will encourage the Whitehall court to physically remove itself to the Strand to be a part of the social action), before bringing into view one of the key gathering points on The Strand which was Cecil's New Exchange. The New Exchange abutted Savoy Palace (former residence of John of Gaunt, now restored as an office of the Duchy of Lancaster), and was also within a stone's throw of the Earl of Bedford's property on the edge of his emergent 'designed' neighbourhood of Covent Garden, of which more in the concluding section.

If Cecil's New Exchange (also known at the time of its opening in 1609 as 'Britain's Burse') with its shopping opportunities and reputation as a site for gossip and trade (numerous plays refer in passing to it, the fleeting nature of these remarks a key indicator in themselves of the building's central position in the cultural imaginary[4]) had been the occasion for theatrical entertainment on its opening, also penned by Jonson, it is equally striking how many of the Strand residences our 1630s pedestrian would have passed en route to the court were themselves linked to theatre both as site and occasion of performance.[5] Henrietta Maria's court at Somerset House (the present-day site of the Courtauld Gallery where, fittingly, several 1630s images hang on the walls) was the site of several high-profile theatrical gatherings and events. The property (formerly known as Denmark House in honour of its previous occupant, James VI and I's Queen Consort Anna) was officially signed over to the recently married and recently arrived

---

[3] Cf. Nora, *Les lieux de mémoire.*

[4] One contemporary example is Davenant's 1636 Blackfriars play *The Wits,* which mentions the New Exchange (ironically as a space for grazing horses) alongside the 'new plantation' in Covent Garden (4.1).

[5] For examples of this kind of comparative reading, see Dutton's previously mentioned introduction to his Revels edition of *Epicene;* and Dillon, *Theatre, Court and City.* Dutton's edition also contains a full text of the James Knowles (ed.), *Entertainment at Britain's Burse* as Appendix B.

Henrietta Maria as her official residence in 1626.[6] John Orrell has gone so
far as to state that, during her residency, Somerset House became the 'chief
London centre for the production of scenic drama until 1640'.[7] Certainly,
both the temporarily converted hall space and the Presence Chamber witnessed several key theatrical productions, masques, and entertainments
during that time. In 1626, just a few weeks after legally receiving the property, Henrietta Maria acted in a private production of Honorat de Racan's
French pastoral *Artenice*. An account by the Tuscan resident Amerigo Sal-
vetti stresses that this was all done 'as privately as possible' because it was
'no normal thing here [in England] to see the queen acting on a stage',
but the production led to other high-profile commissions by the queen,
including Walter Montagu's *The Shepherds' Paradise* in 1633, a revival of
Fletcher's *The Faithful Shepherdess* in 1634, two performances of Heywood's
*Love's Mistress* that year, a further French pastoral *Florimène* in 1635, and
a production of Lodowick Carlell's *The Passionate Lovers* in 1638. Inigo
Jones seemed alert to the theatrical significations of Henrietta Maria's chief
residence in this way when, in his designs for *Artenice*, he incorporated an
image of Somerset House and the Thames by which it was so strongly sited
into the shutters that were deployed at the end of the performance. The
image appeared in full when the shutters were closed in this way, 'ending
the play with an image of the queen's new residence in London'.[8] Jones's
carefully conceived image rendered Somerset House as dramatic space, as
a piece of scenography incorporated into performance along with the city
and the Thames, and in turn he transformed the building into an index of
theatre in a Caroline cultural context.

It is this specific repertoire, then, as well as a more general but nevertheless explicit link between theatricality and the site and space of Somerset
House, which would have been in the public domain when Shirley was
writing *The Lady of Pleasure*. I have written elsewhere of that play's link
to the emergent salon culture imported from Henrietta Maria's native
France. As early as the production of *Artenice*, these salon connections
were being evidenced.[9] Karen Britland has observed how 'The play that

[6] 14 February 1626, *CSPD 1625–6*, p. 561. Cited in Britland, p. 238, n. 35.
[7] John Orrell, *The Theatres of Inigo Jones and John Webb* (Cambridge University Press, 1985), p. 88.
  See also Britland, *Drama at the Courts of Queen Henrietta Maria*, p. 42 for discussion of this
  material.
[8] Britland, *Drama at the Courts of Queen Henrietta Maria*, p. 42.
[9] Julie Sanders, 'Caroline salon culture and female agency: the Countess of Carlisle, Henrietta
  Maria, and public theatre', *Theatre Journal*, 52: 4 (2000), 449–64; see also Erica Veevers, *Images
  of Love and Religion: Queen Henrietta Maria and Court Entertainments* (Cambridge University
  Press, 1989).

Henrietta Maria imported into England in 1626 [. . .] carried with it the traces of *salon* culture, Catholicism, and the French court'.[10] These 'traces' would in turn have linked characters such as Celestina to female members of Henrietta's circle, including Lucy Percy Hay, Countess of Carlisle or Lady Elizabeth Hatton; both of these women were engaged in theatrical activity, not least in the region of the Strand.[11] As well as dancing in several of the court masques overseen by Henrietta Maria, including Jonson's *Chloridia* in 1631 and Townshend's *Tempe Restored* in 1632, the Countess of Carlisle had been explicitly linked to plans for the 'Masque of Amazons' in 1618. Her husband, James, Lord Hay, later Earl of Carlisle, had sponsored entertainments at their Essex House residence on the Strand as early as 1617 and again in 1621.[12] The latter event, the Essex House Masque as it has come to be known, is just one example of a host of theatrical happenings that took place in the Strand neighbourhood in the years between 1619 and 1621, including feasts, ballets, and balls.[13] These particular concurrent seasons from the late Jacobean moment happen to be the best documented in terms of extant material, but there is enough circumstantial evidence in subsequent years to suggest that this kind of performative atmosphere was common on the Strand throughout our focus period.

James Knowles's research has been crucial in establishing for us the 'polycentric' nature of elite culture at this time and what he calls the 'diaspora of masquing culture' in terms of the sheer variants of properties and locations used for theatrical entertainments.[14] However it is, as Knowles indicates, the particular dramatic subgenre of the 'running masque – so-called because it was kinetic performance in two senses, moving between outside street and internal space of the host household in the form of disguised entries, and often between different households on different nights – that provides a particularly suggestive example of the kinetic geography of elite drama at

---

[10] Britland, *Drama at the Courts of Queen Henrietta Maria*, p. 39.

[11] Merritt, *The Social World of Early Modern Westminster*, notes that the Countess of Carlisle rented a house on the Strand at considerable expense in 1634, in the months when Shirley would have been working on his play (p. 149n).

[12] The 1617 performance was Jonson's *Lovers Made Men* and the 1621 production was the so-called 'Essex House Masque' identified in MS form in the late 1990s by Timothy Raylor. See his 'The "lost" Essex House masque (1621): a manuscript text discovered', *English Manuscript Studies*, 7 (1998), 86–130 and *The Essex House Masque of 1621: Viscount Doncaster and the Jacobean Masque* (Pittsburgh, Penn.: Duquesne University Press, 2000).

[13] See Martin Butler, 'Jonson's *News from the New World*, the "running masque", and the season of 1619–20', *Medieval and Renaissance Drama in England*, 6 (1993), 153–78 (153).

[14] James Knowles, 'The "running masque" recovered: a masque for the Marquess of Buckingham (c. 1619–20)', *English Manuscript Studies*, 9 (2000), 79–135 (79, 91).

this time. In the case of the running masque extant from the 1619–20 season, which Knowles speculates is possibly authored by John Maynard and which is certainly linked to the commissioning spirit of George Villiers, Marquess of Buckingham, it appears to have been performed at several properties on or near the Strand over a series of successive evenings. It was staged at the French ambassador's residence on 3 January 1620, at Lady Hatton's household (on the former site of the Bishop of Ely's house) the following day, at the Earl of Exeter's on the next, at the Earl of Warwick's on 7 January, and at James Hay's Essex House on 8 January. It was also intended to be performed at Somerset House (then Denmark House) on 9 January, but this particular performance appears to have been cancelled.[15] The portability and adaptability of the running masques is one important aspect, but it is this visible movement from street to household interior and between properties that concerns me most here in thinking about the Strand as a very particular example of 'street theatre'.[16] The nature of the performance and its use of disguised entries – Knowles suggests that accounts and descriptions provided in letters by John Chamberlain and others indicate that the masquers arrived fully costumed in the street and that, as a result, this street-based section of the masque was 'a major element of the entertainment' – meant that the performance could have been visible to spectators other than those officially invited to these 'private performances'.[17] It renders them curious but pertinent examples of the public theatre of an area like the Strand. The map, as well as the pedestrian experience, of the street that we considered earlier, the significance of the proximity of these symbolic courtiers' residences, and their interrelation as a result in the production of cultural meaning, is realized physically through the performances of running masques.

Correspondence from the period suggests that there were certainly many more household and 'amateur' theatrical events than those for which we have extant texts. The transitory and sometimes ad hoc nature of some of these 'shows' may not have contributed to their survival in manuscript form. For example, in 1636 alone, in the midst of complex diplomatic and ambassadorial negotiations around the visit of Charles Louis the Palatine

---

[15] I am indebted to Knowles, 'The "running masque" recovered', for these geographical details. See, in particular, p. 83.

[16] Another was certainly projected in 1628 though no firm records of its performance have been identified. For full details of these masques in relation to other courtly and provincial masque commissions in this period, see the detailed timeline provided as an appendix to Butler, *The Stuart Court Masque*.

[17] Knowles, 'The "running masque" recovered', p. 91 and see also Appendix 1.2 in the same article which reproduces extracts from Chamberlain's correspondence.

Prince, Martin Butler notes that there were at least two household masques presented by Lady Elizabeth Hatton, possibly authored by commercial playwright Henry Glapthorne, who had a family connection.[18] What we need to bear in mind, then, is a deeply enriched version of 'household theatre' not only as it operated in a provincial or regional context, as was explored in Chapter 3, but as it operated in the Strand and surrounding streets of the capital, where there were multiple aristocratic houses which were more than capable of staging complex theatrical performances.[19]

There were others ways too in which a performative and, by extension, literary culture was made visible in this neighbourhood. Arundel House, which sat in between the symbolic sites of Essex House and Somerset House, had a strong reputation as a literary salon, an intellectual gathering space. Both Thomas Howard, the Earl of Arundel and Lord Marshall at Charles's court following the death of Buckingham in 1629, and his wife Alathea Talbot were experienced patrons of the arts, and sculptors, poets, artists, and architects (not least Inigo Jones) had strong links to the communities that regularly gathered at their Strand residence. Celestina appears to aim for something similar at her Strand household in Shirley's drama:

> I'll have
> My house the academy of wits, who shall
> Exalt it with rich sack and sturgeon,
> Write panegyrics of my feasts, and praise
> The method of my witty superfluities;
> (1.2.84–8)

Richard Cust has recently suggested that Arundel House served occasionally as the surrogate hearing space for the Court of Chivalry.[20] The main site of this civil law court, which had its origins in medieval times, was the Palace of Westminster but smaller cases were probably heard at Arundel House, adding to our growing sense of the Strand as a febrile environment for all kinds of activity, literary, theatrical, political, and legal.

There is also an intriguing connection between the Strand as a theatrical location and one of the most spectacular instances of 'street theatre' in the Caroline period, Shirley's *The Triumph of Peace*. Staged in 1634 by the Inns

---

[18] Butler, *The Stuart Court Masque*, p. 326.
[19] See Knowles, 'The "running masque" recovered', p. 93.
[20] See 'Introduction', in R. P. Cust and A. J. Hopper (eds.), *Cases in the High Court of Chivalry, 1634–1640* (Harleian Society, new series, vol. 18, 2006); see also www.court-of-chivalry.bham.ac.uk/newcourt.htm [date accessed 15 December 2009].

of Court as a form of apology to the monarch following the trenchant attack
of one of their members William Prynne on the theatrical indulgences of
the court in his *Histriomastix* a year previous, Shirley's masque began on
the evening of its first performance (the bulk of the performance was at
Whitehall; it was repeated at the Merchant Taylors' Hall just ten days
later) with 'a cavalcade through the city streets to Westminster' led by
twenty footmen and a hundred men on horse each with attendants in
trains, followed up by a further two hundred halberdiers (compare the
kind of street scene this would have heralded with the image of Marie de
Medicis's 1637 entry into Cheapside reproduced earlier at Figure 4).[21] There
was a series of extensive and experimental anti-masques, some of which
handled topics of law enforcement and parish officialdom in ways that
offer suggestive links to plays such as *A Tale of a Tub*, that had been staged
in the months preceding the masque's creation. The main masque went on
to explore the related topics of law and peace, and, by extension, Caroline
policy during the years of the so-called Personal Rule; similar concerns
have already been registered in the interest in local community and ideas
of authority in a number of the plays examined in the previous chapter.[22]
*The Triumph* has tended to be read by scholars in the context of Stuart
masquing culture, sometimes to the isolation of its more public-facing
elements and episodes. Thousands of spectators lined the streets for the
aforementioned cavalcade and contemporary diaries and correspondence
indicate the considerable and sometimes contradictory effect that the event
had on those present.[23] Shirley's masque should be seen, then, as a part of
a wider envisioning of the cultural and theatrical performance of the built
environment of the city in the early to mid seventeenth century and that
move can inform our understanding of the Strand, in particular, as a spatial
signifier.[24] Running masques were merely a miniaturized form of this kind
of civic spectacular, which both referred to and embodied its mobile site(s)
of performance.

The Strand did participate in *The Triumph of Peace* in one significant,
if not fully visible, way, since Hatton House, the site, as we have seen,
of various kinds of theatrical performance throughout our focus decades,

---

[21] Butler, *The Stuart Court Masque*, p. 299.
[22] For related discussions of drama's response to the Personal Rule, see Butler, *Theatre and Crisis*; Julie
Sanders, *Caroline Drama* (Plymouth: Northcote House, 1999); and Atherton and Sanders (eds.),
*The 1630s*.
[23] See Butler, *The Stuart Court Masque*, pp. 299, 307.
[24] For fuller discussions of *The Triumph of Peace*, see, for example, Butler, *The Stuart Court Masque*,
esp. pp. 298–310; and Wiseman, *Drama and Politics in the English Civil War*, pp. 116–22.

served as a rehearsal space for the performers;[25] but it is as a further example of the ways in which drama of varying kinds sought to harness public space, the literal streets, buildings, and neighbourhoods of the capital, that I invoke Shirley's text in this context. That the playwright was working on this event in the year prior to the first staging of *The Lady of Pleasure* means that their juxtaposition as texts and events can prove instructive. The elite culture of the Strand, performed in its most public sense through occasions such as running masques, from the late Jacobean period onwards, is the cultural and geographical context for Shirley's play and can give us access to the ways in which social space operates within its dramaturgy.

It is the Strand neighbourhood's particular association with leisure activities and with entertainment culture, primarily but not exclusively theatrical in the 1620s and 1630s, then, that I wish to concern myself here. Further traces of that entertainment culture can be registered in exchanges between Bornwell and Aretina in *The Lady of Pleasure* when he berates her for her profligate expenditure, since they have come to live, at her express request, in the town. In the process, Bornwell has abnegated his responsibility to his country estate and this is also a reflection of social actuality. In 1632, Charles I had issued an edict ordering the gentry to quit the distractions of the capital and return to their provincial estates. Bornwell is therefore acting against official government policy by relocating his family in this way. What he describes in the process, however, brings to life the sights and sounds of the Strand at this moment in time.

> Another game you have, which consumes more
> Your fame than purse: your revels in the night,
> Your meetings called the ball, to which appear,
> As to the court of pleasure, all your gallants
> And ladies thither bound by a subpoena
> Of Venus [ . . . ]                    (1.1.112–17)

Bornwell's additional comment that 'There was a play on't' (l. 119), that is to say on this theme of 'revels in the night', is a knowing metatheatrical reference to Shirley's own play *The Ball* (1632), which in Jean Howard's words 'advertises the emerging cult of the ball'.[26] As this reference indicates, then, it was not only official court- or even courtier-sponsored theatre that defined the heady theatrical atmosphere of this street and

---

[25] The point is made in the appendixed materials to Knowles, 'The "running masque" recovered', p. 121.

[26] Howard, *Theater of a City*, p. 183.

neighbourhood, but the wider sense of 'cultural capital' that the Strand marketed and promoted.[27]

In thinking about the implicit theatricality of the Strand and its surrounding environs, it is equally important to think about the ways in which its spatialities, sights, and sounds were reproduced in mainstream drama. Along with the resonant locales of aristocratic households, the New Exchange, as already indicated, was a key point of reference. One of the commodities with which the exchange was particularly associated was china – as indicated by the Boy's lines in Jonson's 1609 entertainment for the building's inauguration:

> What do you lack? What is't you buy? Very fine China stuffs, of all kinds and qualities? China chains, China bracelets, China scarves, China fans, China girdles, China knives, China boxes, China cabinets, [ . . . ] China dogs and China cats? (50–6)

*The Sparagus Garden* in a series of internal references makes clear to its audience that a number of scenes, in particular those relating to the Brittleware family house and china shop, are set close to the Strand. The locational deixis of the Brittleware's shop here rather than within the shuttered arcades of the New Exchange would indicate to audiences that theirs is a lower status establishment, in part explicating the multitasking undertaken by the household in terms of renting rooms to Sir Hugh Moneylacks (who has been present in their house for several years and, as a result, is witness to the intimacies of the couple's troubled marriage), and in the form of John's moonlighting in his former trade as a barber surgeon.[28]

It is when, in the fourth act, Rebecca escapes from her husband's overweening surveillance in a sedan chair that the proximity of the Strand is made explicit. Samuel Touchwood informs a distraught John that he has just seen his wife disappearing down the street: 'If your wife be the gentlewoman o' the house, sir, she is now gone forth in one of the new hand-litters: what call ye it, a sedan?' (4.1. 946). He then adds that she was headed 'Down towards the Strand [ . . . ]' (4.1. 953). As already registered, sedans were a reasonably novel feature of Strand life, one to which several plays at this time alluded; the modes of transport by which people carried themselves down the Strand were themselves being actively realized and

---

[27] The phrase is Howard's from *Theater of a City*, p. 165.
[28] There is an obvious link between the Brittlewares and *Epicene*'s china shop owners near the Strand, the Otters, but, while it is clear that Brome is here both invoking and imitating his mentor, there are also contemporary points being made in the location of the Brittlewares' china shop in this particular part of London in 1635.

represented on the Caroline stage. Rebecca's flight forms part of wider reflections on the way in which increased mobility was contributing to the breakdown of neighbourhood loyalties (though in the end, Rebecca's escape will turn out to have been a piece of street theatre itself).

Brome makes plot capital from the multiple possible exits offered by early modern Strand households, with their alternate streetside and waterside points of access. The landing stairs that enabled householders to acquire quick access to their boats and to the alternate roadway of the Thames (the remnants of which can still be seen today) are regularly mentioned in his plays (and note their presence on the map produced at Figure 10). It is, for example, from landing stairs or the 'water-gate' that Pate is able to escape in the guise of the doctor in *The Northern Lass*. He needs to make a swift exit from the property in which Sir Paul Squelch has ensconced his melancholic niece, having just facilitated (against Squelch's wishes) her elopement with a newly divorced Sir Philip Luckless. The couple escapes via the street-side in a coach with shutters that will conveniently shield their identity from the JP when he arrives at the house. As the clerk states when he re-enters, having been sent off in pursuit of the 'doctor': 'he went forth now at the water-gate and took boat in haste' (5.1.[872.5]). Those same stairs or watergates were an architectural feature of the built environment that also played a role within the social landscape depicted by plays like *The Lady of Pleasure*; in the 1630s the newly appointed painter to the court of Charles I, Flemish artist Anthony Van Dyck, was given a property with a landing stairs at Blackfriars to enable the King and his courtiers easy access to the painter's studio to have their images rendered in oil. This image returns us to the social world in which Aretina and Celestina are both so clearly located at the start of Shirley's Strand-set play. It is Aretina who makes explicit reference to the activity of having one's portrait painted, which, judging by the sheer output of Van Dyck's studio in the 1630s, was a popular pastime when this play was staged:

> It [discourse] does conclude
> A lady's morning work: we rise, make fine,
> Sit for our picture, and 'tis time to dine.
> (1.1.321–3)

Drama set in and around the neighbourhood of the Strand at this time becomes, then, a means of understanding the actual experience of the city and one particular area. Through attention to detail in this way, we can begin to reconstruct, albeit partially, how streets were walked and how buildings and sites were not just perceived or imagined but physically embodied and practised. The commercial plays of Brome and Shirley, but also the running masques hosted by the same aristocratic households that those commercial dramas sought to stage and represent, realize the Strand locale that Richard Dutton helpfully described in relation to Jonson's *Epicene*: 'Between the fashionable residences and the elevated emporia, this was a place of seeing, being seen, of buying, selling, performing social rituals; in short, a place of activity and noise'.[29] It is not stretching a point to claim that all of that activity and noise can be heard again in 1630s drama in all its rich variety.

### MAKING SPACE IN COVENT GARDEN

Jean Howard has written eloquently about the shifting of the geographical fulcrum of London westward in the early seventeenth century and the emergence of the area known as the 'Town'. She notes that:

As London expanded geographically westward, so did the drama in the sense that the plays began to be set in sites in the emerging West End, such as Hyde Park, Tottenham Court, and Covent Garden. In staging these places, the theatre helped to turn them into significant social spaces associated with a defined set of privileged behaviours and social actors.[30]

There has already been much fine scholarship on these social spaces in relation to early modern, and, in particular, Caroline, drama and some of these sites have featured in earlier discussions.[31] I am particularly interested in this concluding section in the agency of drama in the creation of the notion of 'neighbourhood' that I have hitherto been suggesting was central to early modern understandings and practice of the built environment of the metropolis. Covent Garden is the perfect case study in this regard, since, rather than being a fully established area when 1630s drama by Brome, Nabbes, and others sought to deploy it as a stage setting, it was still emergent, in the ongoing process of formation.[32] Drama can therefore be seen to play a key role in shaping public perception of this area, as well as offering modes of practice to be undertaken within its streets and locales.

---

[29] Dutton, *Epicene*, p. 12.      [30] Howard, *Theater of a City*, p. 162.
[31] Butler's pioneering work in *Theatre and Crisis*, pp. 151–8, is of particular note; see also Howard, *Theater of a City*, *passim*; Steggle, *Richard Brome*, pp. 46–53. See also Zucker, 'London and urban space'.
[32] See, for example, Smuts, 'The court and its neighbourhood'; D. Duggan, '"London the ring, Covent Garden the jewell of that ring": new light on Covent Garden', *Architectural History*, 45 (2001), 140–61.

Covent Garden was, in the early 1630s, a site in transition and therefore one which necessarily contained memories of its past usage and function as well as predictive signs of its intended future. A twenty-acre area known as the 'great pasture' was intended by Francis Russell, Earl of Bedford, to become through the building scheme undertaken by Inigo Jones a site of architectural and spatial innovation, but also a thoroughly 'designed' neighbourhood, representing, as it would, gentry values and excluding less desirable elements of society. Julia Merritt has noted that the site deliberately eschewed the narrow alleys and tenements that defined more mixed communities that lived on the fringes of the Covent Garden area (in Long Acre and in streets connecting the Strand such as Falcon Alley and Vinegar Yard).[33] As well as enforcing strict regulation of the building materials to be deployed in constructing the elegant townhouses that would frame the central piazza – itself an innovative spatial phenomenon based on similar squares in Italy, in particular Venice – the site would benefit from piped water and proper sewage. Bedford clearly aimed for his architecture and spatial design to have a civilizing effect on the locale, though the proximity of other more diverse communities and neighbourhoods, where tradespeople lived in close proximity to courtiers, immediately complicated that picture. While efforts were made to exclude the poor from the piazza itself by heavy-handed policing and there were ongoing efforts by the crown and parish authorities to limit the burgeoning number of taverns and alehouses in the immediate region, beggars still tended to congregate at the gateways and entrances to the district in order to ask charity from passing aristocrats and gentry.[34] What is interesting about the ways in which commercial drama responded to Bedford's attempts to construct a neighbourhood is that it responds to the project when it is still in evolution, when the ways in which Covent Garden will operate and be practised were, to all intents and purposes, still under negotiation. In this way, we can argue that drama contributes in a very direct way to the public understanding of Covent Garden and its future interpretation as a space and site.

The opening scenes of Brome's *Covent Garden Weeded* (*c.* 1632–3) and Nabbes's *Covent Garden* (1632–3; pub. 1638) encouraged contemporary audiences to imagine the building site that was the contemporary piazza through the eyes of the characters on (the largely bare) stage. Exactly where these plays were first performed is open to speculation, but there is a case to be made that they were staged at Salisbury Court or the Cockpit, playhouses

---

[33] Merritt, *The Social World of Early Modern Westminster*, p. 196.
[34] Merritt, *The Social World of Early Modern Westminster*, p. 279.

which stood in close physical proximity to the geographical neighbourhood being explored in the drama.[35] Nabbes's opening stage direction reads in the printed text as follows: '*Enter* Dungworth, Ralph, *and* Dobson, *as newly come to Towne by the right scoene*' (1.1. sig. B1r). Dungworth is the owner of a country estate and Ralph and Dobson are his servants. They are shocked by the rough and ready state of the landscape they encounter at Long Acre and begin to lament the neglect of their responsibilities back home:

DOBSON: But all the while the Plough stands still.
RALPH: Sha, Dobson, thy mind's upon nothing but dirt.
DOBSON: Indeed, heer's store of it, anckle deepe.                    (1.1. sig. B1r)

The phenomenological invocation of the actual mud of the developing area is beautifully contrasted here with the symbolic quality of the acreage ploughed and worked by Dungworth's tenant farmers back on his country estate – an estate and neighbourhood (tenant farmers were alternatively referred to as 'neighbours' in plays of this period[36]) representative of those whom Charles I worried were being neglected by the ever increasing interest by the gentry in taking lodgings in London for large parts of the year. The impact of this on audience imaginations might have been further enhanced by the idea that they could have crossed nearby the half-built buildings being described in the play en route to watch the drama that very evening.

   Brome also captures the sense of a building site full of property developers' signs and advertisements selling their new lodgings 'off-plan' with the promise of future wealth to be gained from rents. Rooksbill, an architect-cum-local landlord and property speculator, is showing around the Middlesex suburban JP Cockbrain, boasting in the process of the financial investment his bricks and mortar represent: 'I have piled up a leash of thousand pounds in walls and windows there' (1.1.7). Cockbrain is suitably impressed: 'I like your row of houses most incomparably' (1.1.6) although there is also a clue to the audience about the unfinished state of affairs in that he describes the scene as 'something like! These appear like buildings!' (1.1.4). There is a provisionality implicit here which would give more sceptical members of the audience pause. The Covent Garden project had at the time of these plays yet to be fully realized and also clearly runs the risk of disappointing those, not least the commissioning spirit of the Earl

[35] On the problems with dating and locating the first performances, see the more detailed analysis in Steggle, *Richard Brome*, pp. 43–5.
[36] See the working examples in 1.1 of Nabbes's *The Bride*.

of Bedford, who projected such high ambition for the space and what it would come to represent. Rooksbill praises the beauty of the 'Surveyor's' design, but hints that the clientele and usage of the semi-finished site is already falling rather short of expectations: 'If all were as well tenanted and inhabited by worthy persons [ . . . ]' (1.1.9). Cockbrain hints at something similar when he reflects: 'What new plantation was ever peopled with the better sort at first?' (1.1.10). He clearly intends to try and introduce a desirable clientele into the area as soon as possible, by providing Rooksbill with a prospective tenant for his rented rooms: the West Country gentleman, Crosswill, and his family, who arrive onstage at that moment from their temporary lodgings in Hammersmith (1.1. s.d. 14).

Rooksbill's allusion to the 'Surveyor's' work here is, of course, to the Surveyor of the King's Works, Inigo Jones, who had been predominant in the conception and design of the area and, in particular, its central Italianate piazza and church. Steggle suggests that this opening scene is located on or very nearby the piazza, since the church of St Paul's on its western side is clearly visible to the characters.[37] As well as having a distinctly Protestant aesthetic in its external appearance and internal layout, indicative of Bedford's own complicated religious sympathies (Archbishop Laud would subsequently standardize the placement of the altar in the church), the church was also central to plans to establish Covent Garden as a parish in its own right, as a neighbourhood with all of the established sense of identity and belonging as well as official and jurisdictional frameworks that Jonson was exploring in his dramatic version of parish politics in *A Tale of a Tub*.[38] It would, however, take another fourteen years following Brome's and Nabbes's plays before the parochial status of the area was fully established and therefore, at the time of the building work, it was still part of the wider district of St Martin's and reliant on the constabulary of that parish to regulate and maintain order in the district. With their scenes of the magistracy raiding taverns, both plays engage with this idea and suggest certain failures in or limitations to the official systems in the process.[39] What they also do, I would argue, is try to predict the ways in which this designed neighbourhood might be lived and practised by its residents and

---

[37] Steggle, *Richard Brome*, p. 49.

[38] Cf. Steggle, *Richard Brome*, p. 47. Steggle notes that in Brome's play Nicholas jokes that the graveyard of St Paul's is not yet licensed to receive bodies (p. 48).

[39] Onstage depictions of the raiding of a tavern by Justice Cockbrain in Act 5 of *Covent Garden Weeded* were echoed by real-life events in 1633, when vintners' wine-stocks were seized by the parish constabulary at taverns including the Goat, which is one of those staged, along with the Paris tavern, in Brome's play. Steggle makes the crucial point that this is less a case of drama reflecting than predicting social reality (p. 51).

visitors. As with the cultural representations and stagings of the Strand that we have just been considering, the contribution of theatre and performance to that geographical imagining should not be underestimated.

The link between Rooksbill and Jones would have been fully apparent to audiences in 1632, which would have further linked Jones's name with the creation of theatrical scenery and designs for court masques. This association served further to blur any clearly demarcated lines between public architecture and its theatrical representation. D. J. Hopkins goes so far as to suggest that Jones's Covent Garden blueprints were in essence 'quotations from the theatrical', reworking in a material architectural context spatial practices and perspectival angles learned from the masquing events that he had staged with Jonson, Townshend, and others over recent decades.[40] The signifying location of St Paul's Church with its dominant viewpoint over the piazza, and the deployment of railings to demarcate certain areas (these are mentioned by Dobson in Nabbes's play, when he enquires their purpose of Ralph, who replies sardonically that they are 'mewes for hawkes': 1.1. sig. B1v) can both be seen to have direct theatrical precedent. The operations of agency and impact are once again seen to be multidirectional in practice. As Hopkins observes: 'new perceptions of theatrical space accelerated the pace of transformation in London's urban practices'.[41] Matthew Steggle makes the point that, until the construction of Covent Garden, balconies had previously had a mostly theatrical existence in England.[42] On the stage, in plays like Brome's *The Novella* and, here, in the opening scene of *Covent Garden Weeded*, where Damyris appears on a balcony carrying a lute and 'habited like a courtesan of Venice' (s.d. 69), balconies as spatial and architectural signifiers had become inextricably linked to prostitution. Brome both invokes these associations by way of further questioning the limits to the civilizing intentions of architecture (Covent Garden would become a resort of prostitutes of varying degree throughout the 1630s) and challenges them. 'Damyris' (really Dorcas) will turn out to be anything but what she seems on this first viewing, and likewise the possibility that Covent Garden's new architectural feature might reinterpret social practice

---

[40] D. J. Hopkins refers to the 'quotations from the theatrical' that Jones made in his designs for Greenwich Palace and Covent Garden; see *City/Stage/Globe: Performance and Space in Shakespeare's London* (London: Routledge, 2007), pp. 184–5.

[41] Hopkins, *City/Stage/Globe*, p. 185.

[42] One of the other precedents for balconies and viewing galleries in the English tradition may be seen in the gardens of larger household estates such as Bolsover Castle, which was explored in Chapter 3. The 'theatricality' of these viewing platforms has in turn been discussed by architectural and garden historians; see, for example, Henderson, *The Tudor House and Garden*, especially pp. 153, 164. See also Zucker's discussion of Brome's balconies in his forthcoming *The Places of Wit*.

and behaviour in the process is at least raised as a possibility. As Steggle notes, 'In this play, the new architecture of Covent Garden is apparently creating new behaviours even in its first day of occupancy. The location is creating the action'.[43] I would go one stage further and suggest that theatre itself is also creating ways of understanding and interpreting that location that will in turn affect action. Certainly it is a performance-led understanding of balconies that informs Lady Celestina's intentions in *The Lady of Pleasure*:

> my balcony
> Shall be the courtier's idol, and more gaped at
> Than all the pageantry at Temple Bar
> By country clients. (1.2.93–6)

Fittingly, the Strand residence of this socially ambitious woman deploys its architecturally innovative features to declare its social position to the world. That the social and theatrical semiotics of balconies were, however, dangerously fraught with seedier sexual connotations was a fact that did not escape the attention of Shirley or Brome when associating their female characters with their sociospatial operations.

In all kinds of ways, then, not least through architectural allusions, Brome's *Covent Garden Weeded* seems to predict (or, at the very least, ruminate upon) the future of Covent Garden, from excessive drinking culture and tavern raids through its plot line of the 'Brotherhood of the Blade'[44] to the mixed social and sexual encounters that the new open layout of the Piazza and its balconied townhouses seems to foster and promote, and through to the rise of Puritanism, figured in particular here through the character of the corrupted Gabriel, who comes to see Covent Garden primarily because of its Puritan associations only to find himself as subject to the effects of alcohol as anyone else. The challenges to Bedford's civilizing project that were to emerge within weeks of the play's first performances are inbuilt into the play's episodic proceedings. In his nervous reference in 1.1 to the present tenants occupying the site of Covent Garden, Rooksbill reveals the ambiguous status of the piazza in its early years, when it was as much associated with taverns, ordinaries, prostitution, and other 'low-life' activities as some of the further flung 'Liberties' across the River Thames in Southwark. While Bedford's architectural dream had been to create a civilizing space on the continental European model, in practice

---

[43] Steggle, *Richard Brome*, p. 50.
[44] On the tavern culture of this period, see the introduction to Michael Leslie's edition of this play for *Brome Online*. See also O'Callaghan, *The English Wits*.

Covent Garden seemingly encouraged exactly the same kinds of itinerant and threateningly mobile behaviour that we have explored elsewhere as sites of spatial and geographical anxiety in this period. We have here, without any doubt, drama operating as a key to reconstructing practice of a particular area of London. Beyond simply charting the emergence of the West End, as plays like these have often been made to do, I would argue that the plays themselves shaped and influenced practice. Drama is in the 1630s responding to and participating in the creation of what Raymond Williams would call in a later age 'structures of feeling', recording but also creating residual, dominant, and emergent modes of being and doing.[45]

Brome makes clear through internal references his play's relationship with a particular Jonsonian precedent that was, on the surface, located in a very different space and place on the northern edges of the city, the Smithfield-set *Bartholomew Fair* (1614). Cockbrain declares his aim to be like the (ill-fated) Justice Overdo in 'weeding' Covent Garden and bringing it into a state of moral reform (1.1.10).[46] The Overdo comparisons confirm for knowledgeable audiences that this is a ridiculous aim; to what extent, therefore, Brome genuinely expected his audiences to react to the anti-idyllic version of the new Town space in his play by genuinely reforming behaviour is highly questionable. In the same ways that plays that represented the new phenomenon of urban walking might also be felt to be contributing directly to the practice (see the discussion in Chapter 4), so it is possible to read these plays as culturally contingent interventions in the ongoing response to the new spatial possibilities of Covent Garden.

If, as has already been established in a previous chapter, one of the key ways in which early modern people, not least Londoners, thought about themselves was as parishioners, it is intriguing to note that it is as a parish that Ralph and Dobson try to comprehend the radical social and architectural innovation that is Covent Garden in Nabbes's play. Dobson, looking around him onstage – another gesture that would have had the quality of inspiring or provoking the theatre audience to imagine themselves *in* Covent Garden at this moment (in truth the area was close to the Cockpit theatre where the play was possibly performed and where, in a moment

---

[45] Raymond Williams, 'Structures of feeling', reproduced in Colin Counsel and Laurie Wolf, *Performance Analysis* (London: Routledge, 2001), pp. 193–8, from *Marxism and Literature* (Oxford University Press, 1977).

[46] Zucker has recently suggested that Nabbes's Covent Garden play is the more conservative in its politics, not least in its resistance to showing us the full troubled picture of the spatial practices of the site as Brome does; see *The Places of Wit*.

of head-spinning metatheatricality, Ralph hopes they will lodge so that he can have easy access to plays) – observes that ''tis a jolly company' (1.1 sig. B1v) but asks a key question about dwelling and habitation: 'Dwell they all here abouts?' (1.1 sig. B1v). The point, of course, is once again about provisionality; many of those who haunt the outer edges of the piazza and cause such consternation to the image-conscious Rooksbill in the Brome play are itinerant visitors, there to make profit and cultural capital from the new social phenomenon. The key concept of 'dwelling' that was at the heart of earlier estate poetry such as Jonson's 'To Penshurst' and to which Brome himself responded through characters loyal to locality such as Oldrents and Randall in *A Jovial Crew* is sacrificed here to the pursuit of the new in the built environment of the city. Ralph's reply to Dobson in the Nabbes play is equally telling: 'I scarce think they are all of one parish, neither do they go to one church. They come only for an evening recreation to see Covent Garden' (1.1 sig. B1v). There is something troubling in this form of social mobility, then, as much as there was in the ever-growing surge of gentry types into well-to-do areas such as Covent Garden and the West End. Older ideas of the parish, of belonging, and of community are under threat from these new kinds of neighbourhood formation. This all serves to confirm the agency of Caroline drama in the making, as well as the representation, of social space and the built environment. Here, in the Brome and Nabbes plays, we have a direct example of how drama responded through its staging of cultural geography to the idea of neighbourhood that we previously saw analysed in contemporaneous plays such as *A Tale of a Tub* through the framework of the parish and in *The Sparagus Garden*, *The Magnetic Lady*, and *The Bride* through the idea of medicalized space. In their understanding of the shaping cultural effects of performance, there are clear kinships between all these plays and the theatricalized understanding of the adjacent area of the Strand as developed in the running masque tradition and in a commercial drama like *The Lady of Pleasure*. In the Covent Garden locale of *Covent Garden Weeded* and *Covent Garden*, however, what we witness, above all, is the prediction of what a neighbourhood might become in that magical moment of potential before it has become fully ossified in its practices and reputations.[47]

---

[47] Other plays have been analysed in relationship to the emergent space and social practices or behaviours of Covent Garden. Jean Howard concentrates on the academies and schools of compliments that were popular and, in particular, Sir Francis Kynaston's Museum Minervae, a training school for boys, arguing for Brome's *The New Academy or The New Exchange* as a direct satire on Kynaston's establishment and its educational manifesto (*Theater of a City*, pp. 184–200). Certainly,

*Coda*

Throughout the version of cultural geography promulgated in this study, my emphasis has been on resisting simple binaries, be they between metropolis and province, London and the regions, city and court, public and private, home and abroad.[48] More often than not, these are concepts that feed off and are mutually informed by each other. Rebecca Ann Bach offers the specific example in the early seventeenth century of the Bermudas as connoting both a space elsewhere – the politically renamed Sommers Islands which were themselves the subject of a body of literature as well as contemporary mapping and surveying exercises[49] – and the red-light district of London; this same locale is invoked at the start of Brome's *The Northern Lass* (1.1.5).[50] This directs us, in turn, towards the complex shared space of the stage in plays such as Brome's *The Antipodes*. There, Peregrine has been overwhelmed by his reading experiences of travel literature (a highly marketable form at the time) and, not least, of Mandeville's *Travels*, to the extent that he appears unable to cope with everyday demands, certainly within the context of his marriage. He is brought to London by his family to be 'cured' by a memorable form of applied theatre: a metropolitan household play directed by the charismatic figure of Lord Letoy that stages a journey to the Antipodes.[51] Peregrine trusts utterly in the veracity of his experiences, having been given a sleeping draught and informed that while he slept, he journeyed to the Antipodes by boat. Once

Kynaston's establishment fostered literary production of its own, including a masque-like entertainment for the school's opening, the *Corona Minervae*. See also Steggle, *Richard Brome*, for its suggestive exploration of the ways in which in the tavern scenes an 'imaginative geography' is imposed onto the buildings and interiors of Covent Garden in Brome's *Covent Garden Weeded* (p. 52).

[48] I am inspired in this form of thinking by Rebecca Ann Bach's mobilization of anthropologists' recent concerns to view the metropole and the colony as sharing a single conceptual space, as coexisting within the same analytic field; see her 'Ben Jonson's "Civill Savages"', *Studies in English Literature* 37: 2 (1997), 277–93 (280).

[49] Bach, 'Ben Jonson's "Civill Savages"', p. 280. That work was undertaken by Richard Norwood, who had first travelled to the Islands in 1613 in his capacity as the Virginia Company's pearl diver. He produced and published maps and surveys of the region. He returned as a schoolmaster in 1637, keeping a series of journals during that time. These have been published as Wesley Frank Craven and Walter B. Hayward (eds.), *The Journals of Richard Norwood, 1639–40* (New York: Scholars Press Facsimiles, 1945). He is also renowned for his practical work *A Sea-Man's Practice* (London, 1637). For a useful discussion of Norwood's 'acute sense of space and place', see Bedford, Davis, and Kelly, *Early Modern English Lives*, p. 81.

[50] Bach offers a cognate reading of Jonson' s poem 'To Sir Edward Sackville' (*Underwood* 13) where London 'pirates' are said to 'Have their Bermudas, and their straits in the Strand' ('Ben Jonson's "Civill savages"', p. 280).

[51] The house, to emphasize this link to the household theatre practices explored in Chapter 3, is referred to as 'an amphitheatre / Of exercise and pleasure' (1.2.115).

'there', he rapidly installs himself as monarch, exposing in the process the false foundations of many comparable colonial projects. The scenes staged in 'The Antipodes' enable biting satire on contemporary London as we encounter honest lawyers and watermen who discourse in courtly rhetoric, but they also collapse the spatial difference between 'here' and 'there' in unsettling ways.[52] *The Antipodes* is just one example of a number of plays that were responding not only to the massive expansion of England's capital city, but simultaneously to the emergence of a new colonial identity, and, with it, a new world geography. In this respect, early modern drama proves as able to take on new territory and terrain within the compass of its cultural geography as the sites of daily practice that have more often formed the focus of this study.

I began by attempting, through textual and dramatic examples, to define cultural geography's importance in relation to understanding and interpreting early modern drama through its capacity to illuminate for us the agency of literature in the creation of the practices and behaviours, the networks and the neighbourhoods, spatial and social, that constitute the daily cartographies of our lives and the lives of our historical subjects. I will close by gesturing to the ways in which fresh readings of the numerous vibrant and exciting plays that were produced and staged after 1620 and before the establishment of the English Republic in 1649 (and I have, of necessity, had to be highly selective, both in opting for that timeframe and in those plays on which I have chosen to focus in detail) can be achieved through a deeper contextualization of those plays within contemporary understandings of space and place.

Cultural geography allows us to comprehend the active practice and understanding of specific milieux and environments within particular historical periods, but, in turn, as a methodology and approach, it reveals, not least in the context of the early seventeenth century, the profound and far-reaching agency of literature and drama. Texts, and, in particular, I would argue, play-texts, not only represent but alter, foster, and enable practices of space, place, and landscape; to understand better the times past with which we seek to engage through reading and restaging early modern drama, we must locate that drama's acts and scenes, its settings and dialogues, its characters and concerns, within the cultural geography of the day.

---

[52] For a more detailed discussion of the satirical aspects of the play, see Richard Cave's critical introduction in *Brome Online*.

# Index

236

Lightning Source UK Ltd.
Milton Keynes UK
UKOW06f1226181115

262980UK00005B/109/P